03/ 100
TECHNOLOGY & CRAFTS

TECHNOLOGIE ET ARTISANAT
TECNOLOGÍA Y ARTESANÍA
TECNOLOGIA E ARTES

WET Lamp 102
Malva 103
Virtue of Blue 104
Cirrata 106
AURA 108
Morning Glory 109
Turbine Lamp 110
Treble Chandelier 112
Solar Lampion 113
Highlights Collection 114
Four Seasons 116
FUNGI Lamp 117
Morph Chandelier 118
Soul Cell 119
Story 120
The Chrysanthemum
Centerpiece 121
Trap Light 122
FYR 124
Kyudo 125
Lightness of Being 126
Halley 127
Ameba 128
Field of Light 130
Dune 132
Lotus 7.0 134
Lunar 135

04/ 136
OTHER ECO APPROACHES

AUTRES APPROCHES ÉCOLOGIQUES
OTRAS TENDENCIAS ECOLÓGICAS
OUTROS ENFOQUES ECO

Tilt Lamp 138
Naïve Shade 139
Mushroom Lamp 140
2D LED 141
Ichi-Go 142
Clover Lamp 143
The Duck Lamp 144
E.T.A. Baby 144
Self Compiling Lamp 145
Liberty 146
Lightmate 147
LIGHT_NESS 148
Lightpaintings 149
Freakshow 150
Storm 152
Structend Light 153
Lace Light 154
CMYK Lamp 155

FRA

RECYCLAGE ET RÉEMPLOI

Troisième composante de la gestion des déchets – les deux premiers étant réduction et réemploi –, le recyclage consiste à trouver des solutions créatives et des procédés technologiques qui permettent d'élaborer, à partir de matériaux de récupération ou d'objets usagés, de nouveaux produits et des œuvres d'art à l'esthétique avant-gardiste ou centrés sur l'aspect naturel des matières. Les luminaires sympathiques et originaux illustrés dans ce chapitre ont tous été élaborés à partir d'objets de récupération ou recyclés, comme des bouteilles en plastique, des attaches de câbles, des boîtes à œufs et des sacs en polypropylène.

POR

RECICLAGEM E REUTILIZAÇÃO

O conceito de reciclagem, um dos elementos essenciais da hierarquia dos resíduos «reduzir, reutilizar, reciclar», implica em dominar a tecnologia e as ideias criativas para processar materiais usados e objetos antigos com a finalidade de convertê-los em novos produtos e em obras de arte, insuflando-lhes nesse processo qualidades estéticas novas ou naturais. As luminárias incluídas nesta seção são fabricadas com diversos materiais reciclados e descartados como, por exemplo, garrafas de plástico, cintas abraçadeiras, caixas de ovos e sacos de plástico de polipropileno, que foram reutilizados para lhes conferir designs modernos e atraentes.

01

08-51

ESP

RECICLAJE Y REUTILIZACIÓN

El concepto de reciclaje, uno de los componentes esenciales de la jerarquía de residuos «reducir, reutilizar, reciclar», implica dominar la tecnología y las ideas creativas para procesar materiales usados y objetos antiguos con el fin de convertirlos en productos nuevos y obras de arte, insuflándoles cualidades estéticas nuevas o naturales en el proceso. Las lámparas que se incluyen en esta sección están fabricadas con diversos materiales reciclados y desechados, como por ejemplo botellas de plástico, bridas, cartones de huevos y bolsas de plástico de polipropileno, que se han reutilizado para ofrecerle diseños modernos y atractivos.

ECO DESIGN

LAMPS
LAMPES
LÁMPARAS
ILUMINAÇÃO

promopress

ECO DESIGN
Lamps / Lampes / Lámparas / Iluminação

Translation: English (revision) / French / Spanish / Brazilian Portuguese:
Tom Corkett / Marie-Pierre Teuler / Juan José Llanos Collado / Élcio Carillo
Layout & cover design: Gemma Alberich

PROMOPRESS is a brand of:
Promotora de Prensa Internacional S.A.
C/ Ausiàs March 124
08013 Barcelona, Spain
Phone: +34 93 245 14 64
Fax: +34 93 265 48 83
info@promopress.es
www.promopress.es
www.promopresseditions.com
Facebook & Twitter: Promopress Editions @PromopressEd

Edited by Dopress

ISBN: 978-84-92810-91-8

Printed in China.

ECO DESIGN

LAMPS
LAMPES
LÁMPARAS
ILUMINAÇÃO

ESP

Es indudable que tanto la ecología como el desarrollo sostenible se encuentran entre las cuestiones más relevantes del mundo moderno, de manera que no es extraño que en los últimos años los diseñadores hayan hecho más hincapié en el diseño ecológico. *Eco Design: Lamps,* el segundo volumen de esta serie de diseños ecológicos, le presenta las últimas creaciones de los equipos de diseño más destacados del mundo en el campo de las lámparas ecológicas, con el fin de que otras personas, sobre todo los diseñadores profesionales, consideren actitudes más respetuosas con el medio ambiente en los procesos y las ideas de sus diseños.

POR

Sem dúvida, tanto a ecologia como o desenvolvimento sustentável estão entre as preocupações mais importantes do mundo moderno e, por isso, é natural que nos últimos anos os designers tenham dado mais ênfase ao design ecológico. *Eco Design: Lamps*, o segundo volume desta série de designs ecológicos, apresenta-lhe as últimas criações das equipes de design mais importantes do mundo na área da iluminação ecológica, para que outras pessoas, sobretudo os designers profissionais, assumam posturas mais respeitosas em relação ao meio ambiente na concepção e no processamento dos seus projetos.

FRA

L'écologie et le développement durable font résolument partie des sujets les plus importants de notre époque et désormais les designers en tiennent compte pour concevoir leurs produits. Le deuxième volume de notre collection sur le design écologique, intitulé *Eco Design: Lamps,* s'attache à présenter les toutes dernières créations des meilleurs designers de luminaires de la planète. Il a également pour but d'encourager les gens, en particulier les professionnels du design, à adopter une démarche écologique lors de la mise au point de produits et de procédés de fabrication.

ECOLOGY AND SUSTAINABLE DEVELOPMENT ARE NOW UNDOUBTEDLY AMONG THE MOST SIGNIFICANT TOPICS IN THE MODERN WORLD, AND IN RECENT YEARS DESIGNERS HAVE BEGUN TO PLACE MORE EMPHASIS ON ECOLOGICAL DESIGN. ECO DESIGN: LAMPS, THE SECOND VOLUME IN OUR SERIES ON ECO DESIGNS, AIMS TO PRESENT THE LATEST ECO-LIGHTING PIECES FROM THE WORLD'S LEADING DESIGN TEAMS, AS WELL AS ENCOURAGE MORE PEOPLE, AND ESPECIALLY PROFESSIONAL DESIGNERS, TO CONSIDER MORE ENVIRONMENTALLY CONSCIOUS APPROACHES TO THEIR DESIGN IDEAS AND PROCESSES.

01/ 08

RECYCLING & REUSE

RECYCLAGE ET RÉEMPLOI
RECICLAJE Y REUTILIZACIÓN
RECICLAGEM E REUTILIZAÇÃO

Bicycle Wheel Reflector Chandelier **10**
Plastic Coke Bottle Lampshade **11**
Woven Cable Ties Lampshade **12**
Clamp **13**
Marie-Louise, Therese & Josephine **14**
Neo3 **16**
The Connect Series **18**
Cloud **19**
Dubbot Modular **20**
Zip Tie Light Kit **21**
Ilham, Lazara & Najah **22**
Trash me **23**
A Flip Flop Story **24**
Cloud Walk & Liquid Winter **26**
Cloud Lamps **27**
19 Pots **28**
Wood Lamp **29**
Wash Lamp **30**
Glass Chandelier **31**
Olegami Lamp **31**
Relumine **32**
Six-Pack Ring Pendant Lights **33**
Beute **33**
Stamen & Petals **34**
Mudlight **36**
Paper Light **37**
Pinha **38**
50% Sawdust **40**
Replay **41**
97% Soap **42**
Aria **43**
Kozo Lamp **44**
B-Chain Lamp **46**
Walker **47**
PulpLamp **48**
Found Object Lamp #1 **49**
Bloom **50**
Bee-Hive **50**
Lighthouse Lamp **51**

02/ 52

NATURAL MATERIALS

MATÉRIAUX NATURELS
MATERIALES NATURALES
MATERIAIS NATURAIS

The Bride Lamp **54**
Zhu Guang **56**
Xuan Lamp **57**
Fan Lamp **58**
Gourd Lamp Bracket V **60**
Standing Lamp XII **61**
Standing Lamp XIII: Thorn Sphere **62**
Standing Lamp XIV: Globe II **63**
CoconMalade **64**
Scrafty **65**
Leone Series 01 **66**
Cherry Moon, Formation, Midnight Sky, Five Stone, Cactus & Jewel One **68**
Desert Storm **70**
Landing 200 Lamp **71**
Just Married **72**
Felted **73**
Cappello **74**
Hobo Lantern **75**
Cloud Softlight Mobile **76**
Tekio Light **77**
Honeycomb Lamp **78**
Icarus **79**
Study of Life **80**
Cone Light **81**
Cocoon Pendant Light **82**
Ondol Lamp **82**
Bloom Pendant Light **83**
Wooden Chandelier **84**
The Gudpaka Lamp **85**
Meshmatics **86**
Up in the Clouds **87**
M_Cocoon **88**
Butterfly Light **89**
Yaya **90**
Floor Chandelier **92**
Volume MGX **93**
Flight To Galway **94**
Duet Noir **96**
Singing Water **98**

RECYCLING & REUSE

One of the key components of the "reduce, reuse, recycle" waste hierarchy, recycling involves harnessing creative ideas and technology to process used materials or old objects and turn them into new products or artworks, creating new or natural aesthetic qualities in the process. The lights that appear in this section have been made by taking various recycled and waste materials, for example plastic bottles, cable ties, egg cartons, and polypropylene plastic bags, and reusing them to make cool designs.

BICYCLE WHEEL REFLECTOR CHANDELIER

DESIGNER
Nick Sayers

PHOTOGRAPHY
Nick Sayers

CLIENT
NickSayers.com

This reflective crystalline chandelier is made from sixty discarded bicycle-wheel reflectors. It's a luxury "glass" chandelier created from scrap!

FRA
Ce lustre réfléchissant, fabriqué à partir de soixante réflecteurs de roue de bicyclette mis au rebut, a l'air d'être
en pampilles de verre.

ESP
Esta araña cristalina reflectante se compone de sesenta reflectantes de ruedas de bicicleta desechados. ¡Se trata de una araña de "cristal" de lujo fabricada con chatarra!

POR
Este candelabro de cristal refletor é composto por sessenta refletores descartados de rodas de bicicleta. É um candelabro de "cristal" de luxo fabricado com sucata!

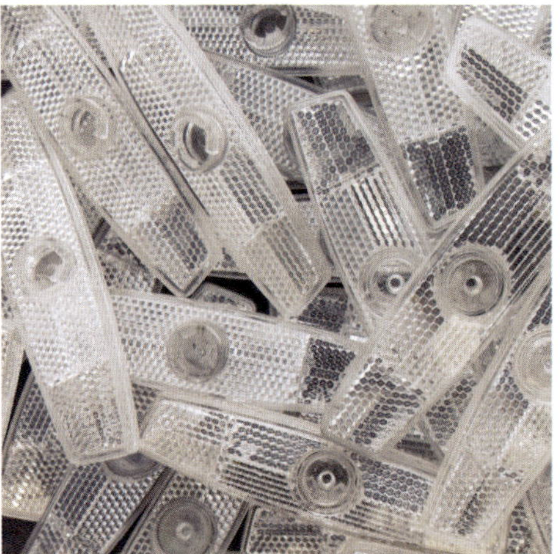

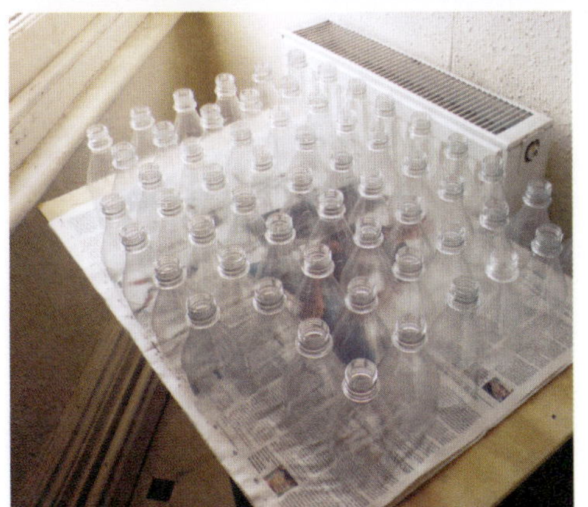

PLASTIC COKE BOTTLE LAMPSHADE

DESIGNER
Nick Sayers

PHOTOGRAPHY
Nick Sayers

CLIENT
NickSayers.com

This glassy lampshade was made from fifty-eight used plastic coke bottles, which were cut by hand and slotted together without using glue.

FRA
Il a fallu 58 bouteilles en plastique de Coca-Cola pour réaliser cet abat-jour. Elles ont été découpées à la main et assemblées sans utiliser de colle.

ESP
Esta pantalla cristalina está hecha con cincuenta y ocho botellas de plástico de Coca-Cola usadas y cortadas a mano que se ensamblan mediante ranuras, sin utilizar pegamento.

POR
Esta cúpula de cristal é feita com cinquenta e oito garrafas de plástico de Coca-Cola usadas e cortadas à mão montadas por meio de ranhuras, sem utilizar cola

WOVEN CABLE TIES LAMPSHADE

DESIGNER
Nick Sayers

PHOTOGRAPHY
Nick Sayers

CLIENT
NickSayers.com

This spherical lampshade was woven by hand, with no internal framework, from 526 cable ties. A standard energy-saving bulb fits inside the hollow central cluster of cable-tie heads.

FRA
Cet abat-jour sphérique, dépourvu d'armature, est composé de 526 attaches de câble tissées à la main. Au cœur de la sphère où convergent les boucles des attaches se trouve une douille standard pour ampoule à économie d'énergie.

ESP
Esta pantalla esférica está hecha a mano con 526 bridas, sin estructura interna de ninguna clase. En el núcleo hueco que forman los extremos de las bridas cabe una simple bombilla de bajo consumo.

POR
Esta cúpula esférica é feita à mão, com 526 cintas abraçadeiras, sem nenhuma estrutura interna. No núcleo vazio formado pelas extremidades das cintas abraçadeiras, cabe uma única lâmpada de baixo consumo.

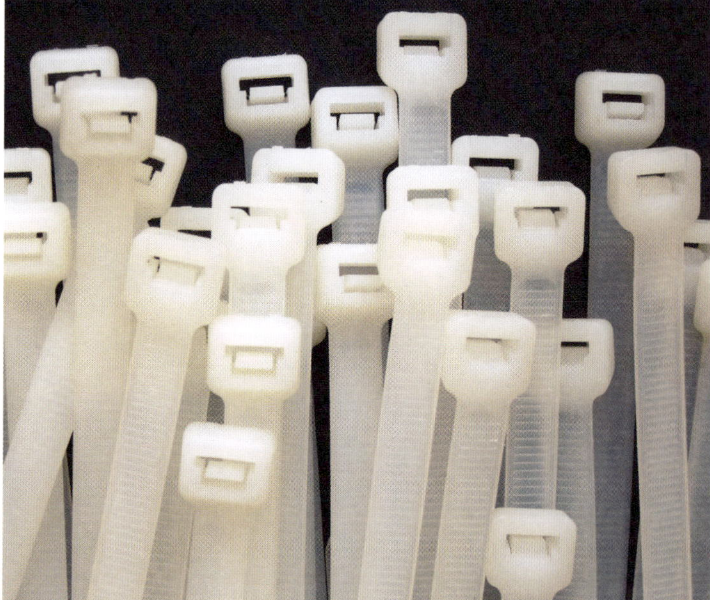

CLAMP

DESIGN FIRM
Enrico Zanolla Design Studio

DESIGNER
Enrico Zanolla

PHOTOGRAPHY
Enrico Zanolla

The inspiration for this suspension lamp comes from the pattern of a Chesterfield sofa. The contrast between the smooth interior and the sophisticated and deep, buttoned exterior is ideal for modern interior spaces with a touch of glamour and classic style. Clamp is made of two aluminum hemispheres—so it is therefore 100 percent recyclable—and natural leather, which decomposes more quickly than artificial plastic leather. A halogen bulb is used because of their energy-saving qualities, efficiency, and lifespan.
Materials: Leather, aluminum.

FRA
Le motif de ce lustre s'inspire du capitonnage des canapés chesterfield. Le contraste entre l'intérieur lisse et le capitonnage profond à bouton de l'extérieur s'intègre parfaitement aux décors modernes auxquels il ajoute une touche de glamour et de classicisme. Clamp est constitué de deux hémisphères en aluminium — il est donc 100% recyclable — et en cuir naturel qui se décompose beaucoup plus rapidement que sa version artificielle en skaï. Clamp utilise une ampoule halogène pour sa faible consommation, son efficacité et sa longue durée de vie

ESP
Esta lámpara colgante se inspira en el diseño de los sofás Chesterfield. El contraste entre la cara interna lisa y la cara externa sofisticada, mullida y abotonada, es especialmente adecuado para espacios interiores modernos con un toque de elegancia y estilo clásico. Clamp consiste en dos hemisferios de aluminio (así que es 100% reciclable) y piel natural, que se descompone mucho más deprisa que la de plástico. Además, utiliza una bombilla halógena, que ahorra energía y es eficiente y duradera.

POR
Esta luminária pendente inspira-se no design dos sofás Chesterfield. O contraste entre a face interna lisa e a externa sofisticada, fofa e com botões, é especialmente adequado para espaços interiores modernos com um toque de elegância e estilo clássico. A Clamp é constituída por dois hemisférios de alumínio (sendo assim 100% reciclável) e couro natural, que se decompõe muito mais rápido que o plástico. Além disso, utiliza uma lâmpada halógena, que economiza energia, é eficiente e duradoura.

MARIE-LOUISE, THERESE & JOSEPHINE

DESIGNER
Sander Mulder

PHOTOGRAPHY
Niels van Veen & Sander Mulder

Made from sixteen transparent contours illuminated by a dimmable fluorescent bulb, this floor lamp provides a modern reincarnation of the traditional ambient lamp. Through the use of special materials and accurate CNC-milling techniques, not only the hood section but the whole body of this fixture emits a magical light. This sophisticated design is part of a series of unique lighting fixtures that are guaranteed to catch the eye in any interior.

FRA
Ce lampadaire, formé de 16 pièces transparentes éclairées par une lampe fluorescente à intensité variable, est une version moderne de l'éclairage d'ambiance. Grâce à la particularité du matériau et à la découpe de précision des pièces au laser, le lampadaire émet une lumière magique aussi bien au niveau de l'abat-jour que du pied lui-même. Ce lampadaire au design très élaboré qui fait partie d'une série de luminaires originaux saura attirer les regards, quel que soit le décor choisi.

ESP
Esta lámpara de pie, confeccionada con dieciséis planos transparentes que se iluminan mediante una bombilla fluorescente regulable, representa la encarnación moderna de la tradicional lámpara de ambiente. Gracias al uso de materiales especiales y la precisión de una fresadora CNC, no solo la sección de la pantalla sino todo el cuerpo emite una luz mágica. Este sofisticado diseño forma parte de una serie de creaciones únicas que sin duda llamarán la atención en toda clase de interiores.

POR
Esta luminária, confeccionada com dezesseis planos transparentes iluminados por uma lâmpada fluorescente regulável, representa a encarnação moderna da tradicional luz ambiente. Graças ao uso de materiais especiais e à precisão de uma fresadora CNC, não só a secção da cúpula, mas todo o corpo emite uma luz mágica. Este sofisticado design faz parte de uma série de criações únicas que, sem dúvida, vão chamar a atenção em todo tipo de interiores.

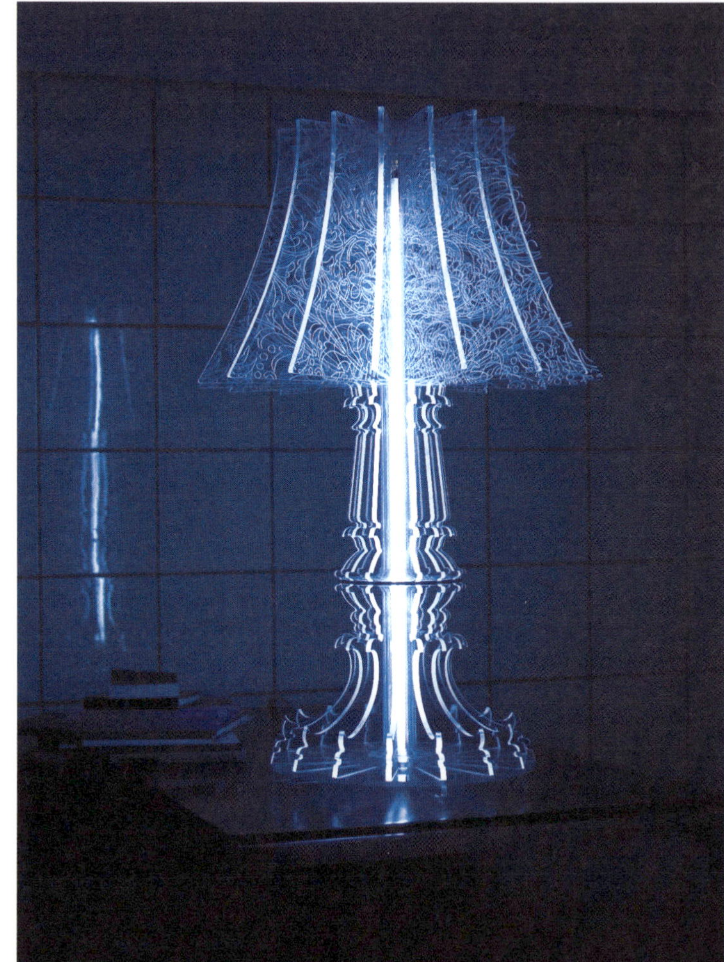

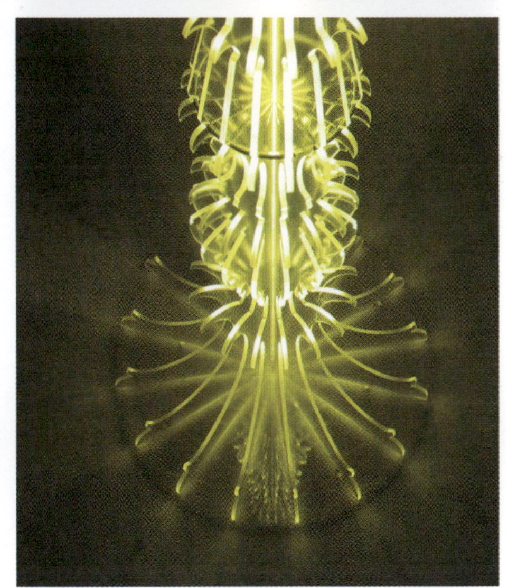

NEO3

DESIGNER
Svetlana Kozhenova

MANUFACTURER
Studio Šimánek Nicro

PHOTOGRAPHY
Dan Friedlaender

The lampshades in this project are made of recycled PCBs from Wi-Fi antennas, which offer high levels of heat resistance and strength as well as the right level of translucency. The PCBs' copper patterns also provide a ready-made technologically themed design. Their shape depends on the frequency the antenna works on and also the manufacturer of the antenna. Once the PCBs are assembled together an unexpected and functional artifact that resembles art styles such as Czech Cubism, Rondocubism, or Art Nouveau is born.

FRA
Les abat-jour présentés ici sont en biphényle polychloré (BPC) recyclé provenant d'antennes wi-fi, qui est une matière solide translucide résistant à la chaleur. Les plaques en cuivre fournissent un motif résolument moderne et prêt à l'emploi. Leur forme varie suivant la fréquence de l'antenne et le fabricant. Après le montage des différents éléments, on obtient un objet à la fois décoratif et fonctionnel dans un style rappelant le cubisme tchécoslovaque, le rondocubisme ou l'art nouveau.

ESP
Las pantallas de este proyecto están hechas con placas de PCB recicladas de antenas Wi-Fi, que tienen una notable fuerza y resistencia térmica, así como la transparencia adecuada. Además, ofrece una estética de inspiración tecnológica gracias a los diseños de cobre de las placas de PCB; estas formas dependen de la frecuencia y el fabricante de la antena. Cuando se ensamblan las placas de PCB nace una creación inesperada y funcional que recuerda a estilos artísticos como el cubismo checo, el rondocubismo o el *art noveau.*

POR
As cúpulas deste projeto são feitas com placas de PCB recicladas de antenas Wi-Fi, que possuem uma grande firmeza e resistência térmica, além de uma adequada transparência. Além disso, oferecem uma estética de inspiração tecnológica, graças aos desenhos de cobre das placas de PCB; estas formas dependem da frequência e do fabricante da antena. Quando se montam as placas de PCB, nasce uma criação inesperada e funcional que lembra estilos artísticos como o cubismo checo, o rondocubismo ou o *art noveau.*

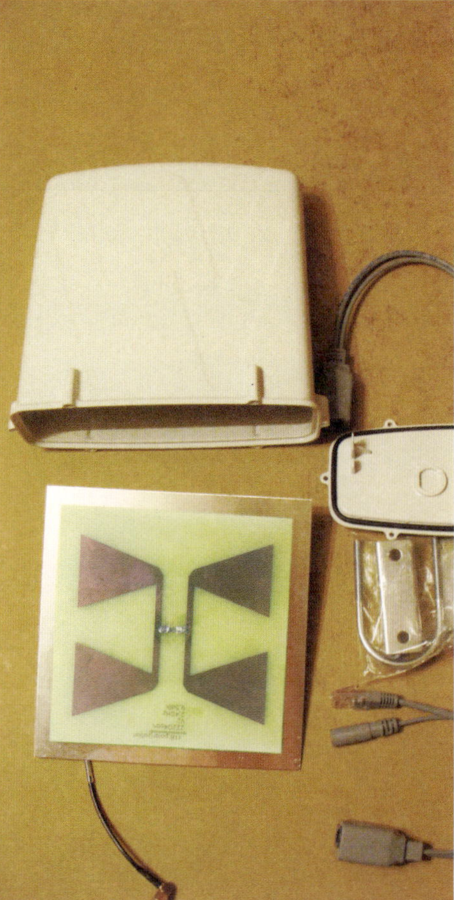

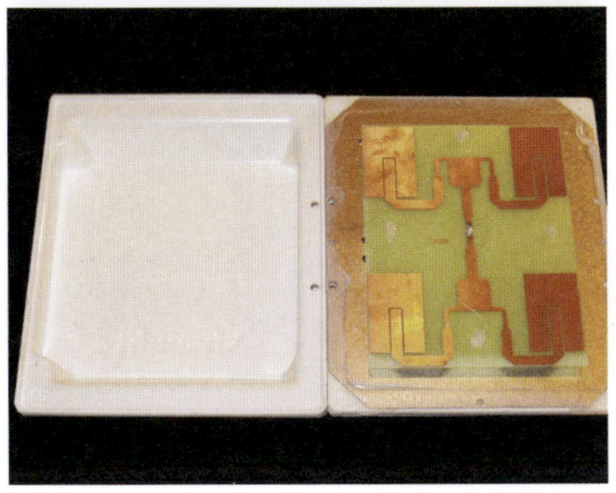

2,4 GHz

THE CONNECT SERIES

DESIGN FIRM
FACARO

DESIGNER
Carolina Fontoura Alzaga

PHOTOGRAPHY
Alan J. Crossley

The Connect Series consists of multiple, functional sculptures that take the form of traditional chandeliers made of recycled bicycle parts. Drawing inspiration from the aesthetics of chandeliers from the Victorian to modern eras, as well as DIY, punk, and bike culture, this developing body of work follows a tradition of using nontraditional art materials. This series addresses class codes, power dynamics, reclaimed agency, and ecological responsibility.

FRA
La série Connect propose différentes sculptures fonctionnelles ou lustres fabriqués à partir de pièces de vélo recyclées. La forme de ces lustres s'inspire de différents courants allant de l'ère victorienne à nos jours, en passant par les tendances punk, motard et « retour aux sources ». La collection combine des styles établis avec des matériaux non traditionnels. Elle mélange habilement codes sociaux, esthétiques ingénieuses et respect de l'environnement.

ESP
La serie Connect se compone de diversas esculturas funcionales que adoptan la forma de las arañas tradicionales, aunque de hecho están confeccionadas con piezas de bicicletas recicladas. Inspirándose en la estética de las arañas desde la época victoriana hasta los tiempos modernos, así como en la cultura DIY o *do it yourself* («hazlo tú mismo»), el punk y las bicicletas, esta serie de trabajos en desarrollo obedece a una tradición de materiales artísticos no convencionales y examina cuestiones tales como los códigos de clase, la dinámica del poder, el medio reciclado y la responsabilidad ecológica.

POR
A série Connect é composta por diversas esculturas funcionais que recebem a forma dos candelabros tradicionais, embora sejam de fato confeccionados com peças recicladas de bicicleta. Inspirando-se na estética dos candelabros desde a época vitoriana até os tempos modernos, como também na cultura DIY ou *do it yourself* («faça você mesmo»), o punk e as bicicletas, esta série de trabalhos em desenvolvimento segue uma tradição de materiais artísticos não convencionais e examina questões como, por exemplo, os códigos de classe, a dinâmica do poder, o meio reciclado e a responsabilidade ecológica.

CLOUD

DESIGN FIRM
Marques & Jordy Ltd

DESIGNER
Yu Jordy Fu

PHOTOGRAPHY
Arts Co London

CLIENT
London Bloomberg

Cloud is made by hand from recycled computer cables and LED lighting. A London Bloomberg commission by Yu Jordy Fu, this floating, thinking cloud sculpture was made with two thousand meters of waste computer cables that came from Bloomberg's London office.

FRA
Cloud est fabriqué à la main à partir de câbles d'ordinateur recyclés et d'éclairage LED. Yu Jordy Fu a utilisé deux mille mètres de vieux câbles d'ordinateurs provenant du bureau londonien de London Bloomberg qui lui avait confié le projet.

ESP
La lámpara Cloud está hecha a mano con cables de ordenadores reciclados y luces LED. Se trata de una escultura con forma de nube flotante y pensante, un encargo de Yu Jordy Fu para Bloomberg, se compone de dos mil metros de cables desechados obtenidos en la oficina de Bloomberg en Londres.

POR
A luminária Cloud é feita à mão com cabos reciclados de computadores e lâmpadas LED. É uma escultura em forma de nuvem flutuante e pensante, uma encomenda de Yu Jordy Fu para a Bloomberg, composta por dois mil metros de cabos descartados que foram obtidos no escritório da Bloomberg em Londres.

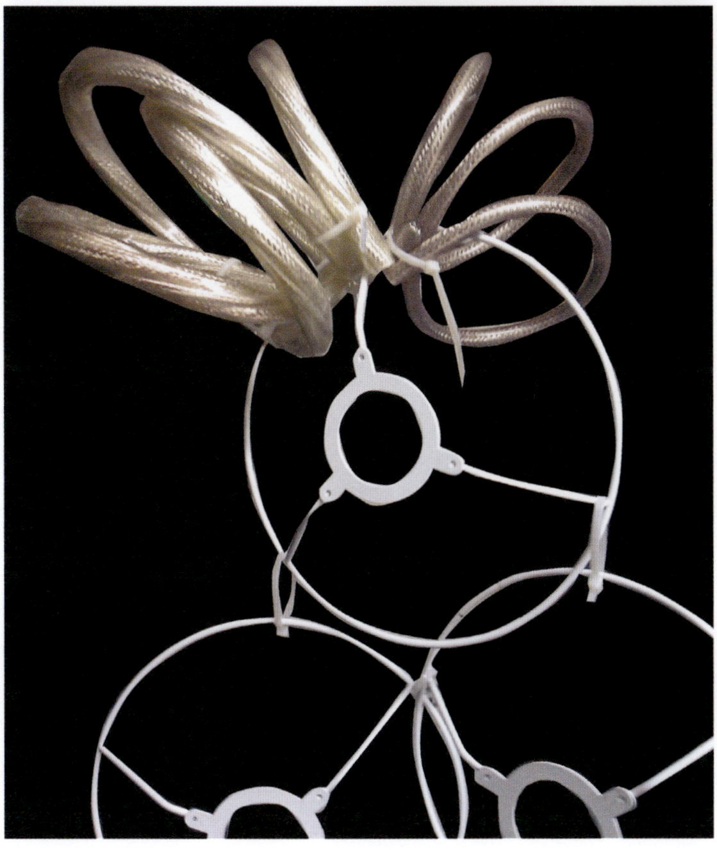

DUBBOT MODULAR

DESIGN FIRM
Steven Haulenbeek Design Concepts Inc.

DESIGNER
Steven Haulenbeek

PHOTOGRAPHY
Angie West

CLIENT
Steven Haulenbeek Design Concepts Inc.

These lights are designed for either deconstruction or deconstruction and reconstruction. They can be customized by their owner again and again to create new and interesting lighting scenarios. Every part, including the thermal-formed sheets and the fasteners used to hold the piece together, is made of one material: polypropylene. This means that when or if the user decides that the piece has reached the end of its life, it can be deconstructed and recycled in one fell swoop.

FRA

Ces lustres sont conçus pour être montés et démontés au gré des besoins et des désirs du client, afin de créer des décors nouveaux et originaux. Tous leurs éléments, y compris les feuilles thermoformées et les attaches qui les assemblent sont en polypropylène. Cela signifie que lorsque le client juge qu'un élément quelconque est arrivé en fin de vie, il peut simplement le démonter et le recycler dans la foulée.

ESP

Estas lámparas están diseñadas para la deconstrucción o la deconstrucción y la reconstrucción. El usuario puede personalizarlas una y otra vez, creándose de esta forma nuevas y sugerentes posibilidades. Hasta el último de los componentes, incluidas las planchas conformadas térmicamente y los corchetes que se emplean para mantenerlas unidas, está hecho exclusivamente de polipropileno, de manera que si el usuario decide que ha llegado al final de su vida puede deconstruirse y reciclarse de un solo golpe.

POR

Estas luminárias são projetadas para a desconstrução ou para desconstrução e reconstrução. O usuário pode personalizá-las várias vezes, criando assim novas e sugestivas possibilidades. Do primeiro até o último componente, incluídas as pranchas conformadas termicamente e os colchetes empregados para uni-las, todos são feitos exclusivamente de polipropileno, de modo que se o usuário decide que chegou ao fim de sua vida útil, pode ser desconstruído e reciclado imediatamente.

ZIP TIE LIGHT KIT

DESIGN FIRM
Steven Haulenbeek Design Concepts Inc.

DESIGNER
Steven Haulenbeek

PHOTOGRAPHY
Steven Haulenbeek

CLIENT
Steven Haulenbeek Design Concepts Inc.

The Zip Tie Light Kit represents the fruition of a conceptual thought process about customization and the involvement of the purchaser in the creation of an object. After purchasing a very reasonably priced, illustrated instruction manual, the purchaser collects the materials, which can be found almost anywhere, and constructs the piece on his or her own. Through this process the value of the lamp and the user's appreciation of it are increased because each one will be a bit different from the next.

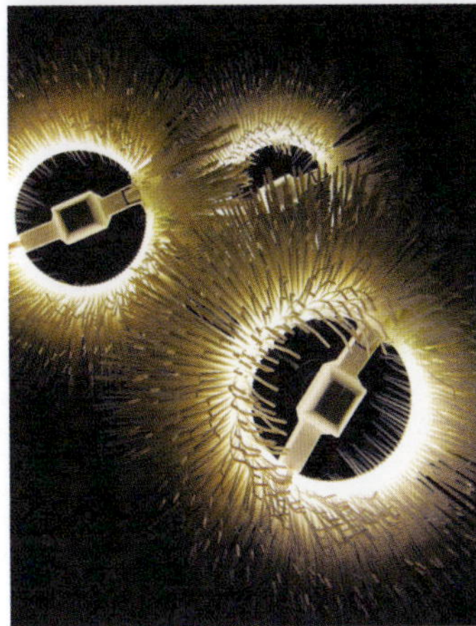

FRA
Le Zip Tie Light Kit est l'aboutissement d'un processus créatif qui laisse au client le soin d'élaborer le lustre de ses rêves, exactement tel qu'il l'imagine. Le client achète le kit à un prix raisonnable, accompagné d'un guide de montage illustré. Il se procure ensuite les différents éléments, disponibles presque partout, et construit le lustre de son choix. L'intérêt est que ce lustre sera d'autant plus apprécié qu'il sera unique en son genre et que le client aura la satisfaction de l'avoir créé lui-même.

ESP
Zip Tie Light Kit representa la culminación de un proceso conceptual sobre la personalización y la implicación del comprador en la creación de un objeto. Así, el comprador adquiere un manual de instrucciones ilustrado a un precio muy razonable, reúne los materiales necesarios, que se encuentran casi en todas partes, y monta la pieza él mismo. Gracias a este proceso aumentan el valor económico y sentimental de la lámpara, ya que cada una es ligeramente distinta de la siguiente.

POR
Zip Tie Light Kit representa o cume de um processo conceitual sobre a personalização e o envolvimento do comprador na criação de um objeto. Deste modo, o comprador adquire a um preço bem razoável um manual de instruções ilustrado, reúne os materiais necessários, que são facilmente encontrados em qualquer lugar, e ele mesmo monta a peça. Graças a este processo, aumentam os valores econômico e afetivo da luminária, já que cada uma delas é levemente diferente da seguinte.

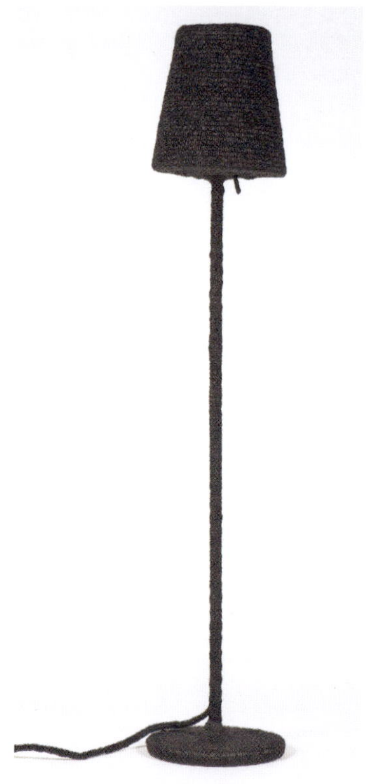

ILHAM, LAZARA & NAJAH

DESIGNER
Anne-Cécile Rappa

PHOTOGRAPHY
Anne-Cécile Rappa

Designed during her studies at the École cantonale d'art de Lausanne, this set of lamps by Anne-Cécile Rappa is created by recycling polypropylene plastic bags. The knits of the lamps are made by a collective of Berber woman in Morocco, while their structures are also made from recycled materials and the lampshades are made of buckets, garbage cans, and bowls. The height of the lamps can also be adjusted.

FRA
Anne-Cécile Rappa a conçu cette série de luminaires à partir de sacs plastiques en polypropylène lorsqu'elle était étudiante à l'École cantonale d'art de Lausanne. Le tricotage est réalisé par un collectif de femmes berbères du Maroc, les structures sont en matériaux recyclés et les abat-jour sont des seaux, des bidons et des bols de récupération. Les luminaires sont réglables en hauteur.

ESP
Esta serie de lámparas de Anne-Cécile Rappa, que las diseñó mientras cursaba sus estudios en la École cantonale d'art de Lausanne, está hecha con bolsas de plástico de polipropileno recicladas. Los nudos son obra de un colectivo de mujeres bereberes de Marruecos, mientras que las estructuras se componen de materiales reciclados y las pantallas están confeccionadas con cubos, papeleras y cuencos. Además, la altura de las lámparas es regulable.

POR
Esta série de luminárias de Anne-Cécile Rappa, desenhadas enquanto ela fazia os seus estudos na École cantonale d'art de Lausanne, é confeccionada com sacos de plástico de polipropileno reciclados. Os nós são obra de um conjunto de mulheres beribéris de Marrocos, as estruturas são compostas de materiais reciclados e as cúpulas são confeccionadas com baldes, cestos para papel e bacias. Além disso, a altura das luminárias é regulável.

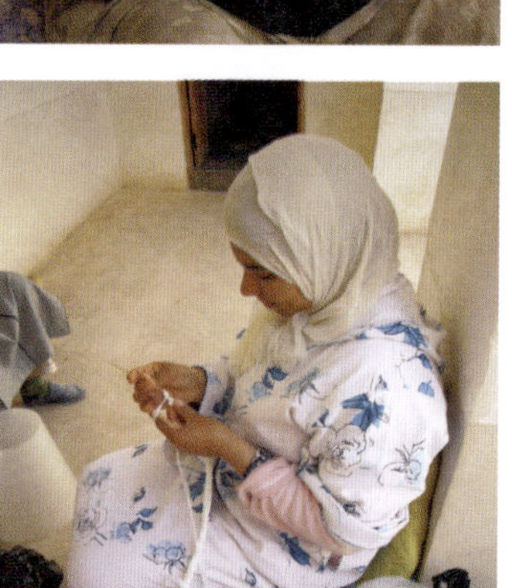

TRASH ME

DESIGN FIRM
The Office of Victor Vetterlein

DESIGNER
Victor Vetterlein

PHOTOGRAPHY
Victor Vetterlein

CLIENT
&Tradition

The intent of the Trash Me lamps project is to create a product that is born from the trash and returned to the trash after a short but useful life cycle. Each Trash Me lamp is created from paper egg cartons that are blended with water and poured over molds. At the end of its life, the Trash Me lamp can be quickly disassembled and the parts reused or recycled to be born again as something new.

ESP
El objetivo del proyecto Trash Me consiste en la creación de un producto que nace de la basura y regresa a ella al cabo de una vida efímera pero útil. Todas las lámparas Trash Me están hechas con cartones de huevo que se mezclan con agua y se depositan en moldes. Al final de su vida, la lámpara Trash Me se desmonta fácilmente y los componentes se reutilizan o se reciclan y renacen como algo nuevo.

FRA
L'idée des luminaires du projet Trash Me était de créer un produit à partir de rebuts qui finira lui-même au rebut après un cycle de vie tout aussi utile que court. Chaque luminaire Trash Me est créé avec du carton de boîtes à œufs mixé avec de l'eau puis versé dans des moules. En fin de vie, le luminaire se démonte aisément, et ses éléments constitutifs peuvent être réemployés ou recyclés pour créer de nouveaux objets.

POR
O objetivo do projeto Trash Me é a criação de um produto que nasce do lixo e regressa a ele ao fim de uma vida curta, porém útil. Todas as luminárias Trash Me são feitas de embalagens de ovos que se misturam com água e são colocadas em moldes. Ao final de sua vida, as luminárias Trash Me se desmontam facilmente e seus componentes são reutilizados ou reciclados e renascem como algo novo.

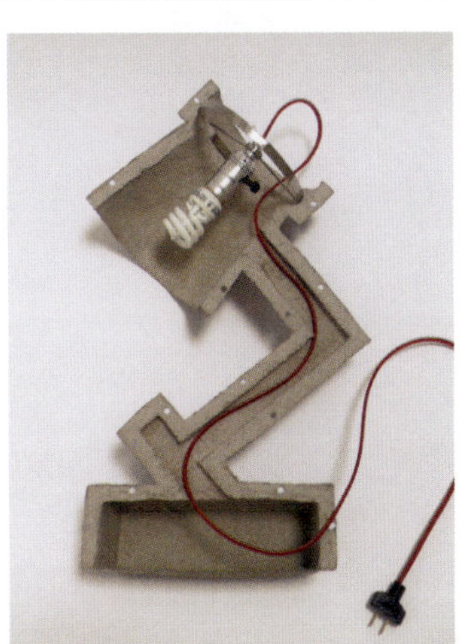

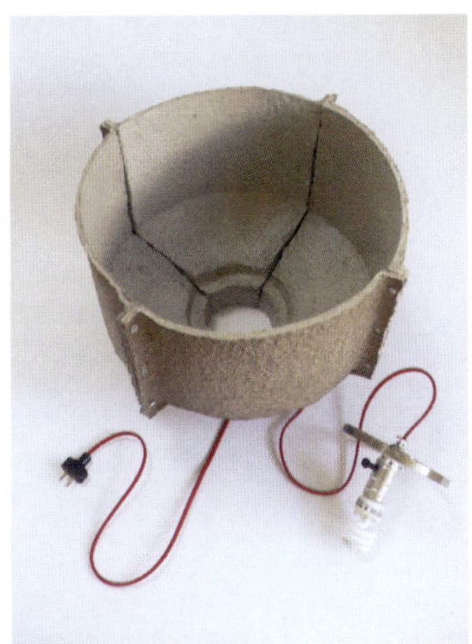

A FLIP FLOP STORY

DESIGN FIRM
Studio Schneemann

DESIGNER
Diederik Schneemann

The A Flip Flop Story collection is made out of lost or discarded flip-flops. Up to thirty thousand kilograms of them per year—mostly blue and pink ones—end up on the shores of Eastern Africa. The UniquEco initiative collects these flip-flops from the beaches, in the process keeping Kenyan beaches clean and helping local Kenyans to make a living. Studio Schneemann supports this initiative by turning, in collaboration with UniquEco, these polluting flip-flops into sustainable design products, ready to start a new life.

FRA

Les luminaires de la collection A Flip Flop Story sont créés avec des claquettes perdues ou mises au rebut. Sur les côtes de l'Afrique de l'est s'échouent chaque année 30 000 kilos de ce type de sandales — surtout des bleues et des roses. L'initiative UniquEco a pour mission de ramasser ces claquettes échouées, ce qui assure la propreté des plages et aide les Kenyans du coin à gagner leur vie. Le Studio Schneemann soutient cette initiative en convertissant ces objets polluants en produits design durables, prêts à démarrer une nouvelle vie.

ESP

La colección A Flip Flop Story se compone de sandalias desechadas o perdidas. Hasta tres toneladas de sandalias (sobre todo azules y rosas) acaban en las costas de África Oriental cada año. La iniciativa UniquEco las recoge y en el proceso mantiene las playas limpias y contribuye a que los kenianos de los alrededores se ganen la vida. Studio Schneemann, en colaboración con UniquEco, apoya esta iniciativa, convirtiendo estas sandalias contaminantes en productos de diseño sostenible con una nueva vida por delante.

POR

A coleção A Flip Flop Story é feita com sandálias descartadas ou perdidas. Cerca de três toneladas de sandálias (principalmente azuis e cor de rosa) chegam a cada ano às costas da África Oriental. A iniciativa UniquEco as recolhe e, nesse processo, mantém as praias limpas e contribui para que os quenianos dos arredores ganhem a vida. O Studio Schneemann, em colaboração com a UniquEco, apóia esta iniciativa, transformando essas sandálias contaminadoras em produtos de design sustentável com uma nova vida pela frente.

CLOUD WALK & LIQUID WINTER

DESIGN FIRM
Marques & Jordy Ltd

DESIGNER
Yu Jordy Fu

PHOTOGRAPHY
Marques & Jordy Ltd

CLIENT
London Design Museum

Cloud Walk and Liquid Winter are both hand made with recycled paper and LED lighting. Cloud Walk is a thirteen-meter-long, white, intricate, horizontal chandelier. It celebrates the spatial relationship between London and its people, as well as the existing, proposed, and imaginary London. Liquid Winter, meanwhile, is a London Design Museum commission that highlights the interplay between nature and the manmade world. The installation is made using identical, lightweight modular "ripples" that are inspired by the views inside and around the Design Museum.

FRA

Cloud Walk et Liquid Winter sont tous deux fabriqués en papier recyclé et équipés de LED. D'une longueur de trente mètres, Cloud Walk est un lustre horizontal blanc, de forme élaborée. Il célèbre la relation spatiale entre Londres et ses habitants, ainsi que celle entre la City réelle et celle que l'on imagine. Liquid Winter, pour sa part, est une commande du London Design Museum qui représente l'interaction entre la nature et les paysages créés par l'homme. L'installation est formée de plusieurs ondulations légères et modulaires identiques qui s'inspirent du décor du musée et du paysage environnant.

ESP

Cloud Walk y Liquid Winter están hechas a mano con papel reciclado y luces LED. Cloud Walk es una intrincada araña horizontal blanca de trece metros de largo que celebra la relación especial que existe entre Londres y sus habitantes, así como el Londres real, el imaginario y el que propone la diseñadora. Liquid Winter, en cambio, es un encargo del Museo de Diseño de Londres que subraya la interacción entre la naturaleza y el mundo manufacturado. La instalación se lleva a cabo mediante ligeras «ondas» modulares idénticas que se inspiran en el interior y los alrededores del Museo de Diseño.

POR

Cloud Walk e Liquid Winter são feitas à mão, com papel reciclado e lâmpadas LED. Cloud Walk é uma intrincada luminária horizontal branca, de treze metros de comprimento, que destaca a relação especial que existe entre Londres e seus habitantes, assim como a Londres real, a imaginária e a que é proposta pela designer. Liquid Winter, por sua vez, é uma encomenda do Museu de Design de Londres, que destaca a interação entre a natureza e o mundo manufaturado. A instalação é feita por meio de suaves «ondas» modulares idênticas que se inspiram no interior e nos arredores do Museu do Design.

CLOUD LAMPS

DESIGN FIRM
Marques & Jordy Ltd

DESIGNER
Yu Jordy Fu

PHOTOGRAPHY
Marques & Jordy Ltd.

Papercutting is a unique art form; Chinese women use this graceful and intricate technique to record the joy and surprises of their lives and decorate their homes. Yu Jordy Fu has developed this ancient technique to create expressive and elaborate forms which break free from the two-dimensional realm into a dreamlike three-dimensional landscape. Cloud Lamps are sustainable; the material is recycled paper, the method of production is handmade, and the product is to be used with energy-saving lightbulbs.

FRA
Le papier découpé est un art à part entière. Cette technique particulièrement élaborée et raffinée est utilisée par les Chinoises pour traduire les joies et les événements marquants de leur vie sous forme d'objets délicats qui décoreront leur maison. Yu Jordy Fu a utilisé cette technique très ancienne pour créer des formes expressives et sophistiquées qui s'échappent du monde en deux dimensions pour réaliser des paysages oniriques en relief. Les luminaires Cloud sont écologiques : elles sont fabriquées à la main avec du papier recyclé et utilisent des ampoules de basse consommation.

ESP
Los recortes son una forma de arte única; mediante esta delicada y compleja técnica las mujeres de China decoran sus casas y dejan constancia de las alegrías y las sorpresas que les depara la vida. Yu Jordy Fu ha desarrollado esta antigua técnica creando formas expresivas y elaboradas que se desmarcan del plano en dos dimensiones para adentrarse en un escenario onírico tridimensional. Las lámparas Cloud son sostenibles; están hechas de papel reciclado, se fabrican de forma artesanal y utilizan bombillas de bajo consumo.

POR
Os recortes são uma forma única de arte; por meio desta delicada e complexa técnica, as mulheres chinesas decoram suas casas e deixam registradas as alegrias e surpresas que a vida lhe traz. Yu Jordy Fu desenvolveu esta antiga técnica criando formas expressivas e elaboradas que se destacam do plano de duas dimensiones e adentram num cenário onírico tridimensional. As luminárias Cloud são sustentáveis; feitas de papel reciclado, fabricam-se de forma artesanal e utilizam lâmpadas de baixo consumo.

19 POTS

DESIGNER
Nir Meiri

PHOTOGRAPHY
Shay Ben Efrayim

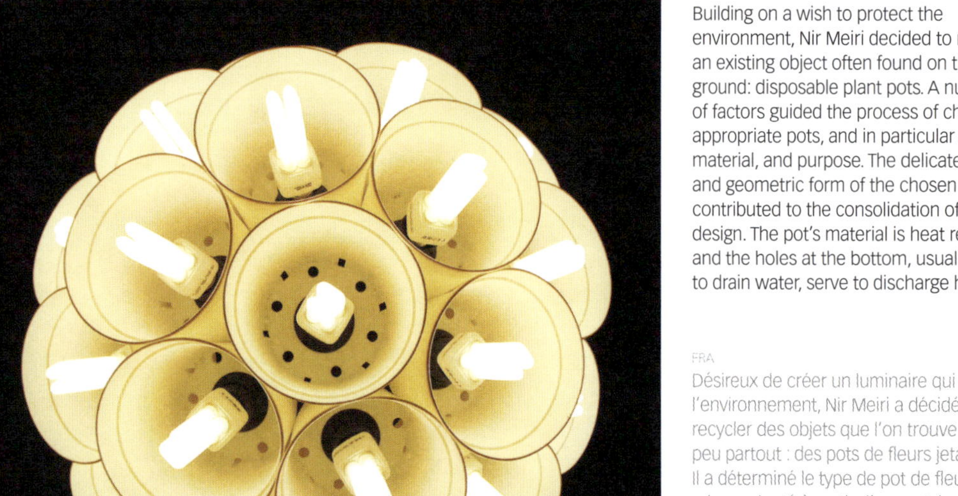

Building on a wish to protect the environment, Nir Meiri decided to recycle an existing object often found on the ground: disposable plant pots. A number of factors guided the process of choosing appropriate pots, and in particular shape, material, and purpose. The delicate and geometric form of the chosen pot contributed to the consolidation of the design. The pot's material is heat resistant, and the holes at the bottom, usually used to drain water, serve to discharge heat.

FRA

Désireux de créer un luminaire qui protège l'environnement, Nir Meiri a décidé de recycler des objets que l'on trouve un peu partout : des pots de fleurs jetables. Il a déterminé le type de pot de fleurs le mieux adapté à partir d'un certain nombre de critères, notamment, la forme, la matière et la fonction. L'aspect délicat et géométrique du style de pot qu'il a choisi s'intègre harmonieusement au design. La matière du pot résiste à la chaleur, et les perforations de sa base qui servent d'habitude à l'écoulement de l'eau permettent d'évacuer la chaleur.

ESP

Movido por el deseo de proteger el medio ambiente, Nir Meiri decide reciclar un objeto existente que suele encontrarse en el suelo: las macetas desechables. Una serie de factores intervienen en el proceso de selección de las macetas adecuadas, en especial la forma, los materiales y la función. La forma delicada y geométrica de las macetas escogidas contribuye a la consolidación del diseño. Los materiales de las macetas tienen una gran resistencia térmica; además, los orificios del fondo, que suelen destinarse al drenaje, sirven para descargar el calor.

POR

Movido pelo desejo de proteger o meio ambiente, Nir Meiri decide reciclar um objeto existente que costuma ser encontrado no chão: os potes descartáveis. Vários de fatores intervêm no processo de seleção dos potes adequados, especialmente o formato, os materiais e a função. O formato delicado e geométrico dos potes escolhidos contribui para consolidação do design. Os materiais dos potes possuem uma grande resistência térmica; além disso, os orifícios do fundo, que costumam servir para a drenagem, servem também para dispersar o calor.

WOOD LAMP

DESIGNER
Nir Meiri

PHOTOGRAPHY
Shay Ben Efrayim

Chipboard is mainly used for products that are perceived as "low-value" ones in terms of the quality of their materials and aesthetics, such as shipping crates. The guiding idea of this project was to reuse chipboard from a shipping crate—at which point it has almost reached the end of its life cycle—in a manner that will upgrade its value and render it usable. The design process prioritized the material's original characteristics and aesthetic fundamentals.

FRA
Le panneau de particules est employé principalement dans la fabrication de produits de qualité médiocre et peu esthétiques, comme les caisses de transport. L'idée directrice du projet était d'utiliser l'aggloméré de caisses de transport — alors qu'il est pratiquement en fin de vie utile —pour revaloriser cette matière et lui trouver un réemploi. La conception s'est focalisée sur la mise en valeur du matériau et l'esthétique.

ESP
El aglomerado se utiliza sobre todo en productos que se consideran «poco valiosos» en cuanto a la estética y la calidad de los materiales, como las cajas de embalaje. La idea que sustenta este proyecto consiste en reutilizar el aglomerado de una caja de embalaje (que en este punto casi ha llegado al final de su vida) de tal manera que se revalorice y adquiera una utilidad nueva. En el proceso de diseño se han respetado las características y los fundamentos estéticos de los objetos originales.

POR
O aglomerado é utilizado, principalmente, em produtos considerados «pouco valiosos» no que se refere à estética e à qualidade dos materiais como, por exemplo, as caixas de embalagem. A ideia em que este projeto se baseia é reutilizar o aglomerado de uma caixa de embalagem (que neste momento quase chegou ao final de sua vida) de tal maneira que se revalorize e adquira uma nova utilidade. No processo de design, respeitaram-se as características e os fundamentos estéticos dos objetos originais.

WASH LAMP

DESIGN FIRM
IDEA Design Studio

DESIGNER
Alex Kovatchev

PHOTOGRAPHY
Martin Kupenov

CLIENT
IDEA

The goal of this project was to create an aesthetically pleasing light fixture using as few new materials as possible. The outcome was the Wash Lamp, made out of the drums of old washing machines. The lamps can be used as a pendant, they can be fixed to a wall, or they can be used as an ottoman with the help of an upholstered seat that designer Alex Kovatchev made using salvaged leftover textiles from tapestry companies.

ESP
El objetivo de este proyecto consiste en la creación de una lámpara estéticamente agradable que utilice el menor número posible de materiales nuevos. El resultado es la lámpara Wash, fabricada con tambores de lavadoras viejas, que puede colgarse del techo, instalarse en una pared y hasta usarse a la manera de una otomana incorporando un asiento tapizado que el diseñador Alex Kovatchev ha confeccionado reciclando telas sobrantes de empresas textiles.

POR
O objetivo deste projeto consiste na criação de uma luminária esteticamente agradável que utilize o menor número possível de materiais novos. O resultado é a luminária Wash, fabricada com tambores de velhas máquinas de lavar, que pode ser pendurada no teto, instalada numa parede e até mesmo ser usada como otomana, incorporada a uma banqueta estofada que o designer Alex Kovatchev confeccionou reciclando tecidos de sobras de indústrias têxteis.

FRA
L'idée de ce projet était de créer un luminaire qui soit esthétique et utilise le moins possible de pièces neuves. Le résultat est Wash, fabriqué à partir du tambour d'une machine à laver : il peut être utilisé comme lustre ou applique murale, ou encore servir de pouf avec l'adjonction d'un coussin galette que le designer Alex Kovatchev a fabriqué à partir de tissus récupérés auprès de fabricants de tapisseries.

GLASS CHANDELIER

DESIGN FIRM
IDEA Design Studio

DESIGNER
Alex Kovatchev

PHOTOGRAPHY
Ivan Kolovoz

CLIENT
Lubomir Vassilev

The Glass Chandelier is an attempt at sleek upcycling. The challenge the client presented IDEA design studio with was to make a light fixture with a luxurious feel; it was designer Alex Kovatchev who added the extra challenge of upcycling as much of the fixture as possible. The concept the firm came up with was to use polished stainless steel for the base, which hides all the electrics, and the client's own wine glasses for the lightshades.

FRA
L'idée du lustre Glass repose sur une solution de recyclage créatif. Le défi proposé par le client à IDEA Design Studio était de créer un lustre écologique d'aspect glamour. C'est le designer Alex Kovatchev qui a choisi de pousser à l'extrême le concept de recyclage créatif. Le cabinet de design a conçu une base en acier inoxydable, qui masque toutes les connections électriques, et a utilisé les propres verres à vin du client comme abat-jour.

ESP
La araña Glass es un ejemplo de sobreciclaje elegante. El reto que ofrece el cliente al estudio de diseño IDEA consiste en la creación de una lámpara que tenga un aire lujoso; en esta empresa el diseñador Alex Kovatchev incorpora el desafío añadido de sobreciclarla todo lo posible. El estudio elabora entonces el concepto de una base de acero inoxidable pulido que oculta todos los componentes electrónicos y confecciona las pantallas con copas de vino del propio cliente.

POR
A luminária Glass é um exemplo de reciclagem elegante. O desafio que o cliente propôs ao Estúdio de design IDEA foi a criação de um candelabro que tivesse um ar luxuoso; neste empreendimento o designer Alex Kovatchev acrescenta o desafio suplementar de reciclar o máximo possível. O estúdio elabora então o conceito de uma base de aço inoxidável polido que oculta todos os componentes eletrônicos e confecciona as cúpulas com taças de vinho do próprio cliente.

OLEGAMI LAMP

DESIGN FIRM
IDEA Design Studio

DESIGNER
Oleg Vladimirov

PHOTOGRAPHY
Ivan Kolovoz

CLIENT
IDEA

IDEA Design Studio wanted to make a light fixture that would represent a break from the wastefulness of normal production processes and would be built from scratch with as few resources as possible. Soon enough a solution was proposed by Oleg Vladimirov. He found an origami shape that was very geometric and modern—ideal for the creation of this lamp. Using a simple recycled paper, the team then began the tedious task of folding each individual star and attaching it to the next without using glue.

FRA
IDEA Design Studio souhaitait mettre au point un lustre qui évite de générer des déchets, comme c'est le cas des méthodes de fabrication classiques, et de créer un produit de toute pièce avec le moins de ressources possibles. C'est Oleg Vladimirov qui a rapidement proposé une solution. Il a trouvé une forme origami à la fois géométrique et moderne qui était parfaitement adaptée au lustre que nous voulions créer. L'équipe a utilisé du papier recyclé pour former chaque étoile individuelle à partir de pliages soigneusement réalisés, les différents éléments étant ensuite fixés les uns aux autres sans employer la moindre colle.

ESP
El estudio de diseño IDEA quiere crear una lámpara que represente una ruptura con el despilfarro que acarrean los procesos de producción habituales y se construya desde cero empleando los menos recursos posibles. Oleg Vladimirov ofrece en seguida una solución, encontrando un diseño origami extraordinariamente geométrico y moderno idóneo para la creación de esta lámpara. El equipo se aplica entonces a la tediosa tarea de doblar cada una de las estrellas de papel reciclado y unirlas entre ellas sin utilizar pegamento.

POR
O Estúdio de design IDEA quer criar uma luminária que represente uma ruptura com o desperdício envolvido nos habituais processos de produção e que seja construída a partir do zero, empregando o mínimo de recursos possível. Oleg Vladimirov logo oferece uma solução, encontrando um origami com desenho extraordinariamente geométrico e moderno, apropriado para a criação desta luminária. A equipe se dedica então à aborrecida tarefa de dobrar cada uma das estrelas de papel reciclado e uni-las entre si, sem utilizar cola.

RELUMINE

DESIGN FIRM
mischer'traxler

DESIGNERS
Katharina Mischer & Thomas Traxler

PHOTOGRAPHY
mischer'traxler

CLIENT
Limited Editions by Engelhorn and Turkiewicz

Relumine plays on the switch from old lightbulbs to new, energy-saving light sources. Each Relumine uses two discarded lamps, which are disassembled, sanded, newly lacquered, and adapted with newer technology, before then being connected together by a glass cylinder that holds a fluorescent tube. By introducing a different type of light source to the old lamps, their look and feel changes completely. And together the two lamps need less energy than each one did in its previous life.

FRA

Relumine joue sur le passage des vieilles ampoules à incandescence aux nouvelles sources d'éclairage de basse consommation. Chaque Relumine utilise deux lampes de récupération qui ont été entièrement démontées, poncées, repeintes et équipées suivant les nouvelles normes électriques. Ces deux lampes sont ensuite réunies par un cylindre en verre contenant un tube fluorescent : ainsi adaptées, elles n'ont plus rien à voir avec ce qu'elles étaient au départ. En outre, toutes les deux ensemble consomment moins d'énergie que chacune d'elle ne le faisait séparément à l'époque des ampoules incandescentes.

ESP

Relumine se inspira en el paso de las antiguas bombillas a los nuevos dispositivos de bajo consumo. Se compone de dos lámparas desechadas que se desmontan, se lijan, se barnizan y se modernizan con tecnología más novedosa, antes de conectarse mediante un cilindro de cristal que contiene un tubo fluorescente. Cuando se introduce una fuente luminosa distinta en las lámparas viejas cambia por completo el aspecto y la sensación que estas transmiten. Y las dos lámparas juntas consumen menos energía que cada una de ellas por separado en su vida anterior.

POR

Relumine inspira-se na passagem das antigas lâmpadas de mesa aos novos dispositivos de baixo consumo. Compõe-se de duas luminárias descartadas que são desmontadas, lixadas, envernizadas e modernizadas com tecnologia mais atual, e depois são interligadas por meio de um cilindro de vidro que contém um tubo fluorescente. Quando se introduz uma fonte luminosa diferente nas velhas luminárias, muda por completo o aspecto e a sensação que elas transmitem. E as duas luminárias juntas consomem menos energia do que cada uma por separado em sua vida anterior.

SIX-PACK RING PENDANT LIGHTS

DESIGN FIRM
Relevé Design

DESIGNER
Bao-Khang Luu

PHOTOGRAPHY
Bao-Khang Luu

The Six-Pack Ring Pendant Lights collection draws inspiration from both modern shapes and natural forms found in plants. Each light uses between one hundred and four hundred postconsumer six-pack rings and weighs between four and twelve pounds. The six-pack rings are hand woven or strung onto metal rings using techniques that took over a year and a half to develop. At the end of its lifecycle, each lamp can be deconstructed easily for recycling or further upcycling.

FRA
La collection Six-Pack Ring s'inspire à la fois des luminaires modernes et des plantes. Chaque lustre utilise entre cent et quatre cents anneaux de canettes pour packs de 6 et pèse entre 1,8 kg et 5,5 kg. Les anneaux sont tissés entre eux à la main ou fixés à des cercles en métal suivant des techniques qui ont demandé plus d'un an et demi de mise au point. Un fois arrivé en fin de vie, chaque lustre peut se démonter facilement pour en recycler les pièces ou les réutiliser de manière créative.

ESP
La colección de lámparas colgantes Six-Pack Ring se inspira tanto en las formas modernas como en las formas naturales que se encuentran en las plantas. Cada una de ellas emplea entre cien y cuatrocientas redecillas de latas y pesa entre dos y seis kilos. Las redecillas se entrelazan artesanalmente o se insertan en anillos metálicos mediante técnicas desarrolladas durante más de un año y medio. Al término de su vida, las lámparas se deconstruyen fácilmente para reciclarlas o sobreciclarlas de nuevo.

POR
A coleção de luminárias pendentes Six-Pack Ring inspira-se tanto nas formas modernas como nas formas naturais encontradas nas plantas. Cada uma delas emprega entre cem e quatrocentas redinhas de lata e tem um peso de dois a seis quilos. As redinhas se entrelaçam artesanalmente ou se inserem em anéis metálicos por meio de técnicas desenvolvidas durante mais de um ano e meio. Ao fim de sua vida, as luminárias são desconstruídas facilmente para serem recicladas ou sub recicladas de novo.

BEUTE

DESIGN FIRM
Herrwolke

DESIGNER
Michael Konstantin Wolke

PHOTOGRAPHY
Michael Konstantin Wolke

In making use of the sort of corrugated cardboard that can only be found in discarded materials, Beute becomes a selection of inimitable light objects. After dissecting the discarded materials, Michael Konstantin Wolke compresses the conquered corrugated cardboard and uses it as raw material with unique characteristics.

FRA
Dans la série Beute fabriquée à partir de carton ondulé de récupération, il n'y a pas deux lustres identiques. Une fois que le carton ondulé a été récupéré sur des objets mis au rebut, Michael Konstantin Wolke le comprime avant de l'utiliser comme matière première d'une indéniable originalité.

ESP
Beute utiliza el cartón ondulado que solo se encuentra en los materiales desechados, convirtiéndose en una selección inimitable de objetos luminosos. Michael Konstantin Wolke disecciona estos materiales, comprime el cartón ondulado y lo emplea como materia prima con características únicas.

POR
Beute utiliza o papelão ondulado que só se encontra nos materiais descartados, convertendo-o numa seleção inimitável de objetos luminosos. Michael Konstantin Wolke disseca estes materiais, comprime o papelão ondulado e o emprega como matéria prima com características únicas.

STAMEN & PETALS

DESIGN FIRM
g.+

DESIGNER
Daisuke Hiraiwa

PHOTOGRAPHY
Daisuke Hiraiwa

The inspiration of these two lampshades came from the structure of flowers and Daisuke Hiraiwa's attempts to construct artificial-flower lighting from everyday objects. Daisuke hit on the idea of using toothpicks to capture the flexible movements of sunflower heads, and also saw in disposable, transparent plastic spoons a resemblance to flower petals. The shapes of both lights can be rearranged after installation.

FRA

Ces deux abat-jour s'inspirent de la structure de certaines fleurs que Daisuke Hiraiwa a essayé d'imiter en utilisant des objets de tous les jours. Le designer a choisi des cure-dents pour représenter le mouvement giratoire du tournesol et des cuillères jetables en plastique transparent qui rappellent des pétales. La forme de ces deux lustres peut être modifiée après installation.

ESP

Estas dos pantallas se inspiran en la estructura de las flores, así como en el empeño de Daisuke Hiraiwa de crear lámparas de flores artificiales empleando objetos cotidianos. Así se le ocurre la idea de capturar los flexibles movimientos de las cabezas de los girasoles mediante palillos. Además, encuentra en las cucharas desechables transparentes una semejanza con los pétalos de las flores. Se puede cambiar la forma de ambas lámparas después de instalarlas.

POR

Estas duas cúpulas inspiram-se na estrutura das flores, bem como na dedicação de Daisuke Hiraiwa em criar luminárias de flores artificiais empregando objetos cotidianos. Desta maneira, ele teve a ideia de capturar os flexíveis movimentos das cabeças dos girassóis por meio de palitos. Além disso, ele enxerga nas colheres transparentes descartadas uma semelhança com as pétalas das flores. Pode-se mudar a forma de ambas as luminárias depois de instaladas.

MUDLIGHT

DESIGN FIRM
Studio Dik Scheepers

DESIGNER
Dik Scheepers

PHOTOGRAPHY
Dik Scheepers

Designer Dik Scheepers's assignment was to make an eco chandelier. These are two words that don't usually go well together. Eco implies a certain awareness of the environment, while a chandelier consumes a lot of energy when in use. In response to the challenge Scheepers chose to make simple models of lampshades out of adobe, a material that does not consume much energy and is available everywhere.

FRA
La mission du designer Dik Scheepers était de créer un lustre écologique. Ce n'était pas gagné d'avance dans le sens ou écologie rime avec économie d'énergie alors qu'un lustre consomme beaucoup de courant lorsqu'il est allumé. La solution trouvée par Dik Scheepers a été de fabriquer des abat-jour de forme simple en adobe, qui est un matériau peu gourmand en énergie et qui est disponible partout.

ESP
El diseñador Dik Scheepers recibe el encargo de crear una araña ecológica, aunque estas dos palabras no suelen casar bien. El concepto «ecológico» implica que se tiene cierta consciencia del medio ambiente y una araña consume mucha energía. En respuesta a este desafío, Scheepers diseña sencillos modelos de pantallas con adobe, un material que no consume demasiada energía y se encuentra en todas partes.

POR
O designer Dik Scheepers recebe a incumbência de criar uma luminária ecológica, ainda que essas duas palavras não costumem casar bem. O conceito «ecológico» pressupõe que se tenha certa consciência do meio ambiente, mas uma luminária consome muita energia. Como resposta a este desafio, Scheepers projeta modelos simples de cúpulas com argila, um material que não consome muita energia e pode ser encontrado em todos os lugares.

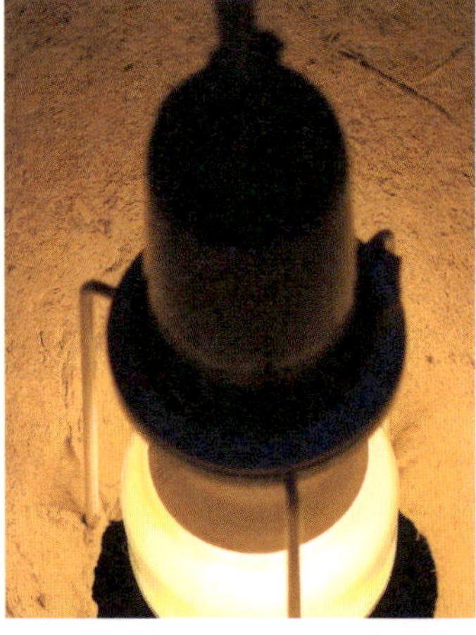

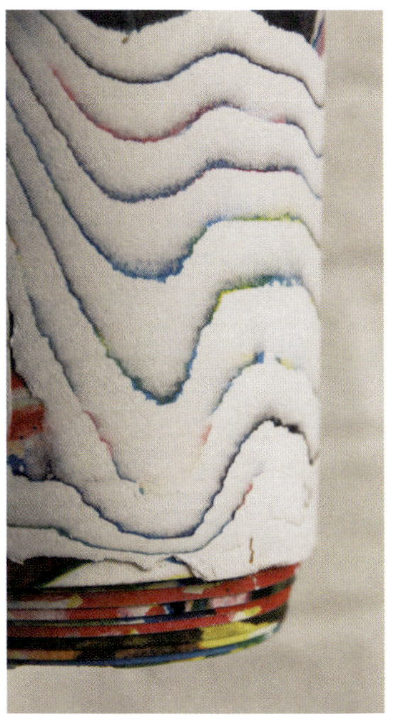

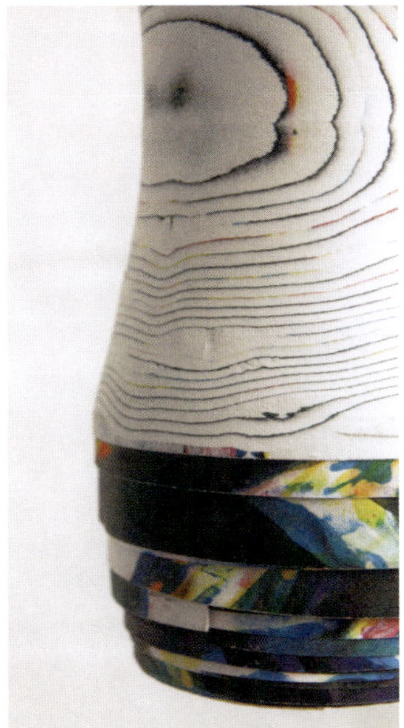

PAPER LIGHT

DESIGN FIRM
Piadesign

DESIGNER
Pia Wüstenberg

PHOTOGRAPHY
Pia Wüstenberg

CLIENT
Utopia and Utility

This project explores the properties of the materials used to make the Paper Light through adopting a variety of processing methods and experimenting with different structural and aesthetic compositions. The Paper Light's aesthetics are as much determined by the paper used to make the light's raw materials as the way those materials are worked. All the paper used in making the Paper Light is collected from paper recycling bins or donated by printing companies. The final piece is made using rolled paper and LED lights.

FRA

Pour ce projet nous avons étudié les propriétés des matériaux intervenant dans la fabrication du lustre Paper Light en testant différentes méthodes de production et combinaisons structurelles et esthétiques. L'aspect du lustre Paper Light dépend autant du papier utilisé comme matière première que de la façon de le travailler. À noter que le papier employé pour fabriquer les lustres Paper Light est collecté dans les conteneurs de recyclage ou donné par des imprimeries. Le produit fini est enroulé au tour puis équipé de LED.

ESP

Este proyecto ahonda en las propiedades de los materiales que se emplean, adoptando diversos métodos de procesamiento y experimentando con distintas composiciones estructurales y estéticas. Así, la estética de la lámpara está determinada por el papel que constituye la materia prima y la forma en la que este se trabaja. Todo el papel que se ha utilizado en la fabricación de Paper Light se ha obtenido en contenedores de papel reciclado o ha sido donado por imprentas. La pieza definitiva está hecha con papel enrollado y luces LED.

POR

Este projeto aprofunda nas propriedades dos materiais empregados, adotando diversos métodos de processamento e fazendo experiências com diversas composições estruturais e estéticas. Assim, a estética da luminária é determinada pelo papel, o qual constitui a matéria prima, e pela forma de trabalhá-lo. Todo o papel utilizado na fabricação da Paper Light foi obtido em recipientes de papel reciclado ou foi doado por gráficas. A peça definitiva é feita com papel enrolado e com lâmpadas LED.

PINHA

DESIGN FIRM
Raw-Edges

DESIGNERS
Yael Mer & Shay Alkalay

PHOTOGRAPHY
Shay Alkalay

CLIENT
Materia Amorim

Pinha proposes a playful approach to lighting through personalization. This hanging lamp consists of a cork outer fixture, to which a printed-paper shade is fastened. You have the last word on how Pinha looks by choosing the shade from different patterns and drawings. In terms of functions, you can also decide on the direction and range of the light, according to where the shade is pinned. Cork's low thermal and electrical conductivity ensures that handling the lamp's shell is perfectly safe.

FRA

Pinha propose une approche amusante qui offre au client la possibilité de personnaliser le lustre. Pinha consiste en une cloche en liège formée de deux parties qui s'emboîtent et sur laquelle vient se fixer l'abat-jour en papier décoré. C'est le client qui choisit la touche finale de Pinha parmi les différents tons et motifs proposés. Il peut également changer l'orientation et la taille du faisceau lumineux suivant l'emplacement choisi. Le liège étant une matière à faible conduction thermique et électrique, la manipulation de la cloche ne présente aucun danger.

ESP

Pinha ofrece una visión divertida de las lámparas a través de la personalización. Esta lámpara colgante consiste en un accesorio externo de corcho al que se incorpora una pantalla de papel estampado. Pero el usuario es quien tiene la última palabra sobre la apariencia de Pinha, puesto que escoge la pantalla entre una serie de ilustraciones y estampados. Además, en términos de funciones, también decide la dirección y el alcance de la luz, en función de la posición en la que se coloca la lámpara. Gracias a la escasa conductividad eléctrica y térmica del corcho, manipular la carcasa es absolutamente seguro.

POR

Pinha oferece uma visão divertida das luminárias através da personalização. Esta luminária pendente é composta por um acessório externo de cortiça ao qual se incorpora uma cúpula de papel estampado. Porém, é o usuário quem tem a última palavra a respeito da aparência da Pinha, pois é ele quem escolhe a cúpula dentre uma série de ilustrações e estampados. Além disso, em termos de funções, ele também decide a direção e o alcance da luz, em função da posição em que a luminária for colocada. Graças à baixa condutividade elétrica e térmica da cortiça, o manuseio da carcaça é algo absolutamente seguro.

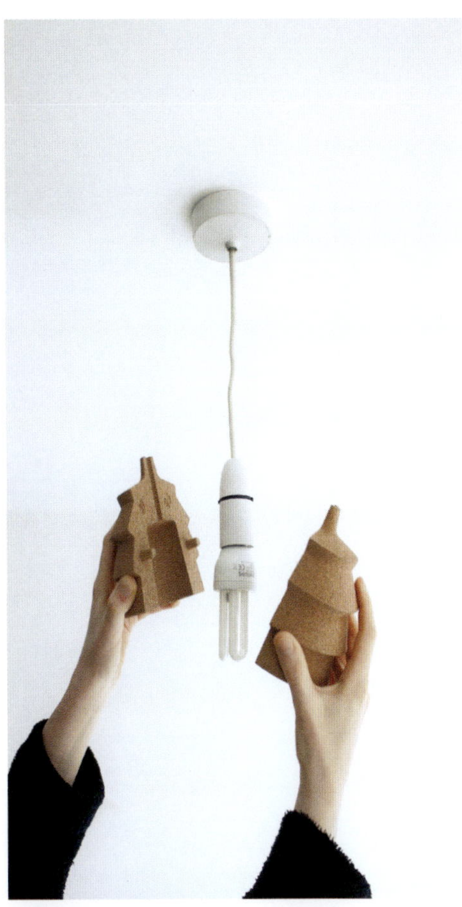

WILLESDEN JUNCTION
Kensal Green
North Acton
East Acton
West Acton
EALING COMMON
ACTON TOWN
Chiswick Park
Turnham Green
Gunnersbury

50% SAWDUST

DESIGN FIRM
Kulla Studio

DESIGNERS
Adi Shpigel & Keren Tomer

PHOTOGRAPHY
Aviv Kurt

Kulla Studio's research into raw materials has led to the development of a new technique that combines two different worlds of waste: wooden sawdust and plastic bags. This new material and its method of production were developed through the manipulation of sawdust in an effort to introduce new qualities to the material. The result of Kulla Studio's innovation is a firm, structurally strong, aesthetically new material that allows the two original materials to be reused, thus prolonging their life.

FRA

Les recherches de Kulla Studio sur les matériaux bruts ont débouché sur la mise au point d'une nouvelle technique qui associe deux produits recyclés complètement différents, à savoir la sciure de bois et le sac en plastique. C'est en cherchant à modifier les propriétés de la sciure que le studio a créé cette nouvelle matière et la méthode de production associée. Le produit résultant est un matériau novateur à la fois solide et esthétique qui permet le réemploi des deux matières d'origine et le rallongement de leur durée de vie.

ESP

La investigación de Kulla Studio sobre las materias primas ha dado como resultado el desarrollo de una nueva técnica que combina dos mundos distintos de residuos: el serrín y las bolsas de plástico. Este nuevo material, así como el método de producción que comporta, se ha desarrollado manipulando el serrín en un intento de aportarle cualidades nuevas. El resultado de la innovación de Kulla Studio es un material estéticamente novedoso, resistente y estructuralmente fuerte que permite que se reutilicen los dos materiales originales, prolongando de esta forma su vida.

POR

A pesquisa de Kulla Studio sobre as matérias primas teve como resultado o desenvolvimento de uma nova técnica que combina dois universos distintos de resíduos: a serragem e os sacos de plástico. Este novo material, bem como o seu método de produção, foram desenvolvidos com a manipulação da serragem, tentando conferir-lhe novas qualidades. O resultado da inovação de Kulla Studio é um material esteticamente inovador, resistente e estruturalmente forte, que permite que se reutilizem os dois materiais originais, prolongando desta forma a sua vida.

REPLAY

DESIGN FIRM
The Office of Victor Vetterlein

DESIGNER
Victor Vetterlein

PHOTOGRAPHY
Victor Vetterlein

This project began by scavenging building materials from a trash dumpster at a local construction site and then reconfiguring the pieces into a useful object. The lamp is composed of oriented strand board (OSB), a concrete brick, and concrete board. A reused standard lighting fixture that accepts screw-in CFL or LED bulbs and a cloth electrical cord with switch and plug complete this new, hybrid design.

FRA
Ce projet a démarré avec la récupération de matériaux de construction dans une benne à ordures d'un chantier voisin et l'assemblage de différentes pièces pour créer un objet utilitaire. Le corps de la lampe est constitué de pièces en panneau de particules orientées et d'une briquette en béton. Il est équipé d'une douille à vis pour lampe fluocompacte ou à LED, d'un cordon électrique recouvert de tissu, d'un interrupteur et d'une prise. Le résultat est un objet hybride particulièrement original.

ESP
Al comienzo de este proyecto se rebuscaron materiales de construcción en los contenedores de basura de una obra cercana y se reconfiguraron estos componentes con el fin de transformarlos en objetos útiles. Así, la lámpara se compone de tableros de tiras orientadas (en inglés, OSB), un bloque de hormigón y un panel del mismo material. Este novedoso diseño híbrido se completa con un casquillo estándar reutilizado que acepta bombillas de rosca CFL o LED y un cable eléctrico trenzado con interruptor y enchufe.

POR
No início deste projeto, cataram-se materiais de construção nos recipientes de lixo de uma obra próxima e se reconfiguraram esses componentes com a finalidade de transformá-los em objetos úteis. Desse modo, a luminária é composta por tabuleiros de tiras orientadas (em inglês, OSB), um bloco de concreto e um painel do mesmo material. Este inovador design híbrido se completa com um soquete padrão reutilizado que aceita lâmpadas de rosca CFL ou LED e um fio elétrico trançado, com interruptor e tomada.

97% SOAP

DESIGN FIRM
d-VISION

DESIGNER
d-VISION

PHOTOGRAPHY
Guy Hecht

LEDs are extremely energy efficient, can last for up to seventeen years, and are also cool to the touch as very little energy is emitted as heat. It was this last quality that enabled d-VISION to create a lamp using a material with a low melting temperature. They came up with the idea of making a lamp out of soap after recognizing its high potential for creating a dimming effect. And as a biodegradable material soap is very environmentally friendly.

FRA

Les diodes électroluminescentes sont écoénergétiques : elles peuvent durer jusqu'à 17 ans, et sont froides au toucher car elles n'émettent que très peu de chaleur. C'est cette dernière qualité qui a permis à d-VISION de créer une lampe dans une matière ayant un point de fusion bas. Ils ont eu l'idée d'utiliser du savon parce que cette matière tamise admirablement la lumière. Par ailleurs, c'est un produit biodégradable et donc respectueux de l'environnement.

ESP

Las luces LED son extremadamente eficientes desde el punto de vista energético, ya que duran hasta diecisiete años, y son frías al tacto porque apenas emiten energía en forma de calor. Gracias a esta última característica, d-VISION ha creado una lámpara con un material que tiene una baja temperatura de fusión. La idea de crear una lámpara de jabón surge cuando los diseñadores reconocen su gran potencial para producir un efecto de atenuación. Y como además es biodegradable, el jabón es muy respetuoso con el medio ambiente.

POR

As lâmpadas LED são extremamente eficientes do ponto de vista energético, pois duram até dezessete anos e são frias ao tato porque quase não emitem energia em forma de calor. Graças a esta última característica, d-VISION criou uma luminária com um material que tem baixa temperatura de fusão. A ideia de criar uma luminária de sabão surge quando os designers reconhecem o seu grande potencial de produzir um efeito de atenuação. E como, além disso, é biodegradável, o sabão é respeita muito o meio ambiente.

ARIA

DESIGNER
Marcel Kieser & Christof Spath

PHOTOGRAPHY
Kristof Lemp

Aria is a classic textile balloon light. The textile creates a warm, atmospheric, and diffuse light suited not only for living and dining rooms but also for bars and lounges. The voluminous textile body is available with crinkled or even surfaces. The body gets its tension through the spring steel between the plastic rings. Aria follows cradle-to-cradle principles and all of its parts can be recycled separately.

FRA
Aria est un lustre fabriqué dans le tissu dont ont fait les aérostats. C'est une matière qui procure une lumière chaude et diffuse convenant aussi bien à un salon ou une salle à manger qu'à un bar ou un café. Le tissu recouvrant le grand volume de l'abat-jour existe en version lisse ou froissé. Les baleines en acier reliées par les anneaux en plastique assurent la tension du tissu. Aria est un lustre écologique dont tous les éléments peuvent se recycler séparément.

ESP
Aria es una clásica lámpara globo de tela. Gracias a esta tela se obtiene una luz cálida, atmosférica y difusa que no solo es idónea para salones y comedores sino también para cafeterías y bares. El voluminoso cuerpo de tela está disponible con superficies rugosas o lisas. La tensión del cuerpo se debe al resorte de acero instalado entre las anillas de plástico. Aria sigue los principios «de la cuna a la cuna» y todos sus componentes se reciclan por separado.

POR
Aria é uma clássica luminária globo de tecido. Graças a este tecido, obtém-se uma luz cálida, atmosférica e difusa, que não só é apropriada para salões e salas de jantar, mas também para cafeterias e bares. O volumoso corpo de tecido está disponível com superfícies rugosas ou lisas. A tensão do corpo é resultante da mola de aço instalada entre os anéis de plástico. Aria segue os princípios «do berço a berço» e todos os seus componentes são reciclados separadamente.

KOZO LAMP

DESIGN FIRM
Kozo Lamp

DESIGNER
David Shefa & Anati Shefa

PHOTOGRAPHY
Guy Gilad

Kozo Lamps are constructed out of galvanized iron, which is best known for its rustproof quality. Designing with upcycled materials is a challenge, but succeeding with doing so brings great satisfaction and benefits both people and our beautiful planet. A beautiful touch of rust may form over time along the edges of the pipes, where the iron is not coated, and add an authentic touch to the unique story of the upcycled design. Kozo Lamps are turned on and off by the innovative faucet light switch, which makes using them authentic and fun.

FRA

Les articles de la collection Kozo sont fabriqués en fer galvanisé, matière connue pour sa résistance à la rouille. La conception des lampes repose sur le recyclage créatif qui pose un certain nombre de défis mais profite à la fois aux individus et à la planète dans son ensemble. Au fil du temps, il est possible qu'un léger voile de rouille apparaisse sur les arêtes des tuyaux, là où le métal n'est pas galvanisé : ce sera une marque supplémentaire d'authenticité signalant l'origine de ces produits issus du recyclage créatif. Pour allumer ou éteindre une lampe Kozo, il faut ouvrir ou fermer le robinet. Voilà un interrupteur amusant, résolument pas comme les autres !

ESP

Las lámparas Kozo están hechas con hierro galvanizado, que como todos sabemos es inoxidable. El diseño con materiales sobreciclados representa un desafío, pero el triunfo reporta una gran satisfacción y es beneficioso tanto para nuestro hermoso planeta como para quienes lo habitamos. Es posible que con el paso de los años se forme un bonito toque de óxido en los contornos de las cañerías, donde el hierro no está recubierto, que aportaría un toque de autenticidad a la extraordinaria historia del diseño sobreciclado. Las lámparas Kozo se encienden y se apagan mediante un novedoso interruptor en forma de grifo, lo que hace que usarlas sea auténtico y divertido al mismo tiempo.

POR

As luminárias Kozo são feitas de ferro galvanizado, o qual, como sabemos, é inoxidável. O design com materiais reciclados implica num desafio, mas o triunfo traz uma grande satisfação e beneficia tanto ao nosso lindo planeta como a todos nós, seus habitantes. É possível que, com o passar dos anos, acabe se formando um bonito toque de óxido nos contornos dos canos, onde o ferro não está recoberto, o que dará um toque de autenticidade à extraordinária história do design reciclado. As luminárias Kozo se acendem e apagam por meio de um inovador interruptor em forma de torneira, tornando o seu uso autêntico e, ao mesmo tempo, divertido.

B-CHAIN LAMP

DESIGN FIRM
dialoguemethod

DESIGNER
Hyung Suk Cho

PHOTOGRAPHY
Hyung Suk Cho

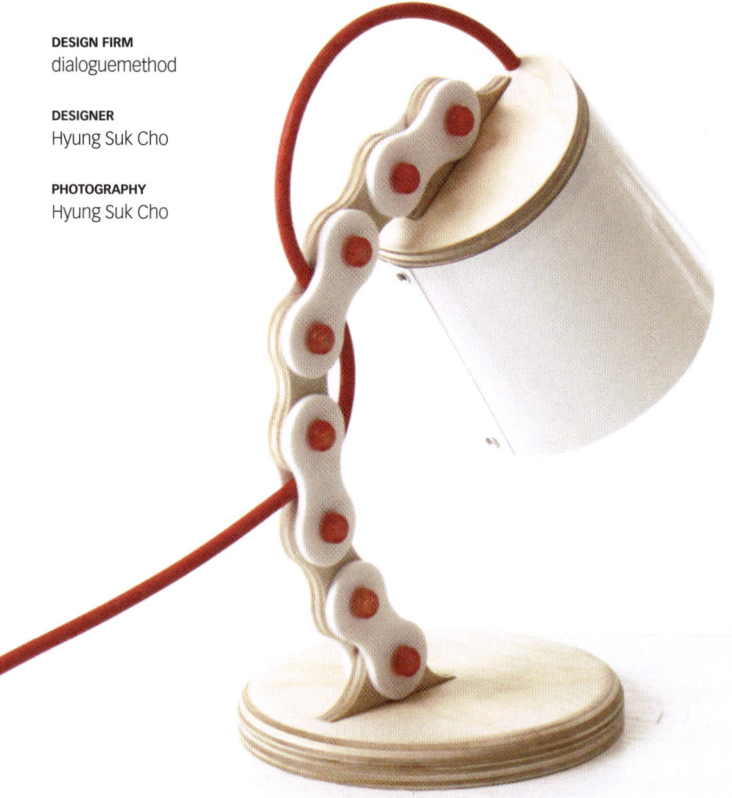

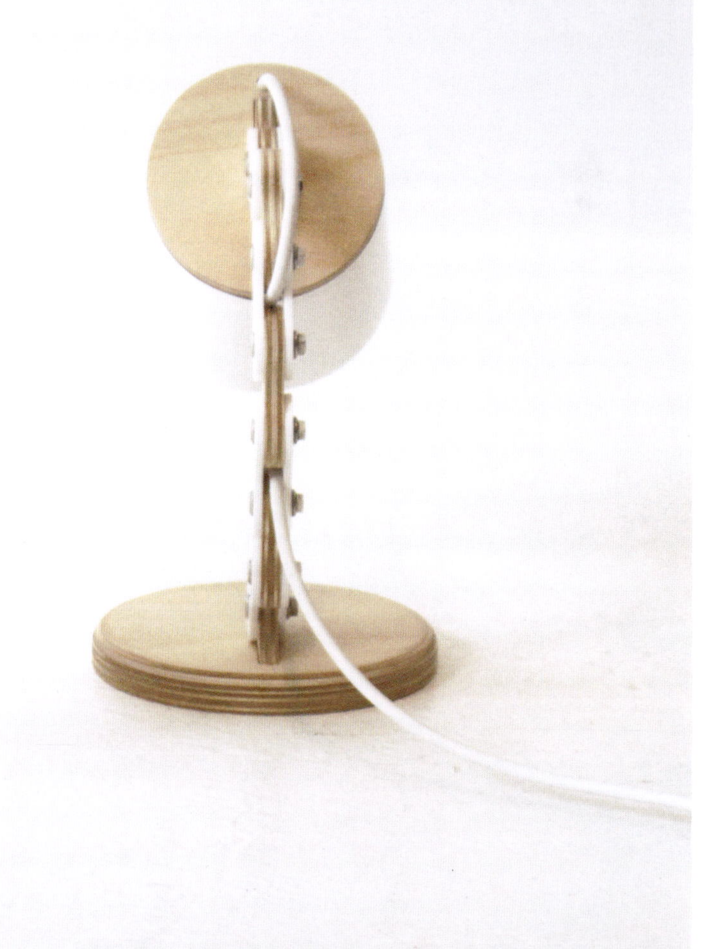

Bicycle chains are highly functional and allow each B-chain Lamp unit to take on unique and complementary shapes. The lamp's eight joints allow it to be shone wherever it is needed. The B-chain Lamp's modular design makes it possible to create whatever length and shape you want. The two sides of the white B-chain Lamp are different, with one featuring the nuts and the other the bolts.

FRA
Les chaînes de vélo sont des mécanismes polyvalents qui confèrent aux lampes B-chain une originalité et une flexibilité hors pair. Les huit rivets de la chaîne permettent d'orienter la lampe en fonction des besoins. De par leur conception modulaire, les lampes B-chain peuvent être créées suivant la forme et la longueur souhaitée par le client. Les deux côtés de la chaîne sont différents : sur une face se trouvent les têtes de boulons et sur l'autre les écrous.

ESP
Gracias a las cadenas de bicicleta, que son notablemente funcionales, la lámpara B-chain adopta formas únicas y complementarias. Además, cuenta con ocho articulaciones con las que proyecta luz allá donde haga falta y un diseño modular con el que se obtiene un sinfín de formas y longitudes. Los dos lados de la lámpara B-chain blanca son distintos; en uno de ellos se observan las tuercas y en el otro los pernos.

POR
Graças às correntes de bicicleta, que são extremamente funcionais, a luminária B-chain ganha formas únicas e complementares. Além disso, dispõe de oito articulações, com as quais projeta a luz onde seja necessário, e possui um design modular, com o qual se pode obter uma infinidade de formas e comprimentos. Os dois lados da luminária B-chain branca são diferentes; num deles aparecem as porcas e no outro os parafusos.

WALKER

DESIGN FIRM
Frankie

DESIGNER
Frank Neulichedl

In addition to being over 90 percent recyclable, Walker literally always stays standing. He will not fall down if you kick him; he will run away. Walker is made using uncoated or processed iron; cotton-covered, PVC-free cables; and ceramic fixtures made according to CE standards. Walker won the European Luminiere Award in 2006 and was hand produced in a limited series.

FRA

Le lampadaire Walker est recyclable à 90 %. D'une grande stabilité, il se maintient debout même si on le bouscule par mégarde. Walker est en fer brut ou galvanisé gainé de coton. Ses câbles sont en PVC et ses composants électriques en céramiques sont conformes aux normes en vigueur. Le lampadaire Walker a gagné le prix du luminaire européen en 2006 et a été produit à la main en séries limitées.

ESP

Walker no solo es más del 90% reciclable, sino que además siempre se mantiene en pie, literalmente. Si le dan una patada sale corriendo en lugar de venirse abajo. Esta lámpara está hecha con hierro procesado sin barnices y utiliza cables desprovistos de PVC y recubiertos de algodón; además, los casquillos de cerámica cumplen todos los requisitos de la UE. Se trata de una serie limitada hecha a mano que ha recibido el premio europeo Luminiere.

POR

Walker não só é reciclável em mais de 90%, mas também fica sempre em pé, literalmente. Se ela recebe um pontapé, em vez de cair sai correndo. Esta luminária é feita de ferro processado sem vernizes e usa fios sem PVC e recobertos de algodão; além disso, os soquetes de cerâmica atendem a todos os requisitos da UE. Trata-se de uma série limitada, feita à mão, que recebeu o prêmio europeu Luminiere.

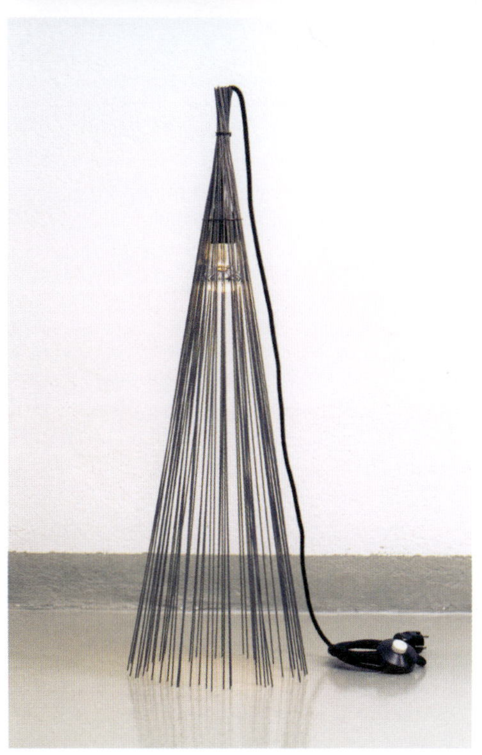

PULPLAMP

DESIGNER
Enrique Romero de la Llana

PHOTOGRAPHY
Ana Cuba

The lamps in the PulpLamp collection are made solely of paper paste from recycled newspapers, which thus acquire a second life. They are not standardized models, and each new creation will have a new shape, color, and texture. All the shapes are made with inflatable molds, which can be deformed to make each lamp unique. Due to the material from which they are made they are living pieces that lightly change their form depending on the environmental and humidity conditions.

FRA
Les lustres de la collection PulpLamp sont fabriqués exclusivement avec de la pâte à papier provenant de journaux recyclés qui entament ainsi une deuxième vie. Il n'existe pas de modèle de base standard et chaque lustre présente une forme, une couleur et une texture différentes. Les formes sont obtenues à l'aide de moules gonflables que l'on peut déformer à l'infini, ce qui explique pourquoi il n'y a pas deux lustres identiques. En raison du matériau utilisé pour leur fabrication, les lustres semblent respirer car leur forme se modifie légèrement en fonction des conditions ambiantes et du taux d'humidité.

ESP
Las lámparas de la colección PulpLamp se fabrican exclusivamente con la pasta de papeles de periódicos reciclados, que de esta forma disfrutan de una segunda vida. Además, como no son modelos estandarizados, cada nueva creación tiene una forma, color y textura diferentes. De hecho, todas las lámparas se hacen con moldes inflables, que se deforman para que cada una de ellas sea única. Gracias a la materia prima con la que se fabrican, son obras vivas que cambian ligeramente de forma en función de la humedad y las condiciones del entorno.

POR
As luminárias da coleção PulpLamp são fabricadas exclusivamente com pasta de papel de jornais reciclados, que desta maneira gozam de uma segunda vida. Além disso, como não são modelos padronizados, cada nova criação tem uma forma, cor e textura diferentes. De fato, todas as luminárias são feitas com moldes infláveis que se deformam para que cada uma delas seja única. Graças à matéria prima com que são fabricadas, são obras vivas que mudam levemente de forma em função da umidade e das condições do ambiente.

FOUND OBJECT LAMP #1

DESIGNER
Darshan Alatar Patel

PHOTOGRAPHY
Darshan Alatar Patel

This eco-conscious lamp is designed from upcycled components that include bamboo plates, glass jars, and drawer lining.
The idea of the lamp is to minimize the impact of having to discard or even recycle refuse by giving it new uses and, in a sense, adding value to it.

FRA
Cette lampe écologique est fabriquée suivant le principe du recyclage créatif à partir de panneaux de bambou, de bocaux en verre et de garnitures de fonds de tiroir. L'idée recherchée est de minimiser la mise au rebut, voire le recyclage de produits usagés et de leur donner une nouvelle vie en les détournant de leur fonction d'origine.

ESP
Aquí tenemos una lámpara respetuosa con el medio ambiente diseñada con componentes sobreciclados, como tablas de bambú, un tarro de cristal y revestimiento de cajones. El concepto de la lámpara se basa en minimizar el impacto de los desechos y hasta el reciclaje de los residuos, dándoles nuevos usos y en cierto sentido revalorizándolos.

POR
Temos aqui uma luminária que respeita o meio ambiente, projetada com componentes reciclados, como tiras de bambu, um frasco de vidro e revestimento de gavetas. O conceito da luminária baseia-se em minimizar o impacto dos descartes e inclusive em reciclar os resíduos, dando-lhes novos usos e, em certo sentido, revalorizá-los.

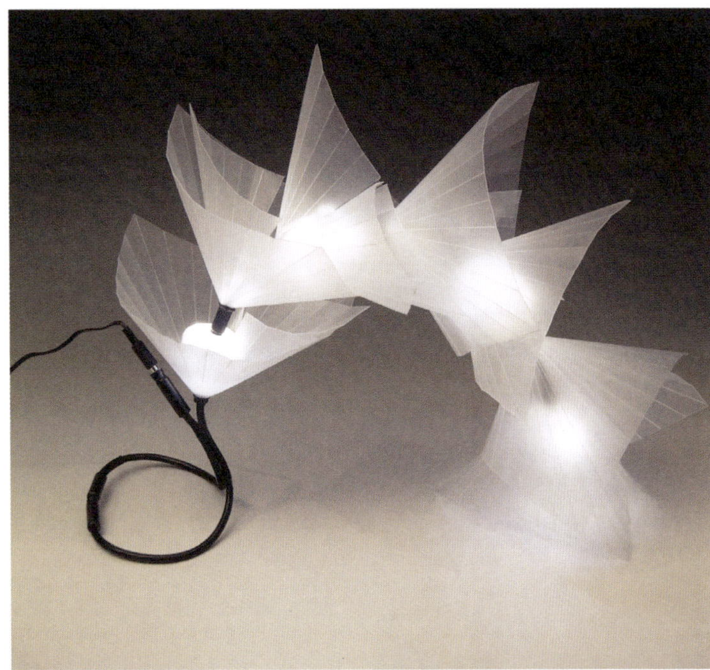

BLOOM

DESIGN FIRM
Ewa Sendecka Design

DESIGNER
Ewa Sendecka

PHOTOGRAPHY
Ewa Sendecka

Bloom lets you use your imagination and create your own lamp according to your mood. Just modify your flexible lamp and invent new shapes! Made from discarded microphones, the main structure is a flexible cable that keeps its shape after being bent. As a result it is possible to hang the lamp or form a base using its cable and position it vertically. LEDs provide the light source. The lamp can be plugged in from either its first or last module.

FRA
Bloom vous permet de donner libre cours à votre imagination et de créer un luminaire dont vous pourrez changer la forme au gré de votre humeur. Les luminaires Bloom sont fabriqués à partir de microphones mis au rebut. Leur structure est un câble souple qui conserve la forme que vous lui donnez. Vous pouvez aussi bien le pendre au plafond pour servir de lustre ou enrouler la structure pour former un socle de lampe ou de lampadaire. Bloom utilise une source d'éclairage à diodes électroluminescentes. Elle se branche au choix à partir du premier ou du dernier module.

ESP
Con Bloom el usuario debe utilizar la imaginación y crear una lámpara propia en función del estado de ánimo del momento. ¡Transforme una lámpara flexible y descubra nuevas formas! La estructura, que se fabrica con micrófonos desechados, consiste en un cable flexible que conserva la forma aunque se doble, así que es posible colgarla o construir una base con el cable para colocarla de pie. La lámpara incorpora luces LED y se enchufa en el primer módulo o en el último.

POR
Com Bloom o usuário deve usar a imaginação e criar uma luminária própria em função do estado de ânimo do momento. Transforme uma luminária flexível e descubra novas formas! A estrutura, fabricada com microfones descartados, consiste em um cabo flexível que conserva a forma em que é dobrado; deste modo é possível pendurar a luminária ou construir uma base para ela com o próprio cabo, para assim colocá-la em pé. A luminária incorpora lâmpadas LED e se conecta no primeiro módulo ou no último.

BEE-HIVE

DESIGN FIRM
Ewa Sendecka design

DESIGNER
Ewa Sendecka

PHOTOGRAPHY
Ewa Sendecka

This lamp is inspired by the shape of a beehive and the interactions that take place between its inhabitants. It is intended as interior decoration for cafés and restaurants. If lamps are placed over a table or a bar people gather around them, just as bees gather around a beehive. The lampshade is made of used polyurethane CO2 tubes. It is fully elastic, unbreakable, and has no metal pieces, and it is safe, easily washable, light, and easy to dismantle.

ESP
Esta lámpara se inspira en la forma de una colmena y las interacciones de sus ocupantes. Está diseñada como adorno de interior para cafeterías y restaurantes; si se coloca encima de una mesa o una barra, los clientes se congregarán en torno a ella, así como las abejas se congregan alrededor de una colmena. La pantalla está hecha de tubos de poliuretano para CO2 usados. Es completamente irrompible y elástica y no tiene piezas metálicas, de manera que es segura y ligera y se desmonta y se lava con facilidad.

FRA
La forme de ce lustre s'inspire d'une ruche et de l'interaction existant entre ses habitants. Il est destiné à l'éclairage intérieur de cafés et de restaurants. Un lustre Bee-Hive suspendu au-dessus d'une table ou d'un comptoir attirera les gens, comme la ruche attire les abeilles. L'abat-jour est constitué de tubes usagés en polyuréthane. Le lustre est entièrement élastique, incassable et dépourvu de pièces métalliques. Il est sûr, léger, et se lave et se démonte facilement.

POR
Esta luminária inspira-se na forma de uma colmeia e nas interações de seus habitantes. Foi projetada como adorno de interiores para cafeterias e restaurantes; se for colocada em cima de uma mesa ou de uma barra, os clientes se reunirão em torno a ela, assim como as abelhas se juntam ao redor da colmeia. A cúpula é confeccionada com tubos de poliuretano para CO2 usados. É totalmente inquebrável e elástica e não tem peças metálicas, de maneira que é segura e leve, podendo ser desmontada e lavada com facilidade.

LIGHTHOUSE LAMP

DESIGN FIRM
Dimitrios Stamatakis

DESIGNER
Dimitrios Stamatakis

PHOTOGRAPHY
Alexis Kanakis & Thomas Mailaender

The Lighthouse Lamp's vertical use of light, which defines its form and design, provides a 360-degree diffusion of light into the surrounding space when it is placed on the top of a tripod. The Lighthouse lamp is made of soft maple or reclaimed poplar wood, borosilicate glass—which is resistant to thermal stress and has greater heat-diffusion properties than any other common glass—and a sixty-centimeter, customized LED tube of white, twenty-four-volt LED strips, as well as an analog rotary dimmer.

FRA

Le lampadaire Lighthouse diffuse la lumière verticalement sur 360° autour du trépied qui constitue son socle. Ce dernier est en érable ou en peuplier de récupération et en verre borosilicaté, dont les propriétés de diffusion de la chaleur et de résistance à la température sont supérieures à celles des autres types de verre. Lighthouse est équipé d'un tube blanc à diodes électroluminescentes spécial, d'une réglette 24 volts et d'un modulateur d'ambiance analogique rotatif.

ESP

Gracias a la luz vertical, que define la forma y el diseño de la lámpara, se obtiene una difusión de 360 grados en el espacio circundante al colocarla en lo alto de un trípode. La lámpara Lighthouse está hecha con arce blanco o madera polar reciclada, vidrio de borosilicato (que es resistente a la presión térmica y tiene una difusión calórica más elevada que el resto de los cristales corrientes) y un tubo personalizado de sesenta centímetros que contiene tiras LED blancas de veinticuatro voltios, así como un regulador rotatorio análogo.

POR

Graças à luz vertical, que define a forma e o desenho da luminária, consegue-se uma difusão de 360 graus no espaço circundante ao ser colocada na vertical de um tripé. A luminária Lighthouse é feita com plátano branco ou madeira polar reciclada, vidro de borosilicato (que é resistente à pressão térmica e tem uma difusão calórica mais alta do que o resto dos vidros comuns) e um tubo personalizado de sessenta centímetros, que contém fitas de LED brancas de vinte e quatro volts, bem como um regulador rotatório análogo.

FRA

MATÉRIAUX NATURELS

Les matériaux naturels sont meilleurs pour l'environnement que les matières synthétiques fabriquées par l'homme, comme le plastique. Pour l'élaboration de produits, les premiers consomment moins d'énergie que les seconds, sans compter que les processus employés pour créer des matières synthétiques polluent généralement l'environnement ou émettent dans l'atmosphère du monoxyde de carbone dangereux pour la santé. C'est pourquoi le choix de matériaux naturels dans l'élaboration de luminaires aide à améliorer et à protéger l'environnement.

ESP

MATERIALES NATURALES

Los materiales naturales son mucho más respetuosos con el medio ambiente que los materiales sintéticos o manufacturados, como el plástico. A la hora de la fabricación, los materiales naturales consumen menos recursos y los procesos que requieren los materiales sintéticos o manufacturados con frecuencia acaban contaminando el medio ambiente o emanando peligrosas emisiones de carbono en la atmósfera. Al decantarse por el uso de materiales naturales en la fabricación de lámparas, los diseñadores contribuyen a la defensa y el enriquecimiento del medio ambiente.

POR

MATERIAIS NATURAIS

Os materiais naturais respeitam muito mais o meio ambiente que os materiais sintéticos ou manufaturados, como o plástico. Na hora da fabricação, os materiais naturais consomem menos recursos e processos que os materiais sintéticos ou manufaturados exigem, frequentemente acabam por contaminar o meio ambiente ou liberar perigosas emissões de carbono na atmosfera. Ao optar pelo uso de materiais naturais na fabricação de luminárias, os designers contribuem para a defesa e o enriquecimento do meio ambiente.

NATURAL MATERIALS

Natural materials are much better for the environment than synthetic or manmade ones such as plastic. When it comes to manufacturing, natural materials are much more likely to consume fewer resources than manmade or synthetic materials, and the processes required to make these latter materials can often end up polluting the environment or releasing dangerous carbon emissions into the atmosphere. By choosing to use natural materials when making lights designers are therefore playing their part in helping to improve and protect the environment.

THE BRIDE LAMP

DESIGN FIRM
mammalampa

DESIGNER
Ieva Kaleja

PHOTOGRAPHY
mammalampa

CLIENT
mammalampa

This bride's "dress" is created from paper and represents an unusual use of this traditional lamp material. Entirely handmade, each bride has her own personality, which is characterized by the unique pattern in which her shade was woven by the personal touch of the weaver who created the pattern. As light shines through the paper, the lamp seems to be infused with an aura of airy lightness and imperceptibility, almost as if it were not subject to the laws of gravity.

FRA

Les luminaires de la collection The Bride Lamp sont en papier. Toutefois, ce matériau utilisé couramment dans la confection d'abat-jour, est exploité ici d'une manière tout à fait inhabituelle. Chaque luminaire est entièrement fabriqué à la main et possède sa propre personnalité qui découle de la façon dont l'abat-jour a été tissé par l'artiste pour former le motif de son choix. La lumière qui filtre à travers le papier produit un effet d'aura, le luminaire semblant flotter en suspension dans l'air au mépris des lois de la gravitation.

ESP

Este «vestido» de novia de papel ofrece un uso insólito de esta materia prima que se utiliza tradicionalmente en la fabricación de lámparas. Cada novia está hecha a mano y tiene un carácter propio, que se caracteriza por el diseño único de la pantalla, en la que se aprecia el toque personal del artesano. Cuando la luz la atraviesa parece que la lámpara está rodeada de una aureola etérea, imperceptible y ligera, casi como si no estuviera sometida a la ley de la gravedad.

POR

Este "vestido" de noiva de papel apresenta um uso inusitado desta matéria tradicionalmente utilizada na fabricação de luminárias. Cada noiva é feita à mão e tem personalidade própria, caracterizada pelo design único da cúpula, na qual se pode apreciar o toque pessoal do artesão. Quando a luz a atravessa, parece que a luminária está rodeada por uma auréola etérea, imperceptível e sutil, quase como se não estivesse sujeita à lei da gravidade.

ZHU GUANG

DESIGNER
Fanson Meng

PHOTOGRAPHY
Fanson Meng

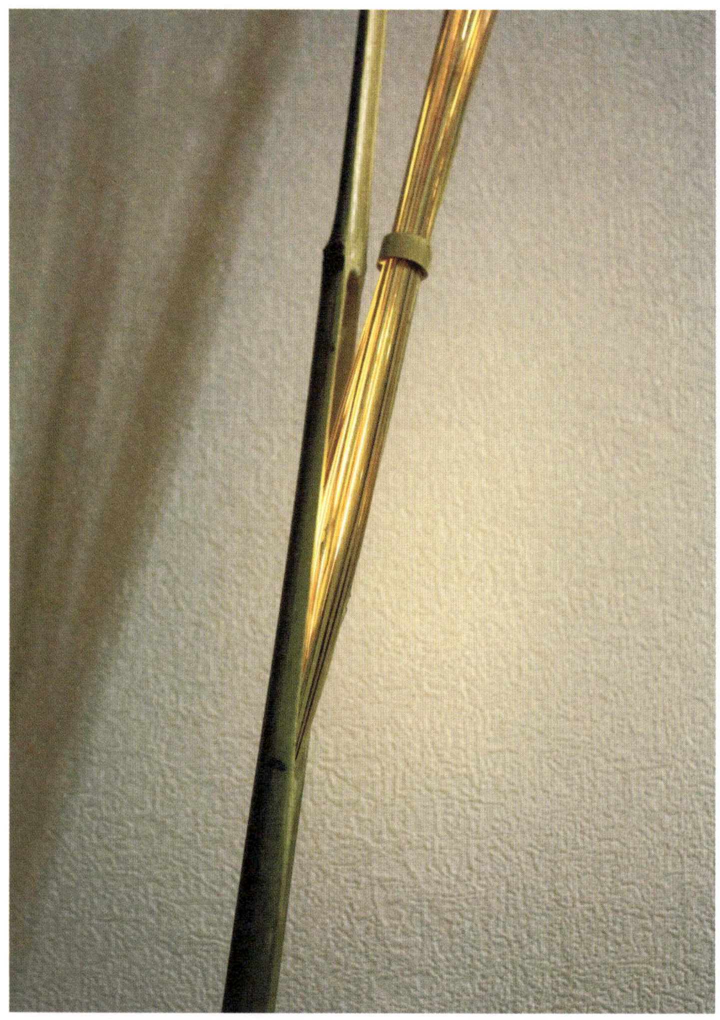

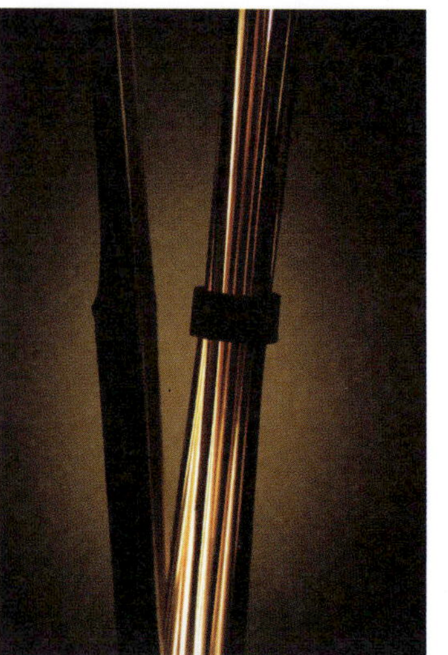

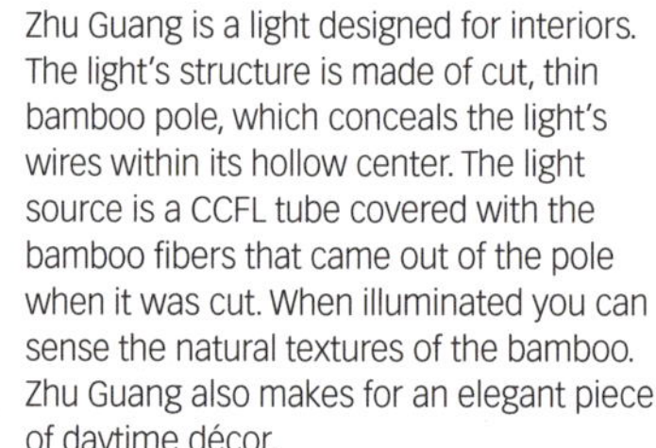

Zhu Guang is a light designed for interiors. The light's structure is made of cut, thin bamboo pole, which conceals the light's wires within its hollow center. The light source is a CCFL tube covered with the bamboo fibers that came out of the pole when it was cut. When illuminated you can sense the natural textures of the bamboo. Zhu Guang also makes for an elegant piece of daytime décor.

ESP

Zhu Guang es una lámpara diseñada para espacios interiores. La estructura consiste en una delgada espiga de bambú cortada que oculta los cables de la lámpara en el centro hueco. La fuente de luz es un tubo CCFL cubierto con las fibras de bambú que se obtienen cuando se corta la espiga. Cuando se enciende se observan las texturas naturales del bambú. Zhu Guang también hace las veces de elegante elemento decorativo durante el día.

FRA

Zhu Guang est un lampadaire d'intérieur. Sa structure consiste en une mince tige de bambou dans laquelle passe le câble électrique qui est donc invisible. La source lumineuse est une lampe fluorescente à cathode froide recouverte par les fibres de bambou qui ont été libérées au moment où la tige a été coupée. Lorsque le lampadaire Zhu Guang est allumé, il met en valeur les textures naturelles du bambou. Dans la journée, Zhu Guang est un objet de décoration particulièrement élégant.

POR

Zhu Guang é uma luminária desenhada para espaços interiores. Sua estrutura é constituída por numa fina espiga de bambu cortada, que oculta os fios da luminária no centro oco. A fonte de luz é um tubo CCFL coberto com as fibras do bambu, obtidas ao se cortar a espiga. Quando se acende, observam-se as texturas naturais do bambu. Zhu Guang também funciona como um elegante elemento decorativo durante o dia.

XUAN LAMP

DESIGN FIRM
Hangzhou PINWU Design Studio

DESIGNERS
Wang Shenghai & Zhang Lei

PHOTOGRAPHY
Zhang Shensen

With its dancing bamboo strands, the Xuan Lamp seems to be guided by the wind. Its raw material is the special kind of bamboo found in China's Sichuan province, which through masterly traditional craftsmanship has been fashioned into smooth, thin strands in a process that also ensures that the bamboo retains its natural color and will remain free of mildew. The Xuan Lamp uses a special low-temperature LED light, which makes it safer to use and saves energy.

FRA
Le lustre Xuan Lamp, constitué d'une tige de bambou dont les brins ont été séparés, semble emporté par le vent. Le matériau utilisé dans sa fabrication est un type particulier de bambou qui pousse dans la province chinoise du Sichuan. Il est travaillé suivant une méthode traditionnelle qui permet de détacher les multiples brins formant sa tige tout en conservant sa teinte originale et en le protégeant contre l'humidité. Pour plus de sécurité, le lustre Xuan Lamp utilise une ampoule LED de basse température spéciale à économie d'énergie.

ESP
Las inquietas hebras de bambú dan la impresión de que el viento mece la lámpara Xuan. La materia prima es el bambú que se encuentra en la provincia china de Sichuán y que los hábiles artesanos tradicionales convierten en finas y suaves hebras mediante un proceso con el que asimismo se aseguran de que conserve el color natural y no se enmohezca. La lámpara Xuan emplea una bombilla LED especial de baja temperatura, de manera que es más segura y ahorra energía.

POR
As inquietas fibras de bambu causam a sensação de que o vento balança a luminária Xuan. A matéria prima é o bambu encontrado na província chinesa de Sichuán e que os hábeis artesãos tradicionais transformam em finas e suaves fibras, através de um processo que garante a conservação da cor natural e impede que embolore. A luminária A Lâmpada Xuan utiliza uma lâmpada LED especial de baixa temperatura, sendo mais segura e economizando energia.

FAN LAMP

DESIGN FIRM
Louie Rigano

DESIGNER
Louie Rigano

PHOTOGRAPHY
Louie Rigano

CLIENT
Louie Rigano

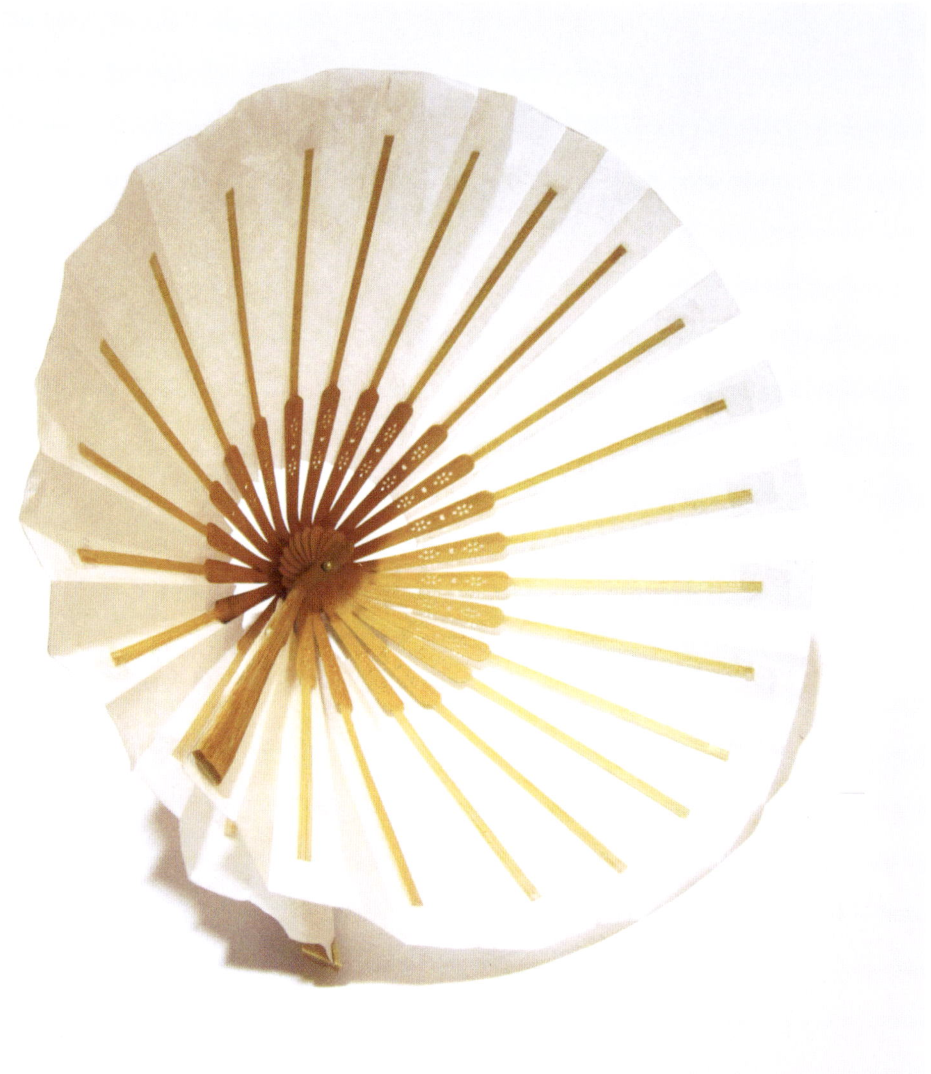

By introducing a single bend into its structure an entirely new function is created for the traditional and ancient Japanese folding fan. Washi paper is the customary material used in folding fans due to its strength and durability; it is also used in lanterns because of its effectiveness in diffusing light. Here, the paper is used to optimum effect, with both of these features being utilized.

ESP
Con la incorporación de un pliegue en la estructura el abanico japonés tradicional adquiere una función completamente novedosa. El papel washi es un material resistente y duradero que suele emplearse en los abanicos plegables, al igual que en los faroles, ya que también es un magnífico difusor de la luz. En esta creación se aprovecha al máximo, pues se emplean estas dos características.

FRA
Avec Fan , Louie Rigano revisite l'éventail japonais traditionnel : en appliquant une légère courbure à sa base, il l'adapte à un usage complètement différent. Le papier washi est ce que l'on utilise habituellement pour fabriquer les éventails parce que c'est une matière à la fois solide et résistante. On l'emploie également pour confectionner des lanternes en raison de sa capacité à diffuser la lumière. Le papier washi est exploité ici de manière optimale, le lustre tirant parti de toutes ses qualités intrinsèques.

POR
Com a incorporação de uma dobra em sua estrutura, o leque tradicional japonês ganha uma função completamente inovadora. O papel washi é um material resistente e duradouro que se costuma utilizar na confecção de leques dobráveis e também de lanternas, pois é, igualmente, um magnífico difusor da luz. Nesta criação, ele é maximamente aproveitado, pois se exploram as duas caraterísticas.

GOURD LAMP BRACKET V

DESIGN FIRM
Calabarte

DESIGNER
Przemyslaw Krawczynski

PHOTOGRAPHY
Przemyslaw Krawczynski

This lamp is created using a Senegalese gourd. Made using just over half a gourd, this particular model was designed to be mounted on a wall, but it is also possible to create versions for use on ceilings. The gourd has a diameter of 21 centimeters at its widest point, while its diameter at the wall is 17 centimeters. The distance between the wall and the bottom tip of the gourd is 16.5 centimeters.

FRA
Cette applique est fabriquée à partir d'une calebasse venant du Sénégal. Dans le modèle présenté ici, on a utilisé un peu plus de la moitié d'une calebasse et réalisé un montage permettant de l'accrocher au mur. Mais on peut aussi adapter le modèle pour disposer d'un lustre qu'on accrochera au plafond. Ici la calebasse présente un diamètre de 21 cm en son point le plus large, celui de l'ouverture en contact avec le mur étant de 17 cm. La distance entre le mur et le fond de la calebasse est de 16,5 cm.

ESP
Esta lámpara está hecha con una calabaza senegalesa. Este modelo en concreto, que utiliza poco más de media calabaza, está diseñado para instalarse en paredes, aunque también es posible crear versiones colgantes. La calabaza tiene un diámetro de 21 centímetros en el punto más ancho y 17 centímetros en la zona de contacto. El punto más bajo de la calabaza se encuentra a 16,5 centímetros de la pared.

POR
Esta luminária é feita com uma cabaça senegalesa. Este modelo, concretamente, que utiliza pouco mais de meia abóbora, foi desenhado para instalar-se em paredes, ainda que também seja possível criar versões pendentes. A cabaça tem o diâmetro de 21 centímetros no ponto mais largo e 17 centímetros na zona de contato. O ponto mais baixo da cabaça fica a 16,5 centímetros da parede.

STANDING LAMP XII

DESIGN FIRM
Calabarte

DESIGNER
Przemyslaw Krawczynski

PHOTOGRAPHY
Przemyslaw Krawczynski

Taking around a month and a half to create, the pattern of Standing Lamp XII is inspired by fractals and nature. The perforations are made by drills of ten different diameters. The base is carved in wood and finished with Italian natural oil. The underside of the base is branded with the Calabarte logo. The supporting stem is finished with black, waxed jewelry string. The lamp is 20 and 22 centimeters in diameter and 39.5 cm high.

FRA

Il faut environ un mois et demi pour réaliser le motif de la Standing Lamp XII qui s'inspire des fractals et de la nature. Les perforations ont été pratiquées à l'aide de mèches de dix diamètres différents. Le socle de la lampe est en bois traité avec une huile de protection venant d'Italie. Le dessous du socle arbore le logo de Calabarte. Autour du bras de la lampe s'enroule une cordelette noire cirée que l'on utilise en bijouterie. La lampe présente un diamètre de 20 et 22 cm et une hauteur de 39,5 cm.

ESP

El diseño de la lámpara Standing Lamp XII, que se desarrolla durante más de mes y medio, se inspira en los fractales y la naturaleza. Los orificios se han realizado con brocas de una decena de diámetros distintos. La base está tallada en madera y acabada con aceite natural italiano. En el anverso de la base está grabado el logotipo de Calabarte. El tallo que sostiene la lámpara está acabado con un hilo de orfebrería encerado negro. La lámpara mide 20 y 22 centímetros de diámetro y 39,5 centímetros de alto.

POR

O design da luminária Standing Lamp XII, elaborado durante mais de um mês e meio, inspira-se nos fractais e na natureza. Os orifícios, de mais de uma dezena de diâmetros diferentes, foram feitos com brocas. A base é entalhada em madeira e recebe um acabamento de azeite natural italiano. No anverso da base está gravado o logotipo de Calabarte. O talo que sustenta a luminária recebe o acabamento com fio negro encerado. A luminária mede 20 e 22 centímetros de diâmetro e 39,5 centímetros de altura.

STANDING LAMP XIII: THORN SPHERE

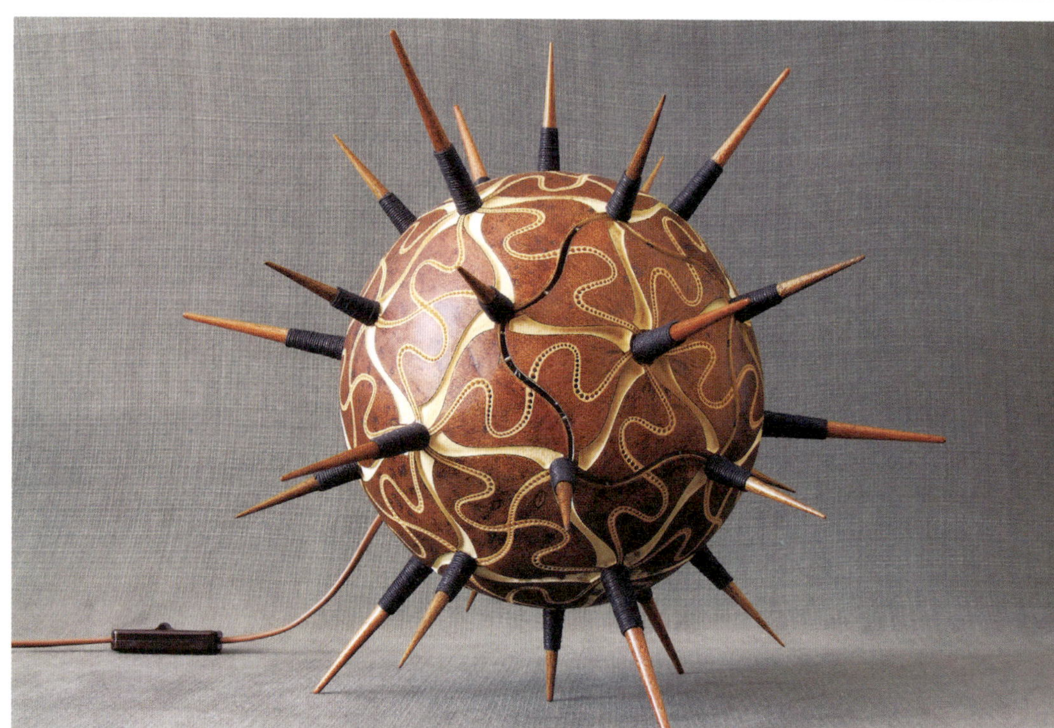

DESIGN FIRM
Calabarte

DESIGNER
Przemyslaw Krawczynski

PHOTOGRAPHY
Przemyslaw Krawczynski

This dodecahedron-shaped piece uses a simpler and flatter pattern than the other lamps in this series. In creating the lamp designer Przemyslaw Krawczynski sought to use single lines of perforation to achieve a sharp lighting effect that steadily diverges within the room. Measuring either six or nine centimeters in length, the thorns are made with oak that has been painted with natural oil and finished using black, waxed string.

FRA

Cette lampe en forme de dodécaèdre arbore un motif moins recherché que les autres luminaires de la série. Le but du designer Przemyslaw Krawczynski était de définir des lignes de perforation simples capables de projeter sur les murs une harmonie d'arabesques de lumière. Sur les pointes de 6 ou 9 cm fabriquées en chêne traité avec une huile spéciale s'enroule une cordelette noire cirée que l'on utilise en bijouterie.

ESP

Esta creación en forma de dodecaedro aplica un diseño más sencillo y liso que las restantes lámparas de la serie. El diseñador Przemyslaw Krawczynski ha tratado de usar líneas de orificios únicas para obtener un acusado efecto luminoso que diverge gradualmente en la estancia. Las espinas de 6 o 9 centímetros de largo están hechas de roble pintado con aceite natural y acabado con un hilo encerado negro.

POR

Esta criação em forma de dodecaedro adota um design mais simples e liso do que as outras luminárias dessa série. O designer Przemyslaw Krawczynski utilizou linhas únicas de orifícios para obter um marcante efeito luminoso que diverge gradualmente no aposento. Os espinhos, de 6 ou 9 centímetros de comprimento, são feitos de carvalho pintado com azeite natural e com acabamento de barbante negro encerado.

STANDING LAMP XIV: GLOBE II

DESIGN FIRM
Calabarte

DESIGNER
Przemyslaw Krawczynski

PHOTOGRAPHY
Przemyslaw Krawczynski

The contours of the continents are faithfully recorded on this lamp, as are lines of longitude and latitude. These lines are perforated, meaning they project their curves into the room when the lamp is lit. The lamp's opening, locked shut using small magnets, is located at the sixty-degree latitude line. The base is carved from wood and finished with natural Italian oil.

FRA
Les contours des continents sont fidèlement reproduits sur cette lampe, ainsi que les cercles représentant les longitudes et les latitudes. Ces cercles sont perforés sur toute leur circonférence, afin que leur ombre se projette sur les murs lorsque la lampe est allumée. La calebasse formant la lampe peut s'ouvrir au niveau du 60ème degré de latitude pour changer l'ampoule. Elle est maintenue fermée à l'aide de petits aimants. Le socle de la lampe est sculpté dans du bois traité avec une huile de protection venant d'Italie.

ESP
Esta lámpara representa fielmente los contornos de los continentes, así como los paralelos y los meridianos, que además están perforados, de manera que proyectan sus curvas en la estancia cuando se enciende la lámpara. La apertura de esta, que se cierra mediante pequeños imanes, se encuentra en la línea de latitud de 60 grados. La base está tallada en madera y acabada con aceite natural italiano.

POR
Esta luminária representa fielmente os contornos dos continentes, bem como os paralelos e meridianos, que também são perfurados, de maneira a projetar suas curvas na dependência quando se acende a luminária. A sua abertura, que é fechada através de pequenos imãs, está na linha da latitude de 60 graus. A base é entalhada em madeira e recebe o acabamento de azeite natural italiano.

COCON MALADE

DESIGN FIRM
Bel&Bo

DESIGNER
Jeannine van Erk

PHOTOGRAPHY
Nina Straßgütle

CLIENT
schubLaden

Cocon Malade and Boule Malade are unique, handcrafted lampshades. Their individuality is achieved through using handmade, specially dyed natural materials. Through the craftsmanship of their Dutch designer, Jeannine van Erk, each lampshade is different. Their special quality is the combination of their warm, atmospheric light and their simple yet contemporary design. Because they are made using natural pigments, which always vary slightly, the color of each order is always slightly different. The lamps are available in seven different colors.

FRA

Cocon Malade et Boule Malade sont des abat-jour fabriqués à la main uniques en leur genre. Leur originalité repose sur l'utilisation de matériaux bruts teintés à l'aide de pigments naturels. Grâce au savoir-faire de Jeannine van Erk, qui a conçu ces abat-jour, il n'y en a pas deux pareils. Ils diffusent une lumière douce et chaleureuse tout en affichant un style contemporain épuré. Comme les pigments sont d'origine naturelle, leur ton varie légèrement d'une commande à l'autre. Les abat-jour existent dans sept couleurs différentes.

ESP

Cocon Malade y Boule Malade son pantallas únicas y artesanales que utilizan materiales naturales hechos a mano y teñidos especialmente. Gracias a las habilidades de la diseñadora holandesa Jeannine van Erk cada pantalla es diferente. La característica más destacada es la combinación de la luz cálida y atmosférica y el diseño sencillo y contemporáneo. Como emplean pigmentos naturales, que varían ligeramente, el color de cada pedido siempre es algo distinto. Las lámparas están disponibles en siete colores diferentes.

POR

Cocon Malade e Boule Malade são cúpulas únicas e artesanais que utilizam materiais naturais feitos à mão e especialmente tingidos. Graças às habilidades da designer holandesa Jeannine van Erk, cada cúpula é diferente. A característica de maior destaque é a combinação da luz cálida e atmosférica e o desenho simples e contemporâneo. Como utilizam pigmentos naturais, que variam ligeiramente, a cor de cada encomenda é sempre um pouco diferente. As luminárias estão à disposição em sete cores diferentes.

SCRAFTY

DESIGN FIRM
decorkuznetsov

DESIGNERS
Valeriy Kuznetsov & Katerina Kuznetsova

PHOTOGRAPHY
Valeriy Kuznetsov

Wearing warm, knitted clothes such as sweaters is a real pleasure during a cold winter. Scrafty is based on this very garment, with the goal behind the piece being to create a warm and cozy lamp. At its core is a steel ball, which is wrapped in Peruvian wool, an entirely natural and light material. It also features a couple of holes that can be used to either warm up cold hands or change the bulb.

FRA
Il est bien agréable de porter des vêtements en tricot l'hiver. Si les luminaires de la collection Scrafty sont en maille tricotée, c'est justement pour créer une ambiance douillette et chaleureuse. Leur armature en acier est recouverte de laine péruvienne, qui est une matière à la fois douce et légère. Suivant le modèle, des trous sont pratiqués dans l'armature pour que l'on puisse y passer les mains afin de les réchauffer ou de changer l'ampoule.

ESP
Ponerse ropa de abrigo de punto, como un jersey, es un verdadero placer durante un invierno frío. Scrafty se basa en esta prenda y tiene como objetivo la creación de una lámpara cálida y confortable. En el centro hay una bola de acero envuelta en lana peruana, que es ligera y natural al 100%. Además, cuenta con dos orificios con los que el usuario puede calentarse las manos o cambiar la bombilla.

POR
Vestir um agasalho de tricô, como uma blusa, é um verdadeiro prazer durante o inverno rigoroso. Scrafty baseia-se nesse agasalho e tem como objetivo a criação de una luminária cálida e confortável. No centro, há uma bola de aço recoberta de lã peruana, que é leve e 100% natural. Além disso, possui dois orifícios através dos quais o usuário pode aquecer as mãos ou trocar a lâmpada.

LEONE SERIES 01

DESIGN FIRM
Lanzavecchia + Wai Design Studio

PHOTOGRAPHY
Daniel Peh K.L.

DESIGNERS
Francesca Lanzavecchia & Hunn Wai

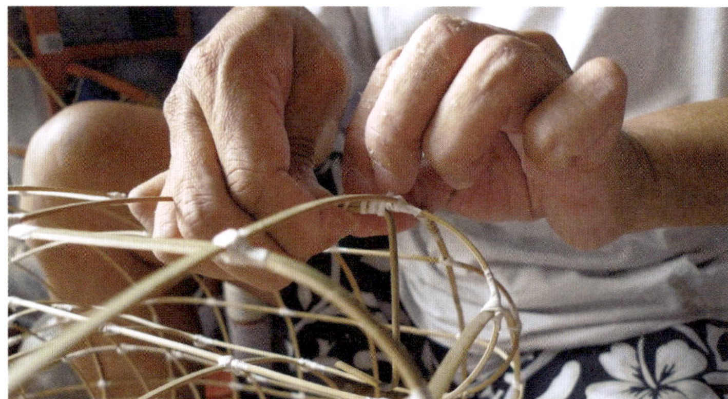

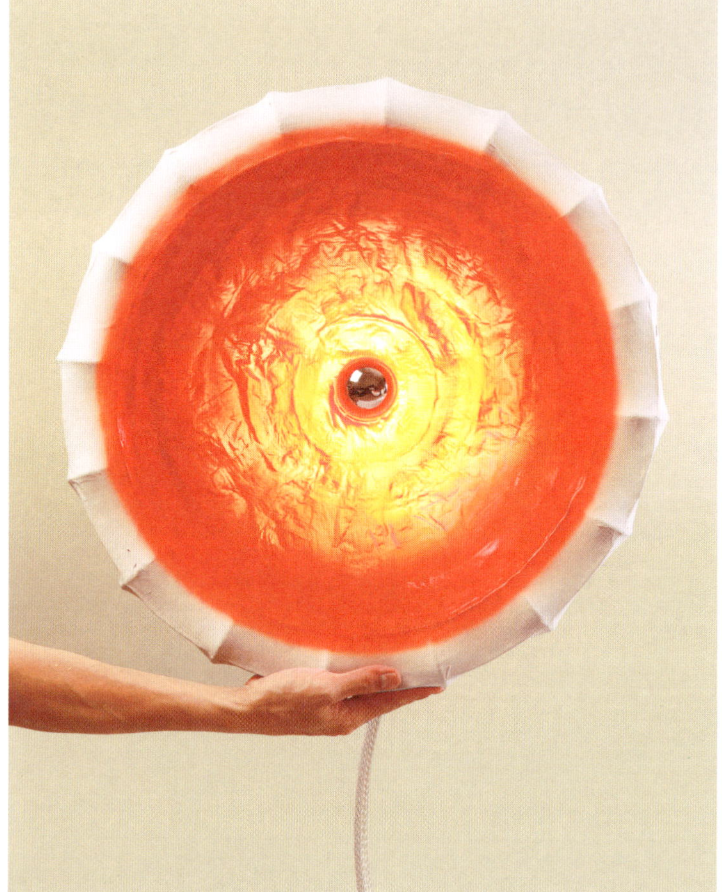

Lanzavecchia + Wai's collaboration with Singapore's last remaining lion-dance mask craftsman has resulted in Leone Lights, a series of lamps that brings the artistry of this rare Southeast Asian trade into the domestic space. Made by hand from lithe strips of bamboo, covered by rice paper, and then painted internally with a fiery orange inspired by traditional livery, these objects bring the lion-dance mask craft back into the public consciousness in a new context and with a new expression.

FRA
La collaboration entre Lanzavecchia + Wai et le dernier sculpteur de masques de la danse du lion de Singapour a donné naissance aux luminaires Leone Series 01 qui ouvrent la porte de nos maisons à un artisanat sud asiatique très particulier. Ces objets sont fabriqués en minces bandes de bambou recouvertes de papier de riz, et leur intérieur est peint dans un orange très vif reprenant la couleur du corps de l'animal mythique. Les luminaires de cette série redonnent vie à la tradition de la danse du lion dans un autre contexte et sous une nouvelle forme.

ESP
La colaboración de Lanzavecchia y Wai con el último maestro de máscaras del baile del león de Singapur ha resultado en Leone Lights, una serie de lámparas que trasladan al espacio doméstico la artesanía de esta insólita tradición del sureste asiático. Hechos a mano con flexibles tiras de bambú, recubiertos de papel de arroz y después pintados por dentro de un naranja intenso que se inspira en los colores tradicionales, estos objetos trasladan la artesanía de las máscaras del baile del león a la consciencia del público en un contexto nuevo y con una expresión novedosa.

POR
A colaboração de Lanzavecchia e Wai com o último mestre de máscaras do baile do leão de Singapura teve como resultado a Leone Lights, uma série de luminárias que transladam para o espaço doméstico o artesanato desta inusitada tradição do sudeste asiático. Estes objetos, feitas à mão com tiras flexíveis de bambu, recobertos de papel de arroz e depois pintados por dentro de uma cor laranja intensa, que se inspira nas cores tradicionais, trazem o artesanato das máscaras do baile do leão à consciência do público num contexto novo e com uma expressão inovadora.

CHERRY MOON, FORMATION, MIDNIGHT SKY, FIVE STONE, CACTUS & JEWEL ONE

DESIGN FIRM
Ango

PHOTOGRAPHY
New Brain Studio

The diffusers used in Ango's lighting are fabricated by hand using natural, highly renewable materials that require minimal energy to process. Their main materials are rattan; silk cocoons; mulberry-tree bark; hand-cast polymer, tapioca skin, or raw silk fiber; freeform silicon lines; and a hand-soldered wire matrix. When the diffuser reaches the end of its life, the light can be used with a new one or reused in some other way.

FRA
Les abat-jour aériens créés par Ango sont fabriqués à la main à partir de matériaux naturels et hautement renouvelables, et leur production nécessite très peu d'énergie. Parmi les principaux matériaux on retrouve : le rotin, le cocon de soie, la fibre de mûrier, le polymère coulé à la main, le tapioca, la fibre de soie naturelle, le fil de silicone souple et une armature métallique soudée manuellement. Lorsque l'abat-jour diffuseur arrive en fin de vie, on peut le remplacer par un autre ou utiliser autre chose à sa place.

ESP
Los difusores de las lámparas de Ango están hechos a mano con materiales naturales y altamente renovables que consumen una energía mínima durante el proceso. Los más destacados son el mimbre, los capullos de seda, la corteza de morera, los polímeros forjados a mano, la piel de tapioca o la fibra de seda en bruto, las líneas de silicona de formas libres y una base de alambre soldada a mano. Cuando llega al final de su vida, se puede cambiar el difusor por uno nuevo o reutilizar la lámpara de otra forma.

POR
Os difusores das luminárias de Ango são feitos à mão com materiais naturais e altamente renováveis, que consomem mínima energia durante o processo. Os mais destacados são o vime, os casulos de seda, a casca da amoreira, os polímeros moldados à mão, a casca de tapioca ou a fibra de seda em bruto, as linhas de silicone de formas livres e uma base de arame soldada à mão. Quando chega ao final de sua vida, pode-se trocar o difusor por um novo ou reutilizar a luminária de outra forma.

DESERT STORM

DESIGNER
Nir Meiri

PHOTOGRAPHY
Shay Ben Efrayim

This project is inspired by sand. The shape of the sand-molded lampshades brings to mind primitive desert structures, while the fixture's overall figure resembles that of plants that blossom on the Mediterranean seashore. The use of sand as the main material plays on the tension between wild nature–sandstorms and vast deserts–and the delicacy of the molded end design. Despite their apparent fragility, the lampshades are sturdy, and their strength partners with that of the fixture's metal pole.

FRA
C'est le sable qui a inspiré ce projet. Les abat-jour façonnés en sable moulé rappellent les structures primitives trouvées dans le désert, la forme générale du luminaire faisant penser à une plante poussant au bord de la Méditerranée. L'emploi du sable comme matériau principal joue sur le contraste entre la nature sauvage – tempêtes de sable et vastes étendues désertiques – et l'aspect délicat du design. En dépit de leur apparente fragilité, les abat-jour sont solides, tout comme l'est leur pied ou bras en métal.

ESP
Este proyecto se inspira en la arena. La forma de las pantallas modeladas con arena nos trae a la memoria las estructuras primitivas del desierto, mientras que la figura de la lámpara se asemeja a la de las plantas que florecen en la costa mediterránea. El uso de la arena como material más importante juega con la tensión existente entre la naturaleza salvaje (las tormentas de arena y los amplísimos desiertos) y la delicadeza del diseño del producto modelado. Aunque parecen frágiles, las pantallas son robustas, al igual que la barra metálica.

POR
Este projeto inspira-se na areia. A forma das cúpulas modeladas com areia nos traz à memória as estruturas primitivas do deserto, enquanto que a figura da luminária se assemelha à das plantas que florescem na costa mediterrânea. O uso da areia como o material mais importante joga com a tensão existente entre a natureza selvagem (as tempestades de areia e os amplíssimos desertos) e a delicadeza do design do produto modelado. Ainda que pareçam frágeis, as cúpulas são robustas, assim como a barra metálica.

LANDING 200 LAMP

DESIGN FIRM
UUN Design Studio

DESIGNER
Kim HyunJoo

PHOTOGRAPHY
Kim HyunJoo

CLIENT
UUN Design Studio

Landing is a lamp carved from solid granite. It's created from nature, and could be returned to dust. Light cannot of course pass directly through stone, and so the lamp is designed so that its light emanates from under its legs. The first version was created using granite, but it could be made with any kind of stone, such as marble or sandstone.

FRA
La lampe Landing est sculptée dans du granit. La pierre est un produit de la nature qui redeviendra poussière un jour. La lumière, ne pouvant bien entendu pas traverser le matériau, se diffuse au niveau des pieds de la lampe sculptés en arrondi. La première version de cette lampe a été taillée dans du granit, mais on pourrait aussi utiliser tout autre type de pierre, comme du marbre ou du grès.

ESP
Landing es una lámpara tallada en granito macizo. Como se ha fabricado con elementos naturales, también puede convertirse de nuevo en polvo. Por supuesto, la luz no atraviesa directamente la piedra, sino que la lámpara está diseñada de tal manera que emane desde debajo de las patas. La primera versión es de granito, pero también puede fabricarse con toda clase de piedras, como el mármol o la arenisca.

POR
Landing é uma luminária talhada em granito maciço. Como é fabricada com elementos naturais, também pode converter-se novamente em pó. Naturalmente, a luz não atravessa diretamente a pedra, mas a luminária é projetada de tal maneira que emane por debaixo das pernas. A primeira versão é de granito, mas também pode ser fabricada com todo tipo de pedra, como o mármore ou o arenito.

JUST MARRIED

DESIGN FIRM
Studio Klass

PHOTOGRAPHY
Marco Coppola

DESIGNERS
Marco Maturo & Alessio Roscini

Just Married lamps are made up of two different parts, the first from ceramic and the second from felt, which are joined together with a red thread. The lamps represent the union of two distant worlds, each so different in their detail that they are seemingly incompatible. The designers deliberately chose to work with ceramic and felt for this very reason; the first of these materials is decidedly cold, shiny, and reflective, while the second is warm, absorbing, and soft.

ESP

Las lámparas Just Married se componen de dos elementos; el primero está hecho de cerámica y el segundo de fieltro, y ambos están unidos mediante un hilo rojo. Estas lámparas representan la unión de dos mundos lejanos, con detalles tan distintos que nos parecen incompatibles. Ese es exactamente el motivo de que los diseñadores se decantaran por la cerámica y el fieltro: la primera es decididamente fría, reluciente y reflectante, mientras que el segundo es cálido, absorbente y blando.

FRA

Les lustres Just Married sont composés de deux parties reliées entre elles par un fil rouge : l'une est en céramique et l'autre en feutre. Ces lustres symbolisent l'union entre deux univers que tout semble opposer. Les designers ont choisi de travailler avec ces deux matières justement parce qu'elles sont foncièrement différentes. La céramique est froide, brillante et réfléchissante alors que le feutre est chaleureux, absorbant et doux.

POR

As luminárias Just Married se compõem de dois elementos; o primeiro é feito de cerâmica e o segundo de feltro, e ambos estão unidos por meio de um fio vermelho. Estas luminárias representam a união de dois mundos longínquos, com detalhes tão diferentes que nos parecem incompatíveis. Esse é exatamente o motivo de que os designers optaram pela cerâmica e pelo feltro: a primeira é, claramente, fria, reluzente e refletora, enquanto o segundo é quente, absorvente e suave.

ESP
Las lámparas de esta colección están hechas de lana y acero inoxidable y son el resultado de una investigación en la que se han explorado diversas formas de combinar ambas cosas. El principio básico que ha adoptado Dana Bachar consiste en seguir la naturaleza de los materiales, absteniéndose de usar elementos externos como pegamento, clavos o tornillos, pues ambos desempeñan una función visible en el objeto y el producto final es el resultado de la combinación de los dos.

FELTED

DESIGNER
Dana Bachar

PHOTOGRAPHY
Hagar Cygler & Dana Bachar

POR
As luminárias desta coleção são feitas de lã e aço inoxidável e são o resultado de uma pesquisa em que foram exploradas diversas formas de combinar ambas as coisas. O princípio básico que Dana Bachar adotou consiste em seguir a natureza dos materiais, abstendo-se de usar elementos externos como cola, pregos ou parafusos, pois ambos desempenham uma função visível no objeto e o produto final é resultado da combinação deles.

The lamps in this collection are made of wool and stainless steel, and are a result of research that explores various ways to combine these two materials. The guiding principle adopted by Dana Bachar was to follow the materials' nature while using no exterior connectors such as glue, nails, or screws. Each one of the materials has a discernible function in the object and combining the two has enabled the final product to be created.

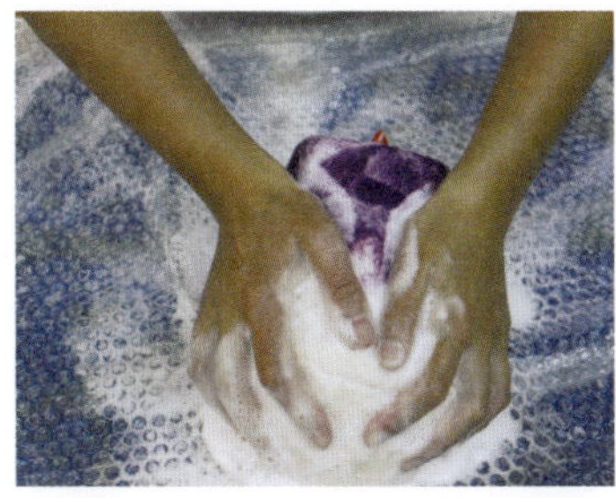

FRA
Les luminaires de cette collection, qui associent la laine et l'acier inoxydable, sont le produit d'une étude qui cherchait à combiner ces deux matières résolument différentes. L'idée directrice de Dana Bachar était de respecter la nature des deux matériaux et de les assembler sans colle ni clou ni vis. Chaque matière joue un rôle bien précis dans ces luminaires et c'est ce qui a permis de les réunir.

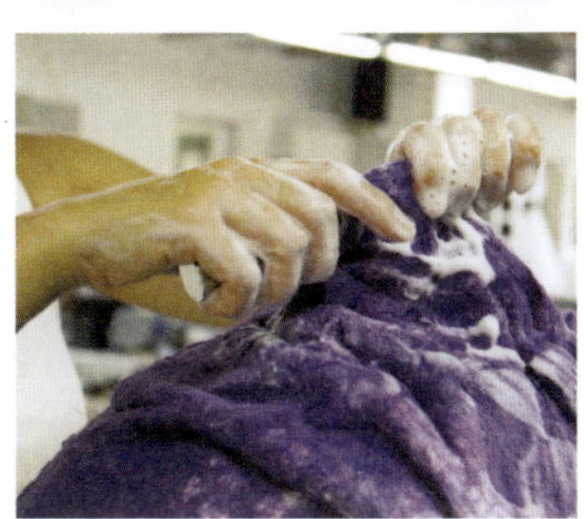

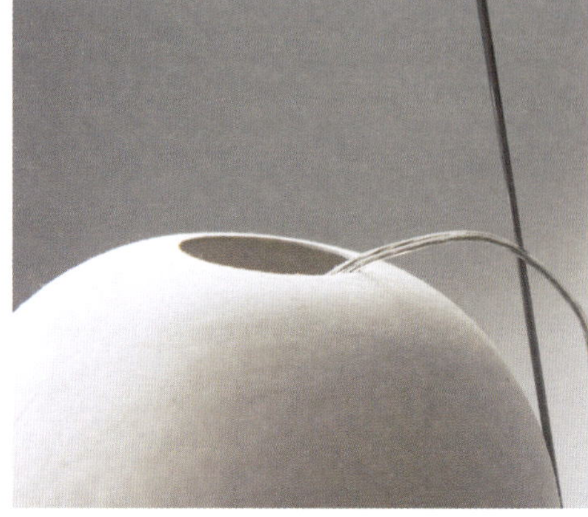

CAPPELLO

DESIGN FIRM
molo

DESIGNERS
Stephanie Forsythe & Todd MacAllen;

CLIENT
molo

Cappello is lit by LEDs and shaded by a paper "cap"—or "cappello" in Italian. Its magnetic connector allows the paper cap to move and tilt, adjusting the direction of the light and giving this little table lamp a gestural, anthropomorphic quality. The wire can leave its perch on the marble base to find another resting spot, and the paper cap with LED can clip to any steel surface using the magnetic connector.

FRA

Cappello utilise une ampoule LED et son abat-jour est une sorte de chapeau (« cappello » en italien) en papier fixé au bras de la lampe par un aimant permettant de l'orienter à loisir pour diriger le faisceau de lumière exactement où l'on veut. Le chapeau donne à la lampe un aspect légèrement anthropomorphe. Le fil électrique, qui repose sur le socle en marbre, peut être placé ailleurs et il est possible de retirer l'abat-jour avec son ampoule pour le fixer sur n'importe quelle surface métallique, grâce à son aimant.

ESP

Cappello se enciende con luces LED y cuenta con una pantalla en forma de «gorro» o capello en italiano, de papel. Gracias al conector magnético, este gorro se mueve y se inclina, modificando la trayectoria de la luz y confiriendo a esta pequeña lámpara de sobremesa características gestuales y antropomórficas. El cable puede retirarse de la guía dispuesta en la base de mármol y dejarse en otra parte, al igual que wel gorro de papel con luces LED puede adherirse a cualquier superficie de acero con el conector magnético.

POR

Cappello se acende com lâmpadas LED e conta com uma cúpula em forma de «gorro» ou *capello* em italiano, de papel. Graças ao conector magnético, este gorro se move e se inclina, modificando a trajetória da luz e conferindo a esta pequena luminária de mesa características gestuais e antropomórficas. O fio pode ser retirado da guia colocada na base de mármore e ser deixado em outro lugar. O gorro de papel com lâmpadas LED também pode aderir-se a qualquer superfície de aço por meio do conector magnético.

HOBO LANTERN

DESIGN FIRM
molo

DESIGNERS
Stephanie Forsythe & Todd MacAllen

PHOTOGRAPHY
molo

This portable bag of light is a piece of pragmatic poetry that can be used as a functional shoulder bag or solely as a lantern. It's perfect for creating extra visibility for pedestrians and cyclists on traffic-heavy city streets or during a romantic walk in the moonlight. At home you can choose to plug the lantern into a regular power outlet or use the included portable battery pack. An energy-efficient LED light source brings the lantern to life with a soft, luminous glow.

FRA

Cette lanterne originale est un objet tout aussi poétique que pragmatique : on peut s'en servir comme sac à bandoulière fonctionnel ou uniquement comme source d'éclairage. Elle permet tout aussi bien de donner davantage de visibilité aux piétons et aux cyclistes dans les rues à forte circulation automobile que d'accompagner une promenade romantique au clair de lune. Pour l'allumer, il suffit de la brancher chez soi sur une prise de courant classique ou d'utiliser la batterie portative fournie. L'ampoule LED de la lanterne est à économie d'énergie et fournit une lumière douce et brillante.

ESP

Esta bolsa luminosa portátil es un ejemplo de poesía funcional que puede utilizarse como farol o como un práctico bolso. Así, es perfecta para los peatones y los ciclistas que recorren las calles congestionadas por el tráfico o un romántico paseo a la luz de la luna. En casa se enchufa a una toma de corriente ordinaria o a la batería portátil que incluye. Entonces cobra vida con el brillo suave y luminoso de una bombilla LED de bajo consumo.

POR

Esta bolsa luminosa portátil é um exemplo de poesia funcional que pode ser utilizada como farol ou como uma prática bolsa. Assim sendo, é perfeita para os pedestres e os ciclistas que percorrem as ruas congestionadas pelo tráfego ou para um romântico passeio à luz da lua. Em casa, conecta-se a uma tomada elétrica comum ou à bateria portátil inclusa. Então, ganha vida com o brilho suave e luminoso de uma lâmpada LED de baixo consumo.

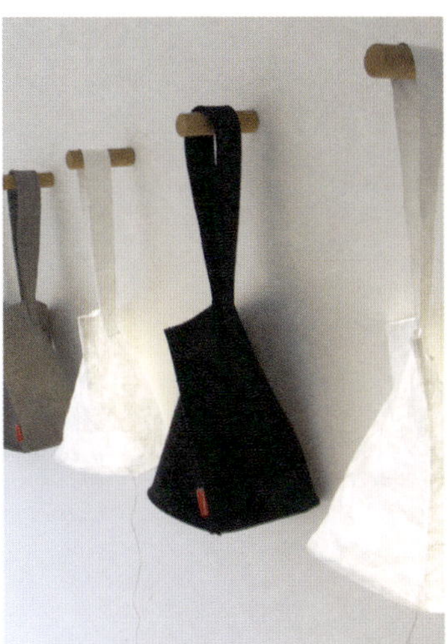

CLOUD SOFTLIGHT MOBILE

DESIGN FIRM
molo

DESIGNERS
Stephanie Forsythe & Todd MacAllen

PHOTOGRAPHY
molo

Cloud Softlight Mobile creates an undulating overhead canopy of soft, luminous forms. The cloud mobiles and pendants can be grouped together to create vast cloudscapes that flow in a unique topography and are tailored to the individual space they are shaping. The hollow cloud forms are internally lit by LED lights, making the sculptural three-dimensional forms mysteriously radiant when viewed from any direction.

FRA
Cloud Softlight Mobile crée une canopée ondulante de formes douces et lumineuses qui semblent flotter comme des nuages. On peut regrouper les mobiles et les lustres pour concevoir un vaste paysage nuageux parfaitement adapté à l'espace choisi. La forme creuse des nuages est éclairée de l'intérieur par des ampoules LED qui transforment les luminaires en sculptures mystérieuses auréolées de lumière, quel que soit l'angle d'observation.

ESP
Cloud Softlight Mobile es un dosel ondulante de formas suaves y luminosas. Los móviles y colgantes de nubes se agrupan creando amplios paisajes nublados que discurren en una topografía única y están hechos a la medida de los espacios individuales a los que dan forma. Las nubes huecas se iluminan desde dentro mediante luces LED, de tal manera que las formas esculturales en tres dimensiones brillan misteriosamente cuando se observan desde todas las direcciones.

POR
Cloud Softlight Mobile é um dossel ondulante de formas suaves e luminosas. Os móbiles e pendentes de nuvens agrupam-se, criando amplas paisagens nubladas que correm numa topografia única e são feitos na medida dos espaços individuais aos quais dão forma. As nuvens ocas se iluminam a partir do interior por meio de lâmpadas LED, de tal maneira que as formas esculturais em três dimensões brilham misteriosamente quando se observam de qualquer direção.

TEKIO LIGHT

DESIGN FIRM
Anthony Dickens

DESIGNER
Anthony Dickens

PHOTOGRAPHY
Anthony Dickens

Tekio is a modular lighting system designed by Anthony Dickens. It takes the idea of the traditional Japanese paper "Chochin" lantern into a new, design-led dimension. Tekio's innovation lies in its flexibility. Inside the paper tube, there is a frame that can be bent from straight to ninety degrees. The sections can also pivot around 360 degrees and are connected using magnets at the end of the paper tubes.

FRA
Tekio est un luminaire modulaire conçu par Anthony Dickens qui s'inspire de la lanterne en papier traditionnelle japonaise « Chochin », à laquelle il a ajouté la flexibilité. À l'intérieur du tube se trouve une armature que l'on peut plier de 0 à 90°. En outre, chaque module peut pivoter sur un axe de 360°. Les modules sont reliés entre eux à l'aide d'aimants placés à l'extrémité des tubes en papier.

ESP
Tekio es un sistema de iluminación compuesto de diversos módulos, obra del diseñador Anthony Dickens, que introduce el concepto tradicional del farol de papel japonés conocido como chochin en una nueva dimensión donde prevalece el diseño. La innovación de Tekio consiste en que es sumamente flexible. Dentro del tubo de papel hay una estructura que puede doblarse hasta un ángulo de 90 grados. Las diversas secciones también giran hasta 360 grados y están conectadas mediante imanes instalados en los extremos de los tubos.

POR
Tekio é um sistema de iluminação composto por diversos módulos, obra do designer Anthony Dickens, que introduz o conceito tradicional do farol de papel japonês conhecido como *chochin* numa nova dimensão onde prevalece o design. A inovação de Tekio consiste na suma flexibilidade. Dentro do tubo de papel há una estrutura que se pode dobrar até o ângulo de 90 graus. As diversas seções também giram até 360 graus e estão conectadas por meio de imãs instalados nas extremidades dos tubos.

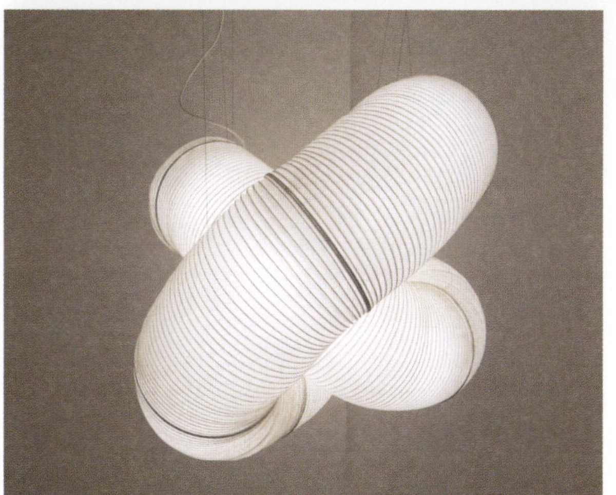

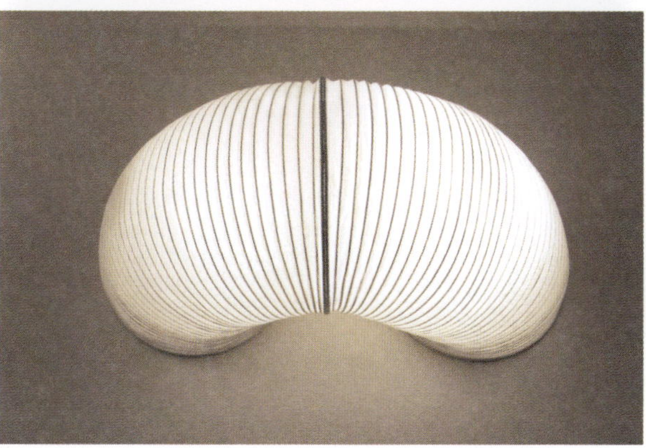

HONEYCOMB LAMP

DESIGN FIRM
Kyouei Design

DESIGNER
Kouichi Okamoto

PHOTOGRAPHY
Yuichi Yamaguchi

In making the Honeycomb Lamp, the fruit of a highly delicate and time-consuming crafting process, Kyouei Design used Denguri paper, a local product of the Shikoku region in Japan. When the lamp is packed up it has a thickness of about two centimeters, transforming into a lamp when you open it and fasten it together with the attached pins.

FRA
La fabrication d'un luminaire Honeycomb demande du temps et un grand savoir-faire. Le matériau utilisé par le cabinet de design Kyouei Design est le papier denguri, qui est produit dans la région de Shikoku au Japon. Dans son emballage, l'épaisseur du luminaire ne dépasse pas 2 cm. Mais une fois déplié et ses deux extrémités réunies à l'aide des attaches intégrées, il se transforme en lampe ou en lustre.

ESP
En la creación de la lámpara Honeycomb, el fruto de un proceso artesanal sumamente delicado y largo, Kyouei Design ha empleado papel denguri, un producto de la región japonesa de Shikoku. Cuando se embala tiene un grosor de apenas dos centímetros, transformándose en una lámpara cuando se abre y se ensambla con los alfileres que se incluyen.

POR
Na criação da luminária Honeycomb, fruto de um processo artesanal sumamente delicado e demorado, Kyouei Design empregou papel denguri, um produto da região japonesa de Shikoku. Quando embalada, tem a espessura de apenas dois centímetros, transformando-se numa luminária quando se abre e se monta com os alfinetes inclusos.

ICARUS

DESIGN FIRM
Latorre Cruz Studio

DESIGNER
Latorre Cruz

PHOTOGRAPHY
Latorre Cruz Studio

Icarus is a collection of handmade paper wings made from mulberry-tree bark. The fronds of the shades take on the appearance of the kind of feathers Icarus would have used to create his wings. The light shining through the wings creates a dreamy effect, achieving ethereality in a contrasting backdrop of gothic romanticism. Made with a low tooling process, the handmade paper is naturally processed.

ESP
Icarus es una colección de alas de papel fabricadas a mano con corteza de morera. Las copas de las pantallas se asemejan a las plumas que habría utilizado Ícaro. La luz que atraviesa las alas produce un efecto fantástico y etéreo que contrasta con el romanticismo gótico del fondo. Apenas se utilizan herramientas en la fabricación y el papel hecho a mano se procesa naturalmente.

FRA
Icarus est une collection d'ailes en papier fabriquées à la main à partir d'écorce de mûrier. Les plis de chaque élément rappellent les plumes qu'Icare aurait pu utiliser pour fabriquer les ailes lui permettant de s'envoler. La lumière qui filtre à travers les ailes distille une ambiance onirique qui contraste avec le motif d'inspiration romantique. Les machines interviennent très peu dans la fabrication du lustre Icare et le papier est produit à la main.

POR
Icarus é uma coleção de asas de papel fabricadas à mão com casca de amoreira. As copas das cúpulas assemelham-se às penas que Ícaro teria utilizado. A luz que atravessa as asas produz um efeito fantástico e etéreo que contrasta com o romantismo gótico do fundo. Quase não se utiliza nenhuma ferramenta na sua fabricação e o papel feito à mão é processado naturalmente.

STUDY OF LIFE

DESIGN FIRM
The Office of Victor Vetterlein

DESIGNER
Victor Vetterlein

PHOTOGRAPHY
Victor Vetterlein

The Study of Life pendant lamp appears to be a raging cyclone of wood caging the calm form of the paper orb. Its strong and flexible main shell is composed of bamboo sticks, sewing thread, and non-toxic wood glue. The inner orb is made from a bamboo rod encased in paper with non-toxic glue. Except for the lighting cord and fixture, which are reusable, the entire lamp is biodegradable after its life cycle.

FRA
Le lustre The Study of Life ressemble à des morceaux de bois emportés par la tempête formant cercle autour d'une boule en papier pour la protéger de la tourmente. Son armature, qui allie souplesse et solidité, est composée de baguettes de bambou et de fil à coudre assemblés à l'aide d'une colle à bois non toxique. La boule est formée de papier enroulé et collé sur une âme en bambou avec de la colle non toxique. Exception faite des composants électriques, qui sont réutilisables, la lampe est biodégradable une fois arrivée en fin de vie.

ESP
La lámpara colgante Study of Life parece un furioso ciclón de madera que aprisiona la forma serena del globo de papel. La estructura fuerte y flexible se compone de espigas de bambú, hilo de coser y pegamento de madera no tóxico. El globo del interior está hecho con una pértiga de bambú recubierta de papel con pegamento no tóxico. Con la excepción del casquillo y el cable eléctrico, que son reutilizables, toda la lámpara es biodegradable cuando termina su vida.

POR
A luminária pendente Study of Life parece um furioso ciclone de madeira que aprisiona a forma serena do globo de papel. A estrutura forte e flexível é composta por espigas de bambu, linha de costura e cola de madeira não tóxica. O globo do interior é feito com uma vara bambu recoberta com papel, com cola não tóxica. Com exceção do soquete e do fio elétrico, que são reutilizáveis, toda a luminária é biodegradável ao terminar a sua vida útil.

CONE LIGHT

DESIGN FIRM
h comma

DESIGNER
Hangyu Kim

PHOTOGRAPHY
Jaekook Suh

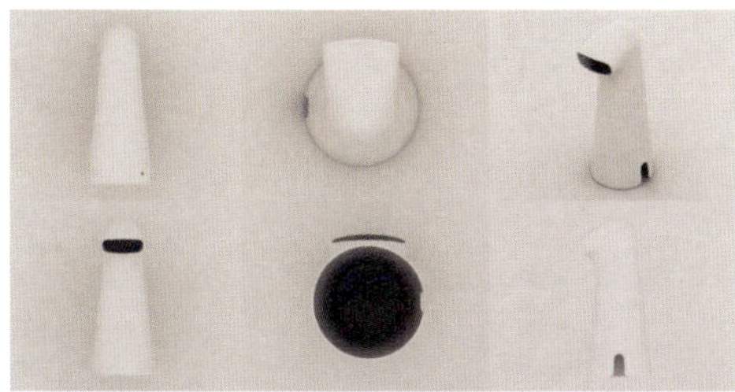

Hangyu Kim tries to integrate the rational and stable structures of outdoor objects into indoor ones. Made using ceramic materials, the Cone Light was designed by using the shape of an orange traffic cone, an item that is seemingly everywhere we look. The light is a free-standing upright form that emits light through a curved, periscope-like opening at its top. It also lights up a space around its base, where small objects can be placed.

FRA
Hangyu Kim s'applique à intégrer l'aspect rationnel et solide des objets conçus pour l'extérieur à ceux créés pour un espace intérieur. La lampe Cone Light, fabriquée en céramique, s'inspire des cônes oranges de signalisation que l'on voie un petit peu partout. La lumière de cette lampe de table est diffusée par une ouverture coudée en forme de périscope située en son sommet, ainsi que par deux évents latéraux placés près du socle, qui permettront de repérer facilement les petits objets posés à proximité.

ESP
Hangyu Kim intenta integrar en los interiores las estructuras racionales y estables de los objetos de exterior. Así, el diseño de la lámpara Cone Light, fabricada con materiales de cerámica, se basa en la forma de un cono de tráfico naranja, un objeto que aparentemente se encuentre allá donde miremos. Esta lámpara cónica, semejante a un periscopio, se sostiene sola y emite luz a través de una apertura combada en la sección más alta. También ilumina un espacio en torno la base en el que pueden depositarse objetos pequeños.

POR
Hangyu Kim tenta integrar nos interiores as estruturas racionais e estáveis dos objetos de exteriores. Deste modo, o design da luminária Cone Light, fabricada com materiais de cerâmica, baseia-se na forma de um cone de tráfego laranja, um objeto que, aparentemente, é encontrado em qualquer que olhamos. Esta luminária cônica, semelhante a um periscópio, sustenta-se sozinha e emite luz através de uma abertura empenada na seção mais alta. Também ilumina um espaço em torno da base, no qual objetos pequenos podem ser colocados.

COCOON PENDANT LIGHT

DESIGN FIRM
MacMaster

DESIGNER
Limahl Asmall

PHOTOGRAPHY
James Champion

CLIENT
MacMaster

The Cocoon Pendant Light utilizes a 2.8mm-thin yet extremely durable three-part timber lamination process to create a strong, elegant, and flexible structure that naturally lends its lightweight properties to elegant and structurally complex lighting applications. The laminations are bonded by an extremely strong resin which increases durability and keeps the thin timber from warping as a result of temperature and humidity changes in the environment.

FRA
Le lustre Cocoon est fabriqué à partir de languettes de bois de 2,8 mm d'épaisseur formées de trois plis, ce qui les rend particulièrement solides. Le résultat est une structure résistante, élégante et souple, qui tire parti de sa légèreté pour procurer une source d'éclairage raffinée et fonctionnelle. Les plis des languettes sont collés à l'aide d'une résine extrêmement forte qui prolonge sa durabilité et empêche le bois de se déformer sous l'effet de la chaleur ou de l'humidité.

ESP
La lámpara colgante Cocoon utiliza un proceso excepcionalmente duradero de laminado de la madera en tres secciones de 2,8 milímetros de grosor con el que se obtiene una estructura que es al mismo tiempo fuerte, elegante y flexible y que contribuye naturalmente con esta ligereza a las aplicaciones luminosas refinadas y las estructuras complejas. Las láminas están unidas mediante una resina extraordinariamente fuerte que no solo hace que sean más resistentes al tiempo, sino que impide que se deformen a resultas de los cambios de temperatura y humedad en el ambiente.

POR
A luminária pendente Cocoon utiliza um processo excepcionalmente duradouro de laminado de madeira em três seções de 2,8 milímetros de espessura e com isso se consegue uma estrutura que é ao mesmo tempo forte, elegante e flexível e que contribui naturalmente com esta leveza para aplicações luminosas refinadas e estruturas complexas. As lâminas são unidas por meio de uma resina extraordinariamente forte que não só faz com que sejam mais resistentes ao tempo, mas também impede que se deformem como resultado das mudanças de temperatura e umidade no ambiente.

ONDOL LAMP

DESIGN FIRM
UUN Design Studio

DESIGNER
Kim HyunJoo

PHOTOGRAPHY
Kim HyunJoo

CLIENT
UUN Design Studio

The Ondol Lamp is made of folding floor paper, which is easy to handle, economical, and difficult to tear or wrinkle. It is used to create the traditional Korean under-floor heating system known as ondol. Korean people may experience a feeling of childhood nostalgia in response to the Ondol Lamp, associating the light emitted through the floor paper with the warmth of an ondol heating system. Overall it's an excellent material for making a lamp.

FRA
Le lampadaire Ondol est fabriqué avec du papier pare humidité pour plancher qui est un matériau économique facile à manipuler et résistant aux déchirures et au froissage. On l'utilise en Corée dans l'élaboration du système de chauffage par le sol traditionnel appelé « ondol ». Les lampadaires Ondol évoqueront chez les Coréens la nostalgie d'une enfance baignée dans la lumière filtrant au travers des lattes chaudes du plancher. Ce type de papier est un matériau idéal pour la fabrication de luminaires.

ESP
La lámpara Ondol está hecha de papel plegable para suelos, que no solo es económico sino que además se manipula sin dificultades y no se rompe ni se arruga fácilmente. Este material se utiliza en el tradicional sistema de calefacción subterránea coreano conocido como ondol; de hecho, es posible que algunos coreanos experimenten cierta nostalgia de la infancia frente a la lámpara Ondol, al asociar la luz que esta emite con el calor que despide el sistema de calefacción del mismo nombre. En términos generales se trata de un material excelente para una lámpara.

POR
A luminária Ondol é feita de papel dobrável para pisos, que não só é econômico, mas também se manuseia sem dificuldades e não se quebra nem enruga facilmente. Este material se utiliza no tradicional sistema de calefação subterrânea coreano, conhecido como *ondol*; de fato, é possível que alguns coreanos sintam certa saudade da infância diante da luminária Ondol, ao associar a luz que esta emite com o calor que libera o sistema de calefação do mesmo nome. Em termos gerais, trata-se de um material excelente para uma luminária.

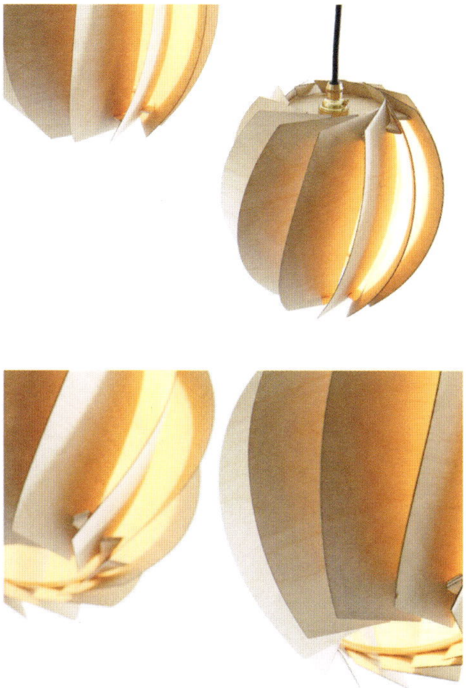

BLOOM PENDANT LIGHT

DESIGN FIRM
MacMaster

DESIGNER
Alex MacMaster

PHOTOGRAPHY
James Champion

CLIENT
MacMaster

The Bloom Pendant Light is made from 100 percent FSC-certified birch plywood, is flat-packable for ease of storage and shipping, and is constructed without glue or external fittings. The curved form that is a signature aesthetic within MacMaster's product range is created here without the use of laminations, instead being formed from flat sheets of lightweight birch aero-ply, which neatly slot into the two columns and thus create the curved form.

FRA
Le lustre Bloom est en contreplaqué de bouleau certifié 100 % FSC fabriqué sans colle ni clou ni vis. On le replie à plat pour le ranger ou l'emballer en vue de son expédition. La forme arrondie, typique de la gamme de produits MacMaster, n'est pas obtenue par laminage : les fines lames de contreplaqué adoptent naturellement ce galbe une fois qu'elles sont insérées dans les rainures.

ESP
La lámpara colgante Bloom está hecha de madera contrachapada de abedul con certificado FSC, es completamente plegable para guardarse y transportarse sin dificultades, y no requiere adhesivos ni accesorios externos en el montaje. La curvatura que constituye la impronta estética de toda la gama de productos de MacMaster se ha obtenido sin el uso de laminados, sino que se consigue gracias a la ligera madera contrachapada, que se inserta fácilmente en las dos columnas, creando así la forma.

POR
A luminária pendente Bloom, feita de madeira compensada de bétula com certificação FSC, é completamente dobrável para ser guardada e transportada sem dificuldade, e não requer adesivos em acessórios externos em sua montagem. A curvatura que constitui a marca estética de toda a gama dos produtos de MacMaster é obtida sem o uso de laminados, mas graças à leve madeira compensada que se insere facilmente nas duas colunas, criando assim a forma.

WOODEN CHANDELIER

DESIGN FIRM
David Krynauw

DESIGNER
David Krynauw

PHOTOGRAPHY
Stef Ernst

As a designer David Krynauw loves to take seemingly worthless pieces of material and transform them into something of great value. Every year an immense amount of trees are cut down by tree-felling companies in urban areas. David's goal was to salvage some of these tree branches to see if he could create inspiring pieces. By using Jacaranda timber he created a series of pendants which is based around eco-friendly, innovative sustainability.

FRA

La passion du designer David Krynauw est de transformer des chutes de matériaux sans valeur en objets de prix. Tous les ans, les sociétés d'abattage coupent des milliers d'arbres dans les zones urbaines. David Krynauw a ramassé des branches abandonnées pour voir s'il pourrait en tirer quelque chose. Parmi les produits écologiques et novateurs en termes de durabilité, il a créé des lustres en bois de jacaranda.

ESP

A David Krynauw le encanta apropiarse de materiales aparentemente ordinarios y transformarlos en algo mucho más valioso. En las zonas urbanas se talan muchos árboles todos los años. David se propone reciclar las ramas de algunos de ellos para crear obras inspiradoras. Así, ha diseñado una serie de lámparas colgantes de madera de jacaranda que se inspiran en el concepto de sostenibilidad innovadora y respetuosa con el medio ambiente.

POR

David Krynauw adora lançar mão de materiais aparentemente ordinários e transformá-los em algo muito mais valioso. Nas zonas urbanas, podam-se muitas árvores todos os anos. David se propõe reciclar os ramos de algumas delas para criar obras inspiradoras. Deste modo, desenhou uma série de luminárias pendentes de madeira de jacarandá que se inspiram no conceito de sustentabilidade inovadora e respeitosa com o meio ambiente.

THE GUDPAKA LAMP

DESIGN FIRM
gt2P

PHOTOGRAPHY
Studio Schkolnick

The Gudpaka Lamp brings together manufacturing and production processes from both the digital and technological fields and artisan and low-tech methods. It is a game of opposites. Besides merging digital and traditional in its manufacturing process, the global and the local also meet in its design process, while it is also a meeting of vegetable and animal in its appearance, smooth shapes and flat faces in its geometry, and northern and southern Chile in the materials it uses.

ESP
La lámpara Gudpaka compagina los procesos de fabricación y producción digitales y tecnológicos con los métodos artesanales y sencillos. Se trata de un juego de opuestos. No solo se funden lo digital y lo tradicional en la fabricación, sino que también se combinan los aspectos globales y locales en el diseño, los contornos vegetales y animales en la apariencia, las formas y las caras planas en la geometría y el norte y el sur de Chile en los materiales que se utilizan.

FRA
Le lustre Gudpaka fait appel à des procédés de fabrication et de production qui combinent technologie numérique et artisanat. Et sa double nature ne s'arrête pas là, puisque son aspect extérieur inspiré du monde animal et végétal contraste avec la forme géométrique de son armature. Les matériaux viennent aussi de points opposés, soit du nord et du sud du Chili.

POR
A luminária Gudpaka compagina os processos de fabricação e produção digitais e tecnológicos com os métodos artesanais e simples. Trata-se de um jogo de opostos. Não só se fundem o digital e o tradicional em sua fabricação, mas também se combinam os aspectos globais e locais no design, os contornos vegetais e animais na aparência, as formas e as faces planas na geometria, e o norte e o sul do Chile nos materiais que se utilizam.

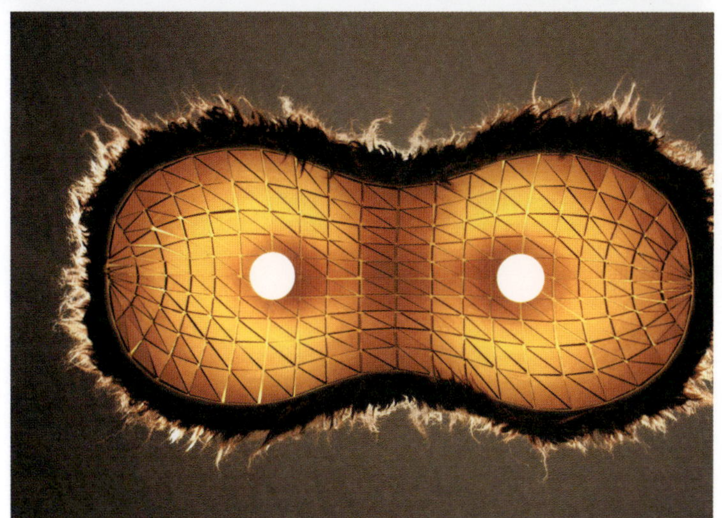

MESHMATICS

DESIGNER
Rick Tegelaar

PHOTOGRAPHY
Rick Tegelaar

The Meshmatics collection focuses on discovering new possibilities and applications for existing materials. It shows how new tools and methods can give even the most banal materials new qualities. All three lamps are made of chicken wire, a material usually without any meaning or value within a design context. When the lamps are turned off one can only see the outer layer of paper. However, when the lamps are lit they reveal the way they are built, creating a vivid light projection.

FRA
L'objectif de la collection Meshmatics est de montrer les possibilités et les applications insoupçonnées que l'on peut tirer de matériaux existants. De nouveaux outils et méthodes de fabrication nous font découvrir les qualités inattendues des matières les plus banales qui soient. Les luminaires de la collection Meshmatics utilisent du grillage de poulailler, qui n'a absolument aucun rapport avec le monde du design. Lorsqu'ils sont éteints, on voit uniquement le papier extérieur de leur abat-jour. En revanche, une fois allumés, on distingue clairement leur armature grillagée qui joue avec la lumière projetée.

ESP
El objetivo de la colección Meshmatics es descubrir nuevas posibilidades y aplicaciones para los materiales existentes, demostrando que empleando herramientas y métodos novedosos se confieren cualidades insólitas incluso a los objetos más banales. Estas tres lámparas están hechas de alambre de gallinero, un material que en el contexto del diseño normalmente no tiene significado ni valor alguno. Cuando se apagan solo se ve la capa externa de papel; sin embargo, cuando se encienden revelan la forma en la que están construidas y proyectan una luz intensa.

POR
O objetivo da coleção Meshmatics é descobrir novas possibilidades e aplicações para os materiais existentes, demonstrando que, ao utilizar ferramentas e métodos inovadores, se pode atribuir qualidades inusitadas inclusive aos objetos mais banais. Estas três luminárias são feitas de tela de galinheiro, um material que no contexto do design normalmente não tem significado nem valor algum. Quando se apagam, só se vê a capa externa de papel; no entanto, quando se acendem, revelam a forma como foram construídas e projetam uma luz intensa.

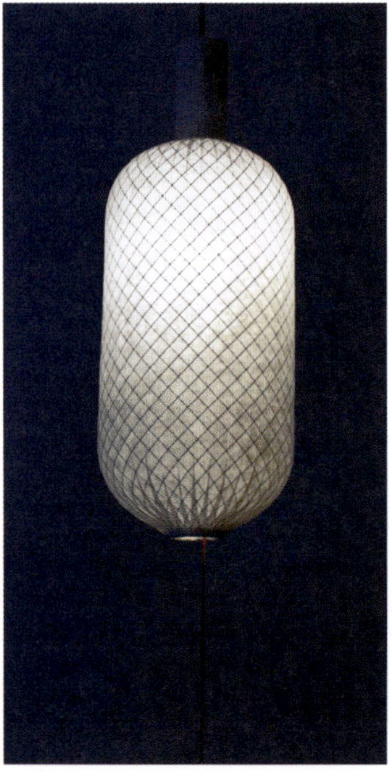

UP IN THE CLOUDS

DESIGN FIRM
Eva Menz Design

DESIGNER
Eva Menz Design Team

PHOTOGRAPHY
Jennifer Pakuls

CLIENT
Ritz Carlton

In 2011 The Ritz Carlton completed their latest hotel. It features the highest spa in the world, on the 116th floor and at 465 meters above ground level. Eva Menz was approached to create a chandelier and wall sculpture that would complement this unique spa experience by utilizing soft, smooth, and natural materials suited to the celestial backdrop of the clouds. The chandelier Menz designed greets guests as they enter the spa for their relaxing and rejuvenating experience.

FRA
En 2011, le Ritz Carlton a achevé la construction de leur tout dernier hôtel, qui possède le spa le plus élevé du monde, situé au 116ème étage et à 465 mètres du sol. Eva Menz a été choisie pour créer un lustre et une sculpture murale qui complèterait harmonieusement cet espace unique en son genre. Elle a utilisé des matières douces, lisses et naturelles pour créer une sculpture qui rappelle les nuages du ciel environnant. Quant au lustre, il accueille les clients qui viennent au spa pour se relaxer et se ressourcer.

ESP
En 2011 se inaugura el hotel Ritz Carlton que alberga el balneario más alto del mundo, instalado en la planta 116, a nada menos que 465 metros sobre el nivel del suelo. Los administradores le encargan a Eva Menz que cree una araña y una escultura mural que complemente la experiencia de este insólito entorno empleando materiales delicados, tersos y naturales, en consonancia con el fondo celestial de las nubes. Ahora, la araña de Menz recibe a los huéspedes cuando estos entran en el balneario para entregarse a una experiencia relajante y rejuvenecedora.

POR
Em 2011, inaugura-se o hotel Ritz Carlton, que possui o balneário mais alto do mundo, instalado no 116º andar, nada menos que a 465 metros acima do nível do chão. Os administradores solicitaram a Eva Menz que criasse um lustre e uma escultura mural que complementasse a experiência deste inusitado ambiente empregando materiais delicados, sóbrios e naturais, em consonância com o fundo celestial das nuvens. Agora, o lustre de Menz recepciona os hóspedes que entram no balneário para se entregarem a uma experiência relaxante e rejuvenescedora.

M_COCOON

DESIGN FIRM
Woodlabo

DESIGNER
Gael Wuithier

M_Cocoon is a new interpretation of the antique chandelier that combines contemporary forms and noble materials. Its silky yet sharp lines allow it to produce an expressive light. M_Cocoon is made of natural birch veneer that comes from sustainably managed Finnish forests.

FRA
M_Cocoon est une interprétation originale des lustres d'autrefois qui associe des formes contemporaines à des matériaux nobles. Ses lignes à la fois galbées et géométriques diffusent une belle lumière. M_Cocoon est fabriqué en contreplaqué de bouleau provenant de forêts finlandaises à gestion durable.

ESP
M_Cocoon constituye una nueva interpretación del concepto de araña que combina las formas contemporáneas y los materiales nobles, emanando una luz expresiva gracias a sus líneas sedosas y acusadas. M_Cocoon está hecha con chapa de abedul natural que se obtiene en bosques fineses gestionados de manera sostenible.

POR
M_Cocoon constitui uma nova interpretação do conceito de lustre, que combina as formas contemporâneas e os materiais nobres, emanando uma luz expressiva graças às suas linhas sedosas e destacadas. M_Cocoon é feito com chapa de bétula natural obtida em bosques finlandeses explorados de maneira sustentável.

BUTTERFLY LIGHT

DESIGN FIRM
Tom Raffield Design

DESIGNER
Tom Raffield

PHOTOGRAPHY
Mark Wallwork

This lamp was inspired by the movement and beauty of a butterfly in full flight. Its form intercepts the light, making intricate shadows and producing a stunning lighting effect in any space. It is handmade in Cornwall from walnut sourced from sustainably managed forests.

ESP
Esta lámpara se inspira en el movimiento y la belleza de una mariposa en pleno vuelo. La forma intercepta la luz, creando sombras intrincadas y produciendo un fascinante efecto luminoso en cualquier espacio. Está hecha a mano en Cornualles con madera de nogal que se obtiene en bosques gestionados de forma sostenible.

FRA
Ce luminaire s'inspire du mouvement et de la beauté d'un papillon en plein vol. Sa forme diffuse la lumière et dessine des ombres qui forment dans l'espace des effets spectaculaires. Il est fabriqué à la main dans le Cornwall à partir de noyer provenant de forêts à gestion durable.

POR
Esta luminária inspira-se no movimento e na beleza de uma borboleta em pleno voo. A forma intercepta a luz, criando sombras intrincadas e produzindo um fascinante efeito luminoso em qualquer espaço. É feita à mão em Cornualles, com madeira de nogueira obtida em bosques explorados de forma sustentável.

YAYA

DESIGNER
Mauro Soddu

PHOTOGRAPHY
Raffaele Vargiu

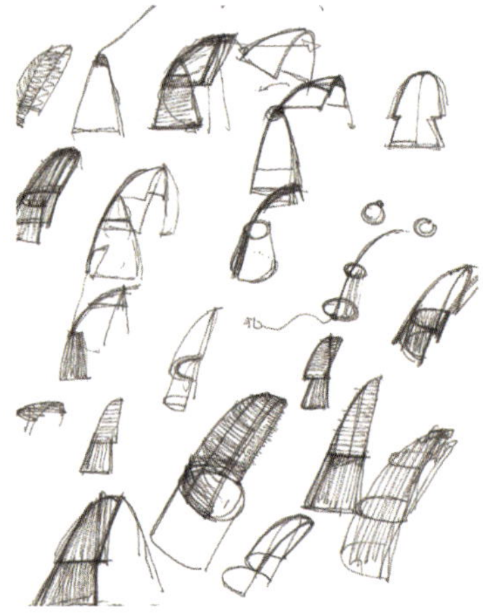

Italian architect Mauro Soddu has created a lamp that celebrates the traditional elderly matriarchs of Sardinia, Italy. The close relationship between Sardinian women and the weaving process influenced his choice of wool as the principal material. Soddu's aim is to evoke the role of the grandmother, which is slowly diminishing in a rapidly modernizing society. The lamp has a very simple and thin iron structure based on five curved elements.

FRA
L'architecte italien a conçu un lampadaire qui célèbre les vieilles femmes de la Sardaigne d'autrefois qui régentaient leur famille. Leur vie était indissolublement liée à la laine qu'elles tricotaient sans relâche. C'est pourquoi le designer a choisi cette matière pour habiller son lampadaire. Mauro Soddu cherche ici à évoquer le rôle de la grand-mère qui a perdu de l'importance dans nos sociétés modernes. L'armature du lampadaire, très épurée, consiste en cinq tubes cintrés en fer.

ESP
El arquitecto italiano Mauro Soddu ha diseñado una lámpara con la que rinde homenaje a las ancianas matriarcas tradicionales de Cerdeña, Italia.
La estrecha relación que mantienen las mujeres corsas con el proceso de tejido ha determinado la elección de la lana como el material más importante.
El objetivo de Soddu consiste en reivindicar el papel que desempeñan las abuelas, que está desapareciendo poco a poco en una sociedad que se moderniza rápidamente.
La lámpara tiene una delgada estructura de hierro muy sencilla que se basa en cinco elementos curvilíneos.

POR
O arquiteto italiano Mauro Soddu projetou uma luminária para prestar homenagem às tradicionais matriarcas anciãs da Sardenha, Itália. A estreita relação que as mulheres corsas têm com o processamento do tecido determinou a escolha da lã como sendo o material mais importante. O objetivo de Soddu consiste em reivindicar o papel que as avós desempenham, que está desaparecendo, pouco a pouco, numa sociedade que se moderniza rapidamente. A luminária possui uma fina estrutura de ferro muito simples, que se apóia em cinco elementos curvilíneos.

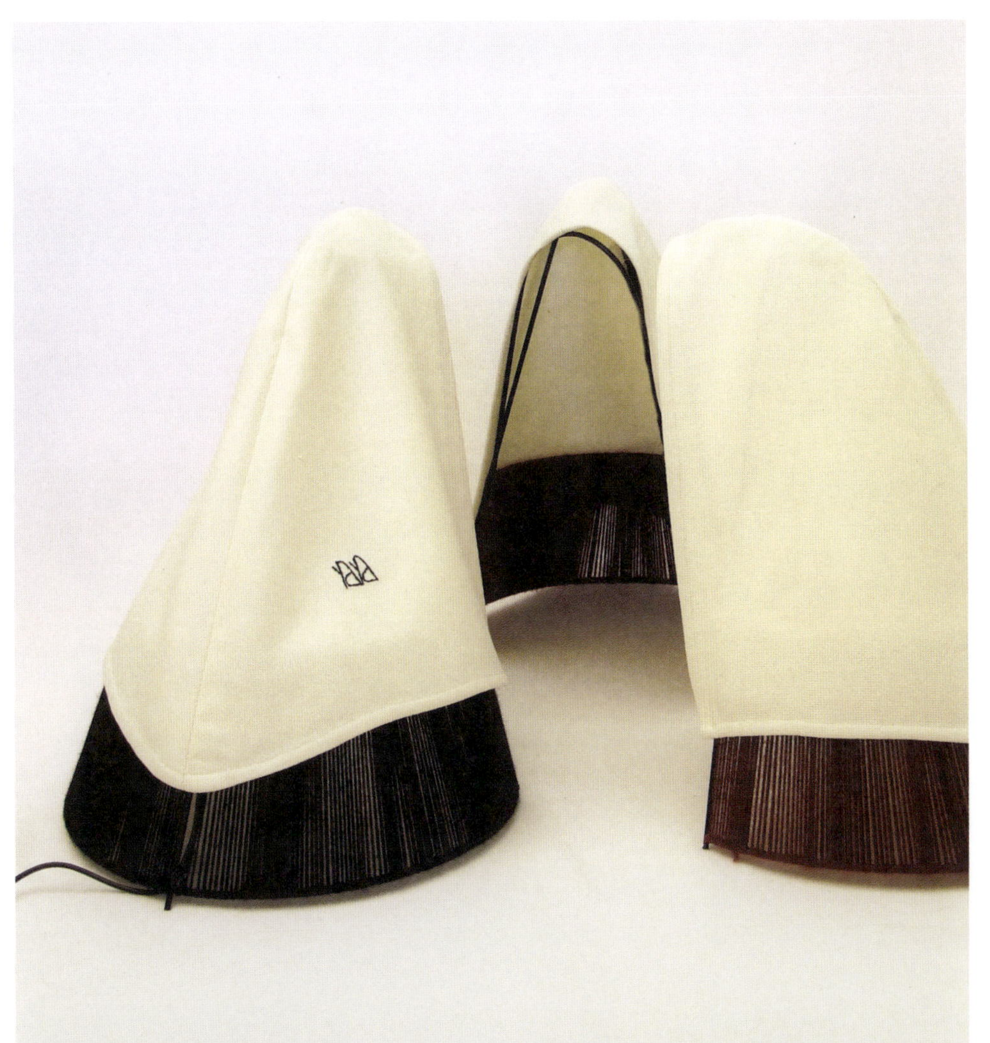

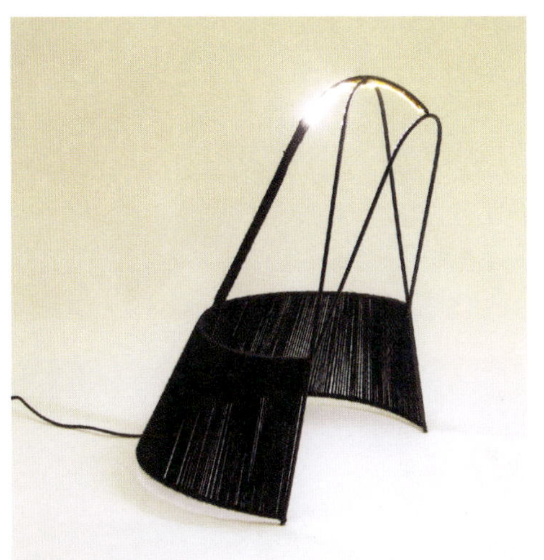

FLOOR CHANDELIER

DESIGN FIRM
DROR

PHOTOGRAPHY
Studio Dror

DESIGNER
Dror Benshetrit

CLIENT
Swarovski Crystallized

This unusual piece displaces the chandelier from the ceiling to the floor. Clear strands weave together 6,400 Swarovski crystals in a grid pattern. When the frame opens, the grid transforms into two sweeping parabolas. The frame itself, a Dror patent, has a self-locking hinge system with no fasteners. Four incandescent strips are placed on the inner walls of the frame, creating a dramatic ambiance as the light glimmers through the curved web of crystals.

FRA
L'esthétique de ce lampadaire rappelle plutôt un lustre en cristal qu'un luminaire à pied classique. Il est constitué de rangs de 6 400 cristaux Swarovski formant un quadrillage transparent. Lorsque l'on écarte les côtés du cadre, il se transforme en deux paraboles harmonieuses. Le cadre est un modèle déposé de Dror. Il est équipé d'un système de charnières autobloquantes dépourvu d'attaches. Quatre tubes incandescents placés sur les chants intérieurs du cadre créent une atmosphère féerique, la lumière traversant les cristaux du maillage.

ESP
En esta insólita obra la araña se desplaza desde el techo hasta el suelo. En una serie de hilos transparentes se enhebran hasta 6.400 cristales Swarovski, componiendo un diseño en forma de cuadrícula. Cuando se abre la estructura, esta cuadrícula se transforma en dos amplias parábolas. La propia estructura, una patente de Dror, cuenta con un sistema de bisagras que se cierran solas, sin la ayuda de fijaciones. Además, en las paredes internas se han instalado cuatro tiras ncandescentes con las que se crea un ambiente dramático cuando la luz atraviesa esta sinuosa telaraña de cristales.

POR
Nesta inusitada obra o lustre se desloca do teto até o solo. Numa série de fios transparentes se enfileiram até 6.400 cristais Swarovski, compondo um desenho em forma de quadrícula. Quando se abre a estrutura, esta quadricula se transforma em duas amplas parábolas. A própria estrutura, uma patente de Dror, conta com um sistema de dobradiças que se fecham por si mesmas, sem a ajuda de fixações. Além disso, nas paredes internas, foram instaladas quatro tiras incandescentes com as quais se cria um ambiente dramático quando a luz atravessa esta sinuosa teia de aranha de cristais.

VOLUME MGX

DESIGN FIRM
DROR

PHOTOGRAPHY
Studio Dror

DESIGNER
Dror Benshetrit

CLIENT
Materialise

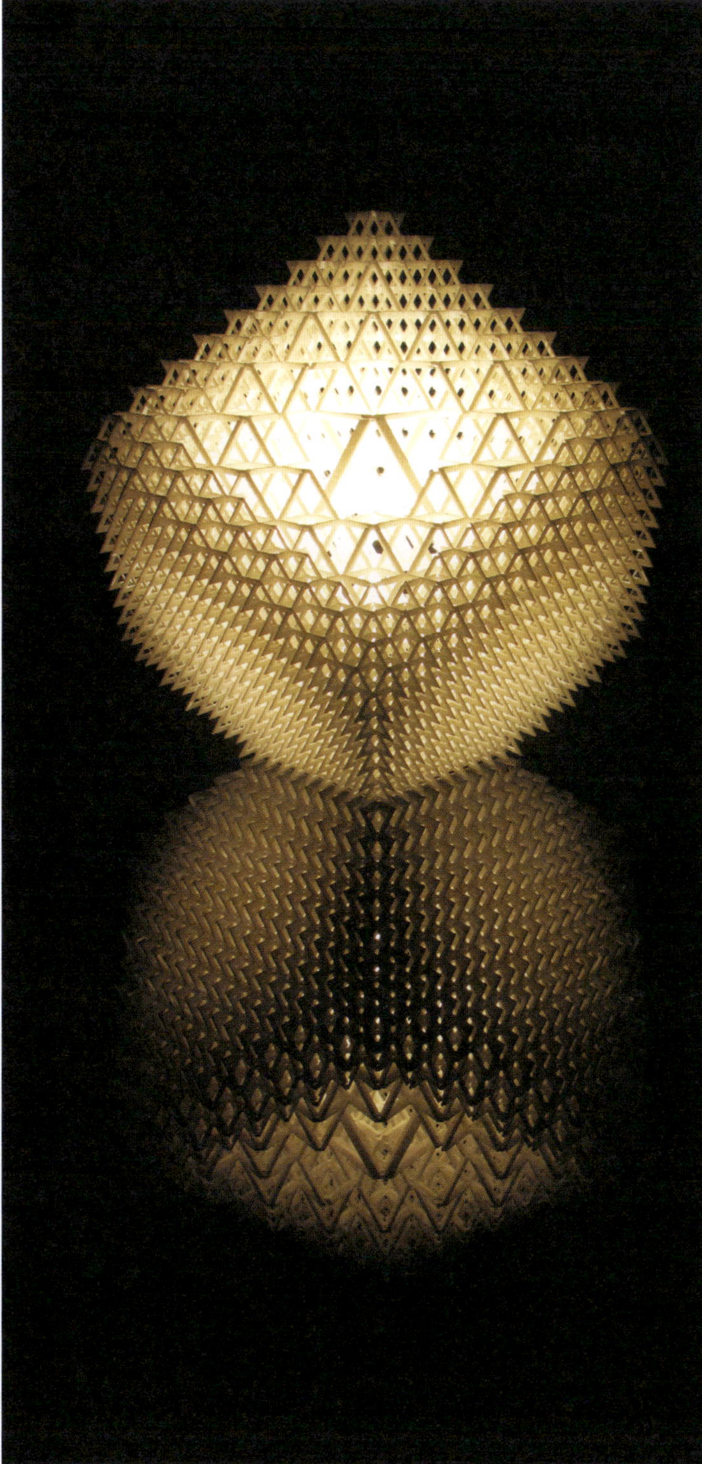

Dror Benshetrit has applied his famed QuaDror geometry to a flat print of interlocking squares to create the three-dimensional Volume MGX. When illuminated, the beautiful complexity of the shape is highlighted through the various effects the light has on the hundreds of squares that make up the collapsible form. The light is diffused in a way that gives the structure a bright, warm glow in the center, which gradually fades into cooler, darker shades at the edges and corners of the cube.

ESP

Dror Benshetrit ha aplicado la famosa geometría QuaDror en esta plancha de cuadrados que se entrelazan, creando las tres dimensiones de la lámpara Volume MGX. Cuando se ilumina, los múltiples efectos de la luz sobre los cientos de cuadrados que componen la estructura plegable subrayan esta forma hermosa y compleja. La luz se difunde de tal manera que el centro de la estructura adquiere un brillo cálido y luminoso que se debilita gradualmente, dando paso a sombras más frías y oscuras en los márgenes y las aristas del cubo.

FRA

Dror Benshetrit a utilisé le motif géométrique de son célèbre QuaDror pour créer la plaque de carrés entrecroisés qui constitue la base du luminaire Volume MGX. Lorsque la lampe est allumée, la lumière diffusée par les centaines de carrés de sa superbe structure alvéolaire, crée des effets magiques sur les surfaces environnantes. Son éclat est plus chaud et soutenu au centre du luminaire et devient plus ténu et plus froid à mesure qu'il s'approche des bords et des angles du cube.

POR

Dror Benshetrit aplicou a famosa geometria QuaDror nesta prancha de quadrados que se entrelaçam, criando as três dimensões da luminária Volume MGX. Quando é acesa, os múltiplos efeitos da luz sobre as centenas de quadrados que compõem a estrutura dobrável destacam esta forma bonita e complexa. A luz difunde-se de tal maneira que o centro da estrutura adquire um brilho cálido e luminoso que se atenua gradualmente, dando lugar a sombras mais frias e escuras nas margens e arestas do cubo.

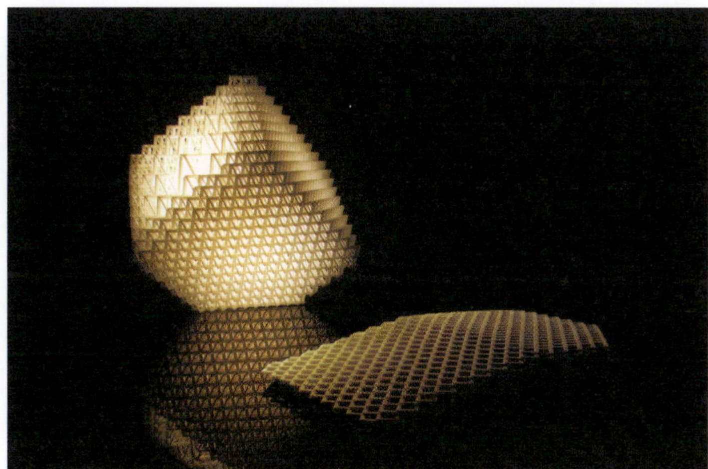

FLIGHT TO GALWAY

DESIGN FIRM
Eva Menz Design

DESIGNER
Eva Menz Design Team

PHOTOGRAPHY
G Hotel

CLIENT
ESPA

Luxury spa company ESPA commissioned Eva Menz to create this installation for their spa in the G Hotel in Galway, Ireland. Origami cranes, which traditionally symbolize long life, health, and prosperity, were meticulously handmade and installed against a backdrop of beautiful slate stone. The installation went on to be named Best European Spa Design in 2006.

FRA
La société de spas de luxe ESPA a confié à Eva Menz la création de cette installation pour leur spa du G Hotel de Galway en Irlande. Les grues en origami, symboles de longévité, santé et prospérité, ont été fabriquées à la main et accrochées de manière à bien ressortir sur le superbe fond en ardoise. Cette installation a remporté le prix du Meilleur design de spa européen en 2006.

ESP
La empresa de balnearios de lujo ESPA encarga a Eva Menz esta instalación destinada al spa del Hotel G de Galway, Irlanda. Las garzas de origami, que tradicionalmente simbolizan la longevidad, la salud y la riqueza, están hechas a mano con gran cuidado y destacan sobre un fondo de hermosa pizarra. Esta instalación recibe el galardón al Mejor Diseño de Spa de Europa en 2006.

POR
A empresa de balneários de luxo ESPA encomenda a Eva Menz esta instalação destinada ao spa do Hotel G de Galway, Irlanda. As garças de origami que tradicionalmente simbolizam a longevidade, a saúde e a riqueza, são confeccionadas à mão com grande esmero e se destacam sobre o fundo de uma linda ardósia. Esta instalação recebe o prêmio de Melhor Design de Spa da Europa em 2006.

DUET NOIR

DESIGN FIRM
Eva Menz Design

DESIGNER
Eva Menz Design Team

PHOTOGRAPHY
Mister Important Design

CLIENT
Mister Important Design

A restaurant by day and dance floor by night, this space required a piece that was translucent yet present. With the changing light, Duet Noir makes for a gentle installation during the day and a mystical ceiling feature at night. This eleven-meter piece contains in excess of seven thousand rocks made of mixed recycled glass, individually suspended over the dance floor. The composition of this piece emulates two large petals engaged in an elegant dance with one another.

FRA

Cet espace qui fait restaurant le jour et piste de danse le soir avait besoin d'un éclairage qui soit à la fois translucide et original. Avec le changement de lumière, Duet Noir qui est une installation sage le jour, devienne un ciel féerique la nuit. Ce luminaire d'une longueur de onze mètres est composé de plus de sept mille obsidiennes artificielles fabriquées dans un mélange de verre recyclé, suspendues chacune au bout d'un fil accroché au-dessus de la piste de danse. L'ensemble ressemble à deux pétales qui dansent gracieusement enlacés.

ESP

Restaurante de día y sala de baile de noche, este espacio requiere una obra translúcida y visible al mismo tiempo. Con la luz cambiante, Duet Noir hace las veces de instalación delicada durante el día y adorno colgante místico durante la noche. Esta obra de once metros contiene más de siete mil rocas de una amalgama de vidrio reciclado, suspendidas una a una sobre la pista de baile. La composición semeja dos grandes pétalos que bailan con elegancia.

POR

Restaurante de dia e salão de baile à noite, este espaço requer uma obra translúcida e, ao mesmo tempo, visível. Com a luz cambiante, Duet Noir faz o papel de instalação delicada durante o dia e de adorno pendente místico durante a noite. Esta obra de onze metros contém mais de sete mil rochas de uma amálgama de vidro reciclado, penduradas uma por uma sobre a pista de baile. A composição assemelha-se a duas grandes pétalas que dançam com elegância.

SINGING WATER

DESIGN FIRM
Eva Menz Design

DESIGNER
Eva Menz Design Team

PHOTOGRAPHY
Mister Important Design

CLIENT
Mister Important Design

Singing Water draws inspiration from the rock shapes and formations found in the natural environment surrounding the nightclub in which it is based in Reno, Nevada. The outcome is an installation of four thousand handmade, crystal-glass pieces that seems to hover above the bar of this spectacular nightspot. With a mesmerizing theatrical effect, the glass pieces are lit by externally projected light.

ESP
Singing Water se inspira en las formas de las rocas y las formaciones de los parajes naturales de los alrededores del club nocturno de Reno, Nevada, en el que se encuentra. El resultado es una instalación de cuatro mil cristales hechos a mano que flota sobre la barra de este espectacular local nocturno. Con un dramático y fascinante efecto, los cristales se encienden mediante una luz que se proyecta desde fuera.

FRA
Le lustre Singing Water tire son inspiration du paysage rocheux environnant le night-club situé à Reno, dans le Nevada. Cette installation qui semble flotter au dessus du bar de cette spectaculaire boîte de nuit comporte quatre mille cristaux de verre fabriqués à la main. Les cristaux éclairés par une lumière projetée ver l'extérieur captivent le regard du public.

POR
Singing Water inspira-se nas formas das rochas e formações dos cenários naturais dos arredores do clube noturno de Reno, Nevada, onde está situado. O resultado é uma instalação de quatro mil cristais feitos à mão, que flutua sobre a barra deste espetacular lugar noturno. Com um dramático e fascinante efeito, os cristais se acendem por meio de uma luz que é projetada de fora.

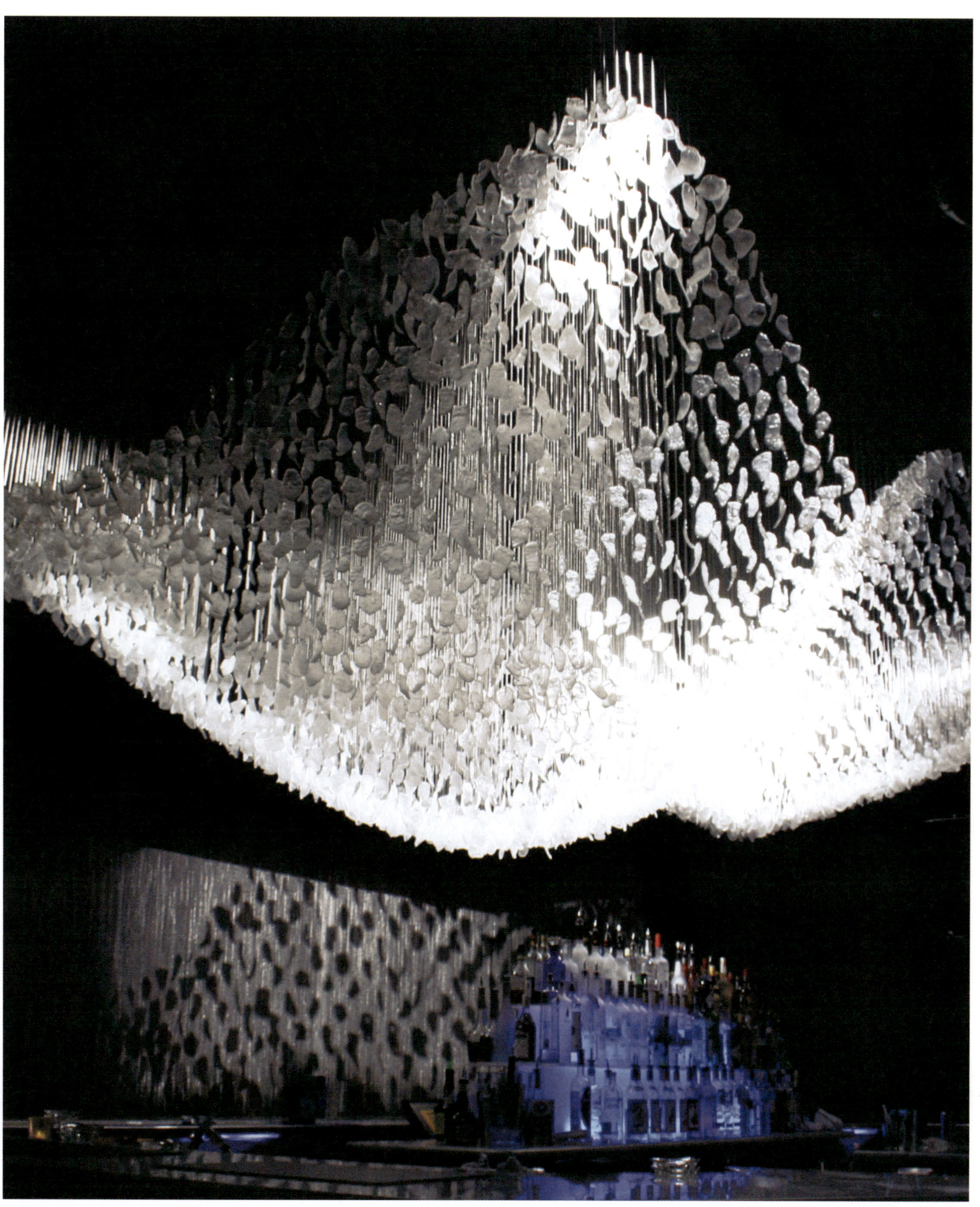

FRA

TECHNOLOGIE ET ARTISANAT

Les nouveaux matériaux issus des technologies de pointe ont toujours occupé une place importante dans les diverses branches du design. De nos jours, on trouve un peu partout des luminaires qui tirent parti de la haute technologie et de concepts ingénieux pour nous faciliter la vie : ils sont originaux, esthétiques et pratiques, et nous procurent un confort accru. Par ailleurs, la technologie peut être tout à fait compatible avec l'écologie. C'est exactement ce que les modèles de luminaires de ce chapitre nous prouvent.

ESP

TECNOLOGÍA Y ARTESANÍA

Los materiales nuevos y avanzados y la tecnología punta siempre han desempeñado una función destacada en todos los campos del diseño. En nuestros días encontramos con cierta frecuencia lámparas que aplican alta tecnología o conceptos ingeniosos a ideas de diseño asombrosas, fantásticas y creativas que hacen que nuestra vida sea más sencilla y confortable. La tecnología manufacturada y la ecología no son necesariamente contradictorias. Por el contrario, las extraordinarias creaciones que se incluyen en este capítulo demuestran que las lámparas ecológicas y creativas basadas en los avances de la tecnología se encuentran a nuestro alcance.

POR

TECNOLOGIA E ARTES

Os materiais novos e avançados e a tecnologia de ponta sempre desempenharam uma função de destaque em todas as áreas do design. Nos dias atuais, encontramos com certa frequência luminárias que aplicam alta tecnologia ou conceitos engenhosos a ideias de design assombrosas, fantásticas e criativas, que tornam nossa vida mais simples e confortável. A tecnologia manufaturada e a ecologia não são necessariamente contraditórias. Pelo contrário, as extraordinárias criações incluídas neste capítulo demonstram que as luminárias ecológicas e criativas baseadas nos progressos da tecnologia estão ao nosso alcance.

TECHNOLOGY & CRAFTS

New and advanced materials and cutting-edge technology have always played an important role in all fields of design. Nowadays it is not difficult to find lights that implement high technology or ingenious concepts in amazingly cool or creative design ideas that make our lives more comfortable and convenient. There need not be a contradiction between manmade technology and ecology. On the contrary, the wonderful works included in this chapter show us how ecological and creative lights based on advanced technology are within our reach.

WET LAMP

DESIGN FIRM
NONdesigns, LLC

DESIGNERS
Scott Franklin & Miao Miao

PHOTOGRAPHY
Coy Koehler

CLIENT
NONdesigns, LLC.

WET is an elegant and playful series of hand-blown glass lamps, each with an alluring water-submerged lightbulb at its center. Putting an exposed lightbulb in water certainly raises some eyebrows, but it also creates an intriguingly simple dimmer switch. Despite its precarious concept, the WET Lamp uses a completely safe and isolated system of low-voltage power and easily replaceable bulbs. People often approach the WET Lamp with caution, but ultimately they can't stop playing with it.

FRA
WET est une série de lampes en verre soufflé aussi élégantes qu'amusantes. L'ampoule repose au fond du globe rempli partiellement d'eau. Le fait de plonger une ampoule sous tension directement dans de l'eau est tout à fait étonnant. Celle-ci est dotée d'un modulateur d'intensité d'une fascinante simplicité. Malgré son concept hardi, WET utilise un système d'alimentation en basse tension parfaitement sûr et sans danger et des ampoules faciles à changer. La première fois qu'une personne voit une lampe WET, elle s'approche avec méfiance, mais une fois qu'elle s'amuse à la faire marcher, elle ne peut plus s'arrêter de l'admirer.

ESP
WET es una elegante y divertida serie de lámparas de cristal soplado a mano con una hipnótica bombilla sumergida en agua en el centro. Una bombilla desnuda bajo el agua suscita cierta suspicacia, desde luego, pero el agua es un reductor de luz tan sencillo que resulta intrigante. A pesar de este arriesgado concepto, la lámpara WET utiliza un sistema aislado y completamente seguro de bajo voltaje y bombillas que se recambian sin dificultades. Los usuarios se acercan a la lámpara WET con cautela, pero no se resisten a jugar con ella.

POR
WET é uma elegante e divertida série de luminárias de vidro soprado a mão, com uma hipnótica lâmpada submersa na água no seu centro. Uma lâmpada nua debaixo d'água, inicialmente, levanta certa suspeita, porém a água é um redutor de luz tão simples que se torna até intrigante. Apesar deste conceito arriscado, a luminária WET utiliza um sistema isolado e completamente seguro de baixa voltagem e lâmpadas que se podem trocar sem dificuldade. Os usuários aproximam-se da luminária WET com cautela, porém não resistem à tentação de brincar com ela.

MALVA

DESIGN FIRM
ett la benn

DESIGNER
Danilo Dürler

PHOTOGRAPHY
diephotodesigner.de

Malva is a series of lights inspired by the natural qualities of cellulose and viscose. The pieces are generated by forming moistened sponge cloth and subsequently hardening it by air drying it on a mold. The translation of this material into individual design pieces through basic processes of forming and drying measures up to the highest demands in sustainability and eco friendliness, with all of the pieces being compostable.

FRA
Malva est une série de luminaires qui tire parti des qualités naturelles de la cellulose et de la viscose. Ses éléments sont fabriqués dans un tissu éponge humide fixé sur une forme qui durcit en séchant à l'air libre. Le processus de fabrication impliquant la mise en forme d'un tissu et un séchage naturel est entièrement écologique et durable. Tous les éléments sont compostables.

ESP
Malva es una serie de lámparas que se inspiran en las características naturales de la viscosa y la celulosa. Estas obras están hechas con una tela esponjosa húmeda que se endurece secándose sobre un molde. Este material, que se traduce en los diseños individuales mediante procesos básicos de formado y secado, cumple todos los requisitos de sostenibilidad y respeto al medio ambiente, ya que todas las obras son compostables.

POR
Malva é uma série de luminárias que se inspiram nas características naturais da viscose e da celulose. Estas obras são confeccionadas com um tecido esponjoso úmido que endurece ao secar-se sobre um molde. Este material, que se traduz nos designs individuais por meio de processos básicos de moldagem e secagem, atende a todos os requisitos de sustentabilidade e respeito ao meio ambiente, já que todas as obras são degradáveis.

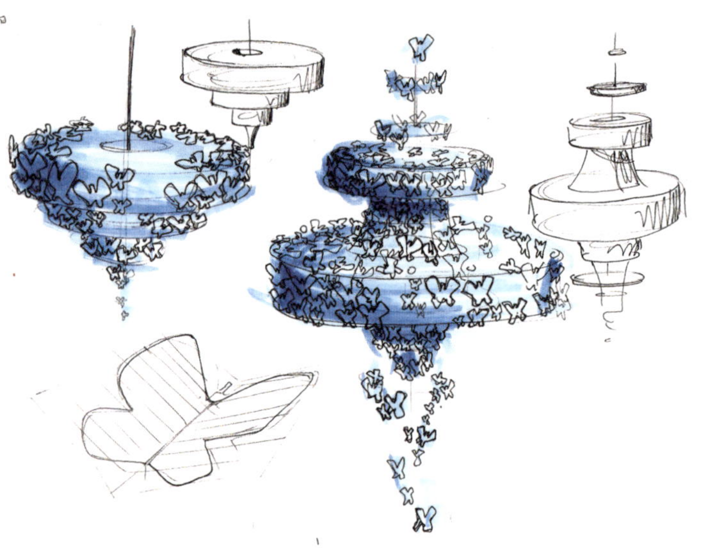

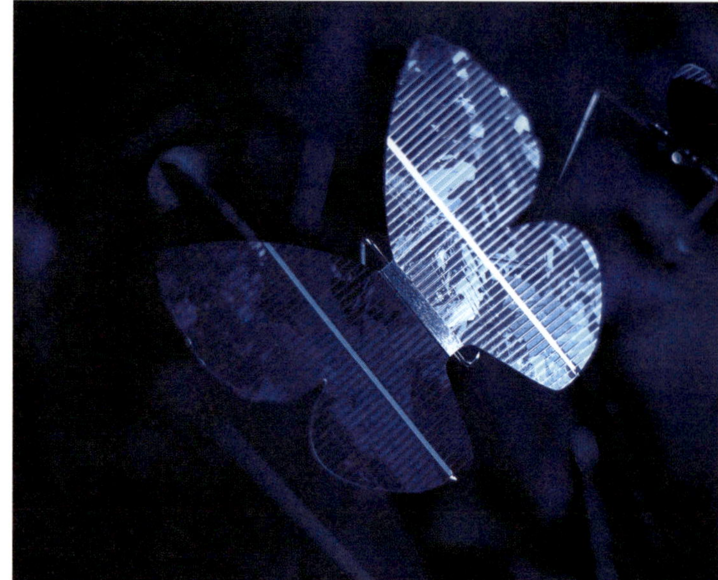

VIRTUE OF BLUE

DESIGNER
Jeroen Verhoeven

PHOTOGRAPHY
Bas Helbers, Giulietta Verdon-Roe & Peter Mallet

Virtue of Blue is a delicate construction featuring five hundred solar-panel cells cut into the shapes of four different breeds of butterfly. These cluster around a flame-like, hand-blown glass bulb, and although they are static, they appear to be in flight. Like real butterflies, which use the rays of the sun to raise their own body temperatures, the wings of the chandelier's butterflies absorb energy during daylight hours to provide power for the light they surround.

FRA
Virtue of Blue est une structure délicate élaborée à partir de cinq cents cellules de panneau solaire découpées suivant la forme de quatre races de papillons différentes. Ceux-ci se rassemblent autour d'une ampoule en verre soufflé, comme attirés par une flamme. On a l'impression qu'ils volent alors qu'ils sont parfaitement immobiles. À l'image des vrais papillons qui utilisent les rayons du soleil pour augmenter la température de leur corps, les ailes du lustre absorbent de l'énergie pendant la journée pour alimenter ensuite la lampe la nuit.

ESP
Virtue of Blue es una delicada construcción de quinientas células de paneles solares recortadas con la forma de cuatro especies de mariposas diferentes. Estas se congregan alrededor de una bombilla soplada a mano en forma de llama y aunque son estáticas da la impresión de que están volando. Al igual que las mariposas auténticas, cuya temperatura aumenta con los rayos del sol, las alas de las mariposas de la araña absorben energía durante las horas de luz y alimentan de energía a la lámpara a la que rodean.

POR
Virtue of Blue é uma delicada construção de quinhentas células de painéis solares recortadas em forma de quatro espécies de borboletas diferentes. Estas congregam-se ao redor de uma lâmpada soprada à mão em forma de chama e ainda que sejam estáticas dão a impressão de que estão voando. Tal como as borboletas autênticas, cuja temperatura aumenta com os raios do sol, as asas das borboletas do lustre absorvem energia durante as horas de luz e alimentam com energia a luminária que elas rodeiam.

CIRRATA

DESIGN FIRM
Markus Johansson Design Studio

DESIGNER
Markus Johansson

PHOTOGRAPHY
Markus Johansson

CLIENT
Markus Johansson Design Studio

Cirrata is a series of lights that challenges preconceptions about what it is possible to achieve with Corian. These brooding lamps also convey the sense of power and menace of the enormous, tentacled sea creatures that lurk at the bottom of the ocean.

FRA

Cirrata est une série de luminaires qui démontre que l'on peut trouver d'autres usages à une matière comme le Corian. Leurs formes tentaculaires évoquent des créatures fantastiques évoluant au fond des océans. La lumière qu'ils diffusent confère une atmosphère de calme et de mystère au décor environnant.

ESP

Cirrata es una serie de lámparas que desafía las ideas preconcebidas sobre las posibilidades del Corian. Además, estas reflexivas creaciones transmiten la fuerza y el peligro de las enormes criaturas marinas armadas con tentáculos que acechan en el fondo del océano.

POR

Cirrata é uma série de luminárias que desafia as ideias preconcebidas sobre as possibilidades do Corian. Além disso, estas reflexivas criações transmitem a força e o perigo das enormes criaturas marinhas armadas de tentáculos que se escondem no fundo do oceano.

AURA

DESIGN FIRM
AURA Studio

DESIGNERS
Océane Delain & Béatrice Durandard

PHOTOGRAPHY
Océane Delain & Béatrice Durandard

The craft of basketry, which has existed for thousands of years, is combined here with LED lights to create a collection of hanging and wall-mounted lamps. Strands of rattan are replaced with flexible strips of LED lights during the weaving process and are worked directly into the structure of the object. AURA is about combining design and craftsmanship in a project that is respectful of the environment and the designer, the consumer, and the manufacturer alike.

FRA

L'art de la vannerie, qui existe depuis des millénaires, associé à un système d'éclairage LED a permis de créer une collection inédite de lustres et d'appliques murales. En cours de tressage, des cannes de rotin sont remplacées par des réglettes LED souples pour faire partie intégrante de l'objet. L'objectif d'AURA est de combiner artisanat et modernité pour produire des luminaires qui respectent non seulement l'environnement, mais aussi le designer, le consommateur et le fabricant.

ESP

El milenario arte de la cestería se combina con las luces LED en esta colección de lámparas colgantes y de pared. Los cables flexibles de luces LED sustituyen a los hilos de ratán en el proceso de tejido, insertándose en la estructura del objeto. AURA trata de combinar el diseño y la artesanía en un proyecto respetuoso con el medio ambiente, el diseñador, el usuario y el fabricante.

POR

A arte milenar da cestaria combina-se com as lâmpadas LED nesta coleção de luminárias pendentes e de parede. As fitas flexíveis de lâmpadas LED substituem os fios de ratam no processo de entrelaçamento, inserindo-se na estrutura do objeto. AURA trata de combinar o design e o artesanato num projeto que respeita o meio ambiente, o designer, o usuário e o fabricante.

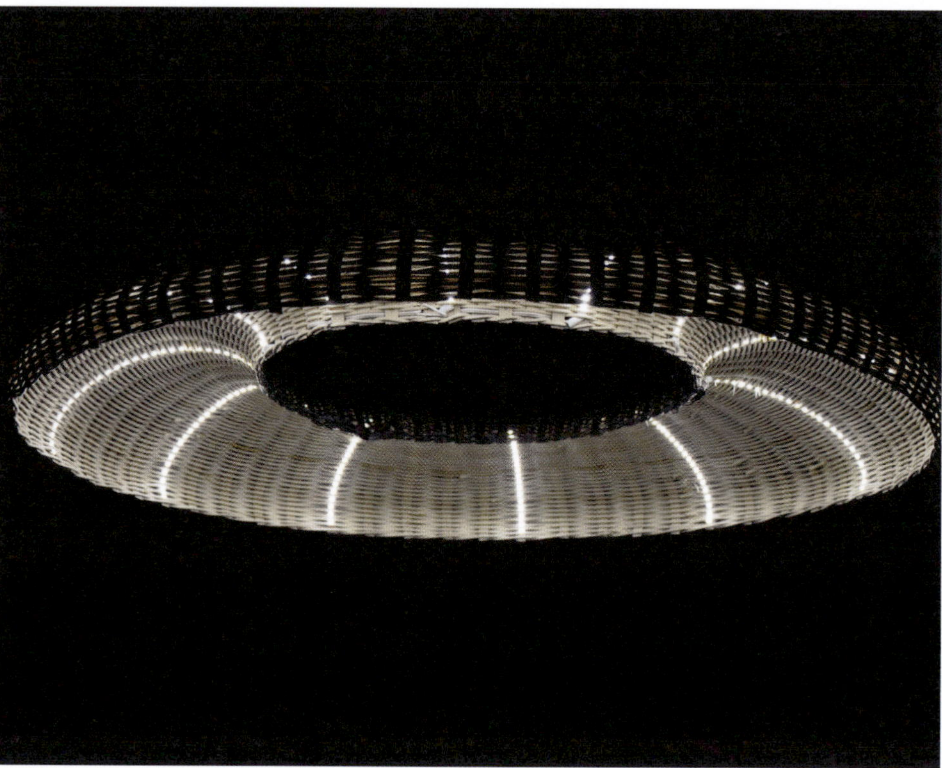

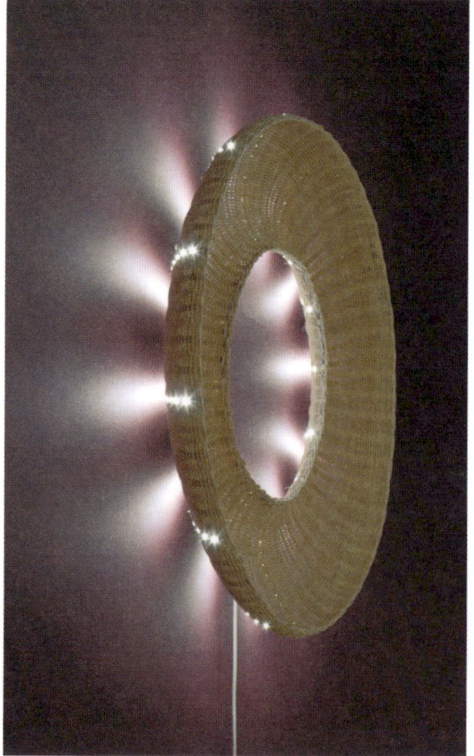

MORNING GLORY

DESIGN FIRM
Studio WM.

DESIGNER
Wendy Legro

PHOTOGRAPHY
Wendy Legro

Our homes are filled with artificial light, and by replacing the sun as a light source we have unintentionally disrupted our biological clocks. Morning Glory brings back an awareness of the fact that the sun is our natural light source. During the day, mechanical flowers on a frame attached to a window are closed, enabling sunlight to come in. When the sun sets, the flowers open and start to emit light.

FRA
Nos maisons sont éclairées par de la lumière artificielle. En remplaçant le soleil, source d'éclairage naturelle, nous avons perturbé sans le vouloir nos horloges biologiques. Morning Glory nous rappelle que le soleil est notre source de lumière naturelle. Pendant la journée, les fleurs mécaniques du lustre, fixé devant une fenêtre, sont fermées pour laisser rentrer le soleil. Lorsque l'astre se couche, les fleurs s'ouvrent et émettent de la lumière.

ESP
Hemos llenado nuestras casas de luces artificiales y al sustituir al sol hemos alterado nuestro reloj biológico sin darnos cuenta. Morning Glory nos recuerda que el sol es la luz de la naturaleza. Durante el día estas flores mecánicas, en una estructura instalada en la ventana, se cierran para que entre el sol, pero cuando anochece se abren y emiten luz.

POR
Enchemos nossas casas de luzes artificiais e, ao substituir o sol, alteramos sem perceber o nosso relógio biológico. Morning Glory lembra-nos que o sol é a luz da natureza. Durante o dia, estas flores mecânicas, numa estrutura instalada na janela, fecham-se para que entre o sol, mas quando anoitece abrem-se e emitem luz.

TURBINE LAMP

DESIGNER
Niels Grubak

PHOTOGRAPHY
Niels Grubak

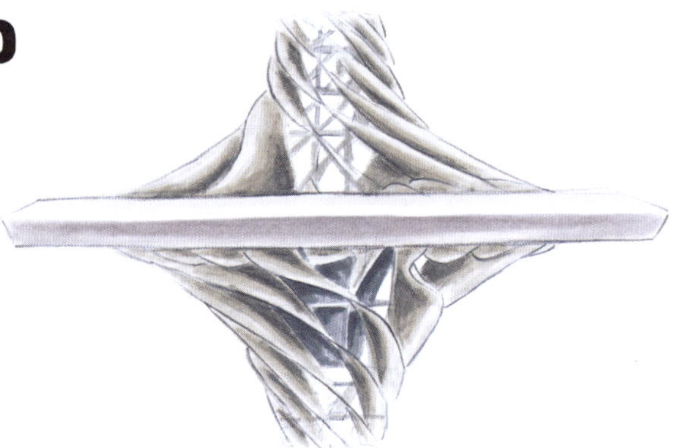

The main idea of the Turbine Lamp is to turn the construction of a traditional lamp inside out. By using LEDs, it is possible to remove the light source from the center of the lamp to its periphery. LED technology is also highly sustainable, as LEDs have a lifespan which is up to fifty times longer than traditional filament bulbs. This luminaire is made from aluminum and polypropylene. Both of these materials are easily recyclable, while the aluminum also serves to cool the LED.

FRA
L'idée du lustre Turbine est d'inverser complètement le principe de base du luminaire en déplaçant la source d'éclairage du centre vers la périphérie, grâce à la technologie LED qui a l'avantage d'être hautement durable. En effet, les ampoules LED durent cinquante fois plus longtemps que celles à filaments. Le lustre est en aluminium et polypropylène, matériaux qui se recyclent facilement, le métal servant par ailleurs à refroidir les LED.

ESP
La idea básica de la lámpara Turbine consiste en darle la vuelta a la construcción de una lámpara tradicional. Gracias a las luces LED, es posible trasladar la fuente de luz desde el centro a la periferia de la lámpara. Además, esta tecnología es altamente sostenible, ya que son hasta cincuenta veces más duraderas que las bombillas de filamentos tradicionales. Este farol está hecho de aluminio y polipropileno, materiales que se reciclan fácilmente; asimismo, el aluminio sirve para que se enfríen las LED.

POR
A ideia básica da luminária Turbine consiste em inverter a construção de uma luminária tradicional. Graças às lâmpadas LED, é possível transladar a fonte de luz do centro para a periferia da luminária. Além disso, esta tecnologia é altamente sustentável, já que elas são até cinquenta vezes mais duráveis que as lâmpadas de filamentos tradicionais. Este farol é confeccionado em alumínio e polipropileno, materiais facilmente recicláveis; ao mesmo tempo que o alumínio serve para que se esfriem as LED.

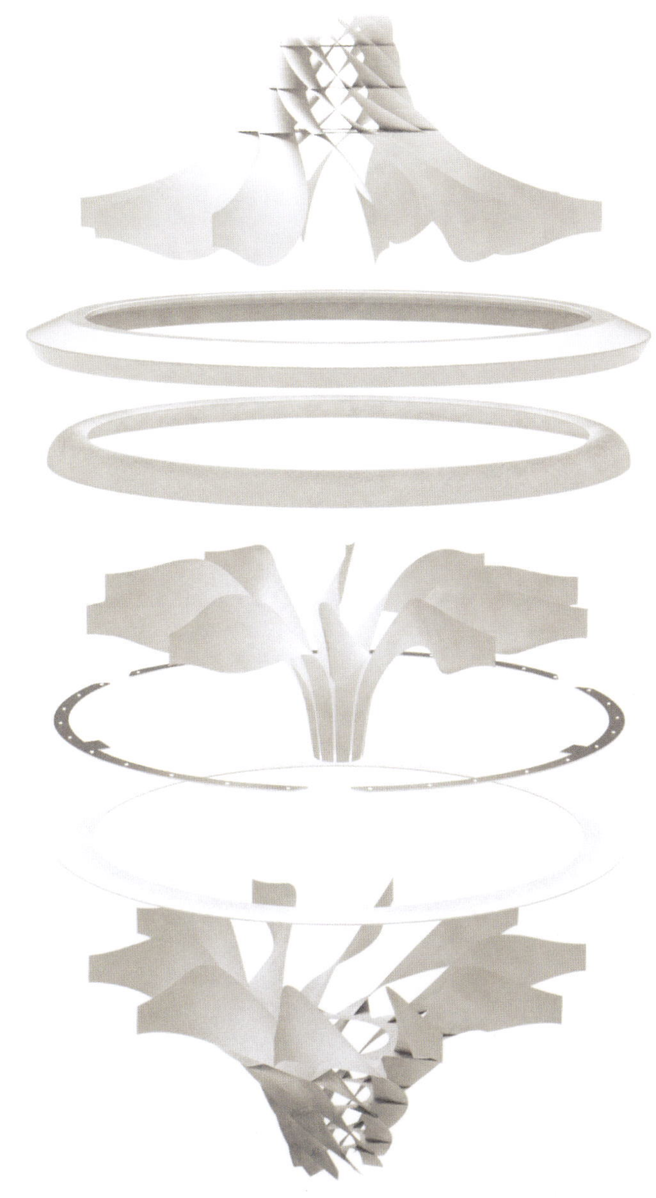

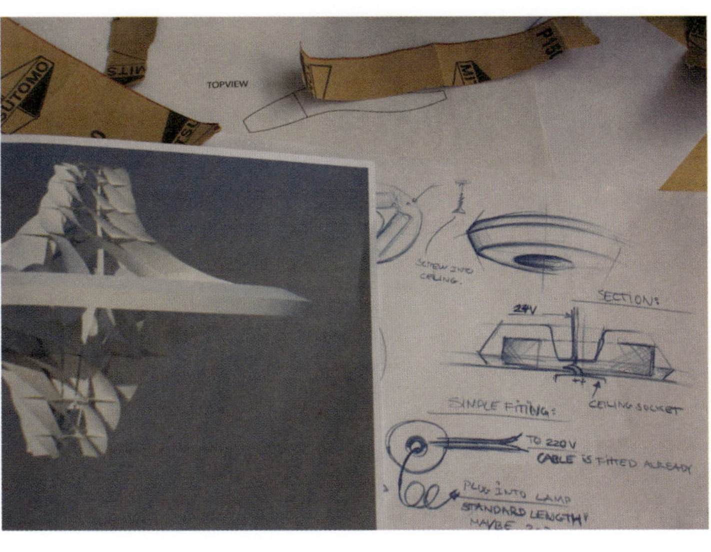

TOPVIEW
SCREW INTO CEILING.
SECTION:
24V
CEILING SOCKET
SIMPLE FITTING:
TO 220V
CABLE IS FITTED ALREADY
PLUG INTO LAMP
STANDARD LENGTH!

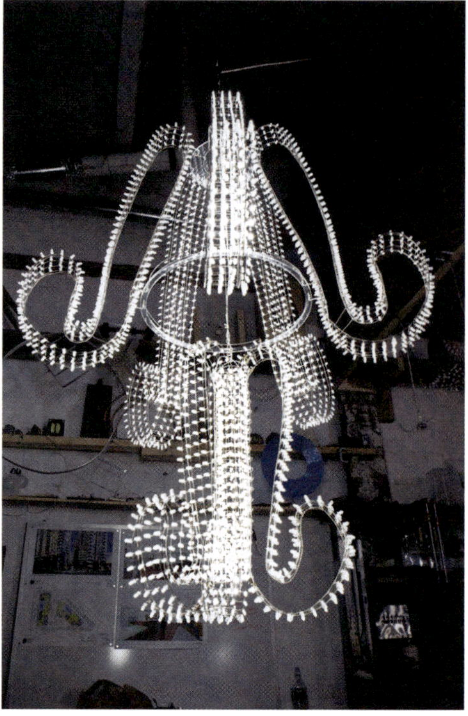

TREBLE CHANDELIER

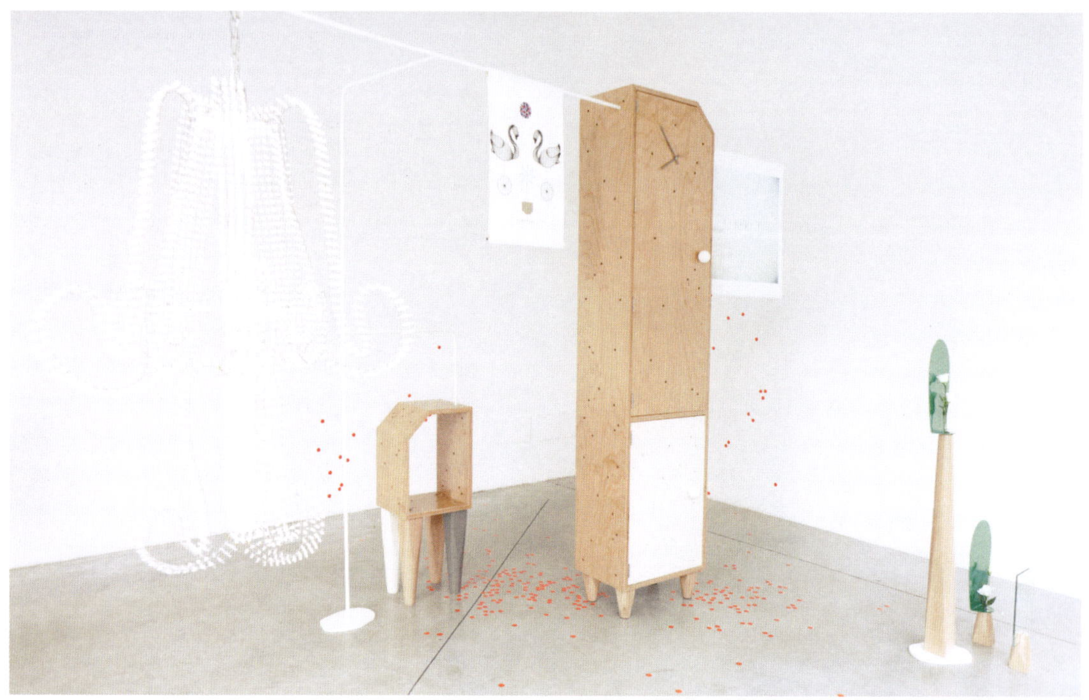

DESIGN FIRM
Jason Krugman Studio with Fabrica

DESIGNERS
Jason Krugman & Sam Baron

PHOTOGRAPHY
Noah Kalina & Gustavo Millon

Treble is a one-of-a-kind LED lighting piece designed as a modern interpretation of the traditional Baroque chandelier. More than three thousand sharp-focus LEDs were soldered together into long ribbons and then formed into the various sections of the chandelier. The combination of the efficiency of the LEDs and the efficiency of design yields a formidable fixture with an energy consumption of under seventy-five watts and a life expectancy of between ten and twenty years

FRA
Treble est un luminaire à LED unique en son genre qui interprète à sa manière le lustre baroque traditionnel. Plus de trois mille diodes électroluminescentes transparentes ont été soudées en longs rubans auxquels on a ensuite donné la forme des différents éléments du lustre. En combinant l'efficacité des LED à l'ingéniosité du design, les designers ont créé un luminaire extraordinaire dont la consommation est inférieure à 75 watts et la durée de vie est de dix à vingt ans.

ESP
Treble es una lámpara LED única concebida como una interpretación moderna de la araña barroca tradicional. Se compone de más de tres mil penetrantes luces LED soldadas en largas franjas con las que se modelan las diversas secciones de la araña. La combinación de la eficacia de las LED y el diseño resulta en una magnífica lámpara que consume menos de setenta y cinco watios y tiene una esperanza de vida de entre diez y veinte años.

POR
Treble é uma luminária LED única, concebida como uma interpretação moderna do lustre barroco tradicional. Compõe-se de mais de três mil penetrantes lâmpadas LED soldadas em largas franjas com as quais se modelam as diversas seções do lustre. A combinação da eficácia das LED com o design produz uma magnífica luminária, que consome menos de setenta e cinco watts e tem uma expectativa de vida de dez a vinte anos.

SOLAR LAMPION

DESIGN FIRM
Damian O'Sullivan Design

DESIGNER
Damian O'Sullivan

PHOTOGRAPHY
Frans Feijen

Damian O'Sullivan, the designer of Solar Lampion, set himself the task of designing a solar lamp whose cells would become an integral part of the design. Design influences were found in traditional Chinese paper lampions but also in structures found in nature, such as the geometric spiraling found in pinecones. The resulting Solar Lampion is, in essence, no more than a bunch of solar cells stuck together. This simplicity makes the lamp unique, as what you see is what it is: a solar lamp made of solar cells!

FRA

Damian O'Sullivan, concepteur du luminaire Solar Lampion, s'était fixé comme objectif de mettre au point une lampe solaire dont les cellules feraient partie intégrante du design. Il s'est inspiré des lampions chinois en papier ainsi que des structures géométriques rencontrées dans la nature, comme les écailles de pommes de pin. Le Solar Lampion est un assemblage de cellules photovoltaïques, et c'est cela qui fait son charme : son originalité réside dans sa simplicité, et on voit du premier coup d'œil de quoi elle est faite.

ESP

Damian O'Sullivan, el creador de Solar Lampion, acomete la tarea de diseñar una lámpara solar en la que las células se convierten en una parte fundamental del diseño. En ella se observan influencias de los tradicionales faroles de papel chinos, pero también de las estructuras que se encuentran en la naturaleza, como las espirales geométricas de las piñas. Así, la Solar Lampion, en esencia, no es más que un montón de células solares adheridas. Esta sencillez hace que sea una lámpara única, pues lo que se ve es lo que hay: ¡una lámpara solar hecha de células solares!

POR

Damian O'Sullivan, o criador da Solar Lampion, empreende a tarefa de desenhar uma luminária solar em que as células se convertem numa parte fundamental do design. Nela se observam influências dos tradicionais faróis de papel chineses, mas também das estruturas que se encontram na natureza, como as espirais geométricas das pinhas. Deste modo, a Solar Lampion, essencialmente, não é outra coisa senão um montão de células solares coladas. Esta simplicidade faz com que seja uma luminária única, pois o que se vê é o que existe: uma luminária solar feita de células solares!

HIGHLIGHTS COLLECTION

DESIGN FIRM
nistor&nistor

DESIGNERS
Gladys & Gabriel Nistor

PHOTOGRAPHY
Voram Reshed

In creating the Highlights Collection Gladys and Gabriel Nistor sought to create pieces that contribute to the quest for a more sustainable lifestyle by creating objects that have a prolonged lifespan in terms of their appeal to the user. This objective is based on the belief that the longer an object speaks to you and surprises you, the longer you will want to keep it, which in turn contributes to reducing waste as well as resource consumption levels.

FRA
Highlights Collection est l'aboutissement d'un projet de Gladys et Gabriel Nistor qui cherchaient à créer un luminaire qui corresponde à un style de vie plus écologique et plaise durablement à ses utilisateurs. Ils sont partis du principe que plus un objet nous charme et nous surprend, moins nous avons envie de nous en séparer, ce qui entraîne une réduction de la production de déchets et de la consommation de produits.

ESP
Con la colección Highlights Gladys y Gabriel Nistor contribuyen a un estilo de vida más sostenible mediante la creación de objetos que mantienen el interés del usuario durante mucho tiempo. Este objetivo se basa en la convicción de que cuanto más expresivo y sorprendente es un objeto, más tiempo deseamos conservarlo, lo que a su vez repercute en la disminución de los residuos y el consumo de recursos.

POR
Com a coleção Highlights, Gladys e Gabriel Nistor contribuem para um estilo de vida mais sustentável mediante a criação de objetos que conservam o interesse do usuário durante muito tempo. Este objetivo baseia-se na convicção de que quanto mais expressivo e surpreendente é um objeto, mais tempo desejamos conservá-lo, o que, por sua vez, repercute na diminuição dos resíduos e no consumo de recursos.

FOUR SEASONS

DESIGN FIRM
Jordi Milà Barcelona

DESIGNER
Jordi Milà

Each of the faces of this piece represents one of the four seasons of the year, and each lets the light through in a completely different way. With a simple stroke of your hand you can turn it around, defining how the light shapes the atmosphere of your room. Four Seasons comes in compact and long-tube versions, as well as gun-metal or satin finishes for the metallic parts.

ESP
Cada cara de esta obra representa una de las cuatro estaciones del año y la luz la atraviesa de una forma completamente distinta. El usuario puede darle la vuelta con un sencillo ademán de la mano, definiendo la forma que da la luz a la atmósfera de la estancia. Four Seasons está disponible en version compacta y de tubo largo, así como con acabados satinados o de pistola en las partes metálicas.

FRA
Chacune des faces du luminaire représente une des quatre saisons de l'année et diffuse la lumière d'une façon complètement différente des autres. Un simple geste de la main permet de le faire pivoter pour changer le mode d'éclairage et l'ambiance de la pièce. Four Seasons existe en format compact ou équipé d'un pied, les parties métalliques étant proposées en bronze ou acier satiné.

POR
Cada face desta obra representa uma das quatro estações do ano e a luz as atravessa de uma forma completamente distinta. O usuário pode dar-lhe a volta com um simples gesto da mão, definindo a forma que a luz confere à atmosfera do local. Four Seasons está disponivel em versão compacta e de tubo longo, como também com acabamentos acetinados ou de pistola nas partes metálicas.

FUNGI LAMP

DESIGNER
Andreas Kowalewski

PHOTOGRAPHY
Andreas Kowalewski

The nature-inspired FUNGI Lamps are made out of nylon webbing that has been bonded together with a special adhesive technique. This unconventional construction method defines the contours and shape of the lamps, with each displaying a tree-like, gradual growth process and revealing traces of imperfections from the process. The illuminated fabric creates a unique and mystical lighting effect.

ESP
Las lámparas FUNGI, que se inspiran en la naturaleza, están hechas con correas de nailon fabricadas mediante una técnica adhesiva especial. Este insólito método define los contornos y la forma de estas lámparas, que experimentan un crecimiento paulatino semejante al de los árboles y revelan indicios de imperfecciones durante el proceso. Además, la tela iluminada crea un efecto extraordinario y místico.

FRA
Les lampes FUNGI s'inspirent directement de la nature. Elles sont constituées de sangles en nylon collées entre elles suivant une technique particulière. Cette méthode de fabrication non conventionnelle imprime sur les luminaires des cernes, sortes de marques de croissance, et des imperfections de surface, comme s'il s'agissait d'arbres ayant poussé dans la nature. Lorsque le luminaire est allumé, le tissu produit un effet d'éclairage absolument magique.

POR
As luminárias FUNGI, inspiradas na natureza, são feitas com cintas de nylon fabricadas com uma técnica adesiva especial. Este inusitado método define os contornos e a forma destas luminárias, que crescem paulatinamente, assim como às árvores, e revelam sinais de imperfeições durante o processo. Além disso, a cúpula iluminada cria um efeito extraordinário e místico.

MORPH CHANDELIER

DESIGN FIRM
Wasielewska

DESIGNER
Alicja Wasielewska

PHOTOGRAPHY
Alicja Wasielewska

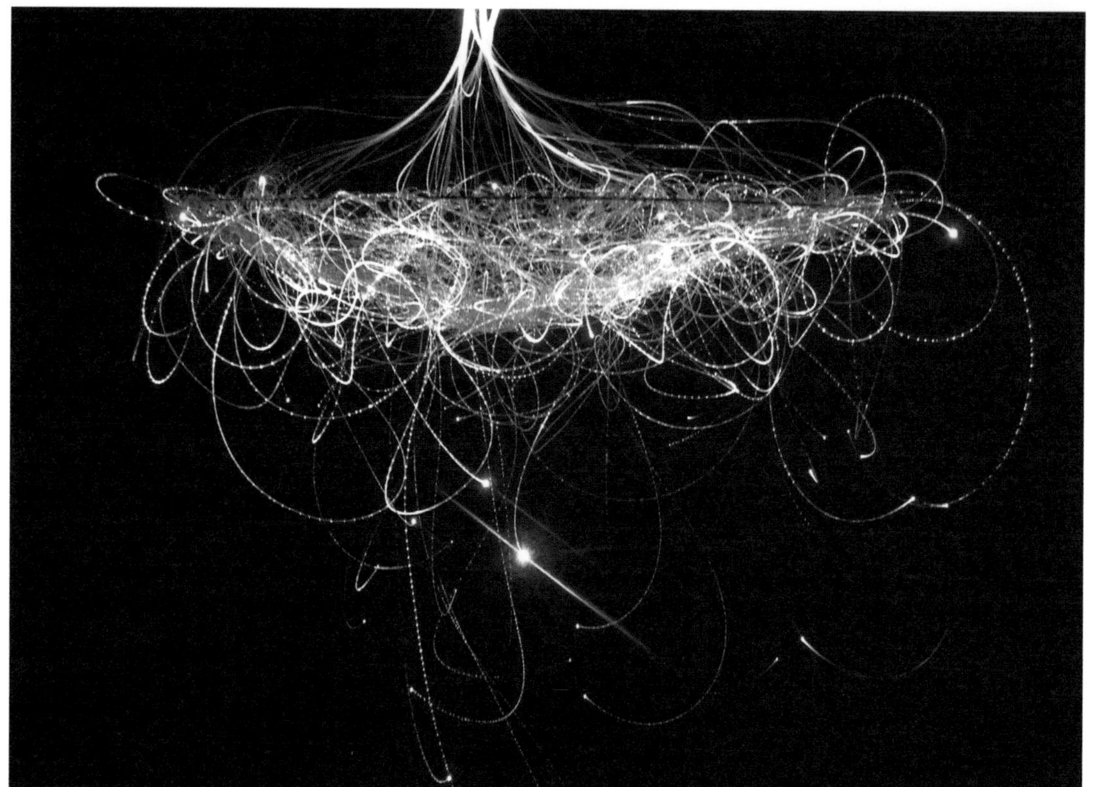

The Morph Chandelier's design is based on the genesis of repetitive transformation patterns through random illuminated lines. In terms of its materials, the piece is created from a set of elastic fiber optics than have been delicately manipulated to form a unique, experimental, and free-flowing chandelier. Traditional techniques for creating fabrics such as knitting or crocheting have been applied in making this design, which also utilizes its LED fiber-optic technology to provide structural support as well as lighting.

FRA
Le lustre Morph est basé sur la formation de motifs répétitifs générés à partir de séries de points qui s'allument de manière aléatoire. Le lustre est fabriqué en fibres optiques élastiques harmonieusement disposées qui lui confèrent son originalité et son aspect aérien. Pour le créer, on a fait appel à des techniques traditionnelles telles que le tricot et le crochet, que l'on a combinées à la technologie LED qui sert à la fois de structure et d'éclairage.

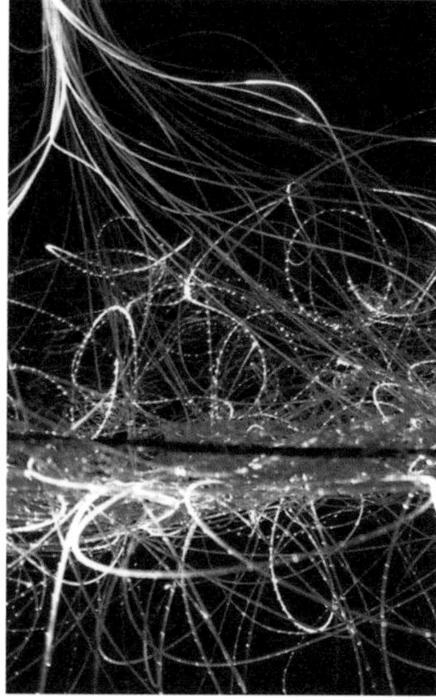

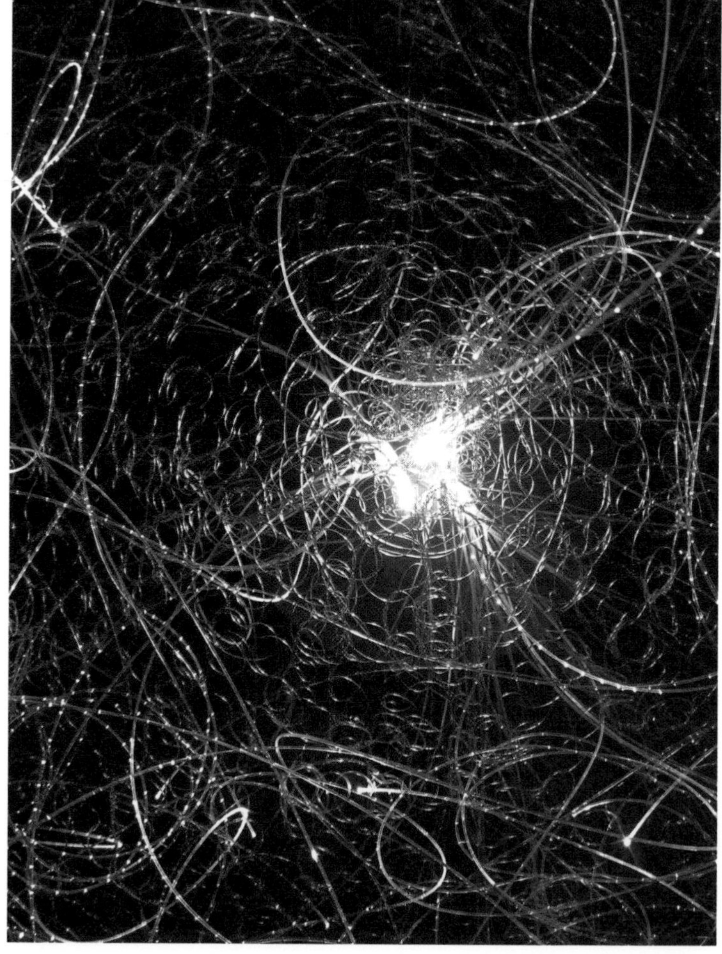

ESP
El diseño de la araña Morph se basa en la génesis de modelos de transformación repetitivos mediante líneas que se iluminan aleatoriamente. En términos de materiales, esta obra se compone de una serie de fibras ópticas elásticas que se manipulan con delicadaza para que formen una araña única, experimental y desprovista de restricciones. Las técnicas tradicionales de creación de tejidos, como el punto o el ganchillo, también se han aplicado en la fabricación de este diseño, que utiliza la tecnología de fibra óptica LED y no solo ilumina sino que ofrece una estructura de apoyo.

POR
O design da luminária Morph baseia-se na gênese de modelos de transformação repetitivos mediante linhas que se iluminam aleatoriamente. Em termos de materiais, esta obra se compõe de uma série de fibras óticas elásticas manipuladas com delicadeza para formar uma luminária única, experimental e sem restrições. As técnicas tradicionais de criação de tecidos, como o tricô ou o crochê, também foram aplicadas na fabricação deste design, que utiliza a tecnologia da fibra ótica LED e não só ilumina, mas também oferece uma estrutura de apoio.

SOUL CELL

DESIGNER
Jesper Jonsson

PHOTOGRAPHY
Jesper Jonsson

The Soul Cell lamp is charged during the day through solar power to provide energy to light up the lamp when it gets dark. To light the lamp, you unfold the shade using a twisting motion. This allows it to be small and portable when you want to carry it with you, but still have a bigger surface on which to project light when needed. A strap with magnets attached allows you to hang the lamp in many different ways.

FRA
La lanterne Soul Cell se charge pendant la journée grâce à l'énergie solaire, ce qui lui permet ensuite de fournir un éclairage la nuit. Pour déplier et allumer la lanterne, il faut écarter les deux plaques en effectuant un mouvement tournant pour tendre le tissu. Lorsqu'elle est fermée, vous pouvez facilement l'emporter partout où vous allez et une fois ouverte, vous disposez d'une grande surface d'éclairage capable de projeter la lumière là où vous en avez besoin. La lanterne est équipée d'une anse munie d'aimants qui permet de l'accrocher de différentes manières.

ESP
La lámpara Soul Cell se carga de energía solar durante el día y alimenta la lámpara cuando oscurece. Para encenderla se despliega la pantalla mediante un movimiento de torsión; gracias a esta característica es pequeña y se transporta fácilmente, aunque tiene una superficie amplia en la que se proyecta la luz cuando es necesario. La lámpara se cuelga de muchas formas distintas gracias a una correa con imanes adheridos.

POR
A luminária Soul Cell é carregada com energia solar durante o dia, que a alimenta quando escurece. Para acendê-la, desdobra-se a cúpula com um movimento de torção; graças a esta característica, ela é pequena e facilmente transportável, ainda que apresente, quando necessário, uma superfície ampla na qual a luz se projeta. A luminária pode ser se pendurada de muitas maneiras distintas, graças a uma correia com imãs colados.

STORY

DESIGNERS
Ida Noemi & Vibeke Skar

PHOTOGRAPHY
Kaja Bruskeland

CLIENT
Leitmotiv

The Story lamp is inspired by Scandinavian traditions and the contrast between cold winter weather and warm clothing and homes. Its pattern, inspired by knitted wool sweaters, melts its icicle form, creating a graceful expression. The rough surface with its translucent, embossed pattern presents the porcelain at its best, while the lamp's mixture of handcrafted production and modern techniques makes it unique and personal.

FRA
Le lustre Story s'inspire des traditions scandinaves où le froid rigoureux de l'hiver est combattu par des vêtements bien chauds. Son motif reprend les dessins des pulls en laine de la région, et sa forme rappelle les glaçons qui se forment lorsque tout a gelé. Sa surface rugueuse translucide décorée du motif ouvragé est un magnifique exemple d'utilisation de la céramique. Le lustre Story fabriqué à la main tire néanmoins parti des techniques modernes. C'est ce qui fait son originalité et lui donne de une vraie personnalité.

ESP
La lámpara Story se basa en las tradiciones escandinavas, así como en el contraste entre el clima frío del invierno, la ropa de abrigo y los interiores cálidos. La figura en forma de carámbano, que se inspira en los jerseys de punto, se funde y crea una expresión delicada. Además, en la superficie áspera con el diseño repujado transparente se aprecian todas las cualidades de la porcelana. Gracias a la combinación de fabricación artesanal y técnicas modernas, se trata de una lámpara única y personal.

POR
A luminária Story baseia-se nas tradições escandinavas, bem como no contraste entre o clima frio do inverno, a roupa de agasalho e os interiores cálidos. A figura em forma sincelo, que se inspira nas blusas de tricô, funde-se e cria uma expressão delicada. Além disso, em sua superfície áspera, com o desenho repuxado transparente, pode-se apreciar todas as qualidades da porcelana. Graças à combinação de fabricação artesanal e técnicas modernas, é uma luminária única e pessoal.

THE CHRYSANTHEMUM CENTERPIECE

DESIGN FIRM
NOMILI

DESIGNER
Dr. Michaella Janse van Vuuren

PHOTOGRAPHY
Dr. Michaella Janse van Vuuren

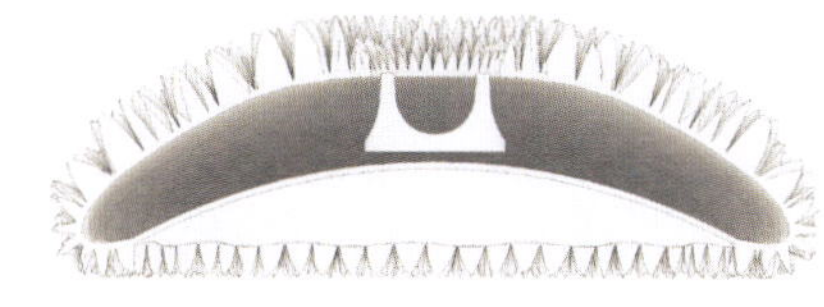

The Chrysanthemum Centerpiece is a multifunctional design that can be used as either a bowl or a candleholder, depending on which side of the design faces upwards. The product is manufactured using three-dimensional printing, which allows for on-demand production from any location in the world. By supporting low-volume and local manufacturing it further eliminates the waste, expensive transportation, and costly tooling required by traditional processes.

FRA
Le Chrysanthemum Centerpiece est un objet multifonctionnel qui peut servir de coupelle ou de bougeoir, selon la face que l'on présente. Il est fabriqué grâce à la technologie d'impression 3D, ce qui permet de le produire à la demande, depuis n'importe quel endroit dans le monde. Comme il est fabriqué localement en petit volume, sa production ne requiert aucun usinage coûteux, ne génère pas de déchet et élimine les frais de transport onéreux.

ESP
El centro de mesa Chrysanthemum es una creación multifuncional que hace las veces de cuenco o candelabro en función de la cara del diseño que se encuentra visible. Se fabrica mediante una impresión en tres dimensiones a petición de los clientes desde cualquier parte del mundo. Además, favorece la producción local a pequeña escala, eliminando los residuos, el transporte caro y las herramientas caras que requieren los métodos tradicionales.

POR
O centro de mesa Chrysanthemum é uma criação multifuncional que faz o papel de tigela ou candelabro em função da face do desenho que está visível. É fabricado por meio de uma impressão em três dimensões, a pedido dos clientes de qualquer parte do mundo. Além disso, favorece a produção local em pequena escala, eliminando os resíduos, o transporte caro e as ferramentas caras que os métodos tradicionais requerem.

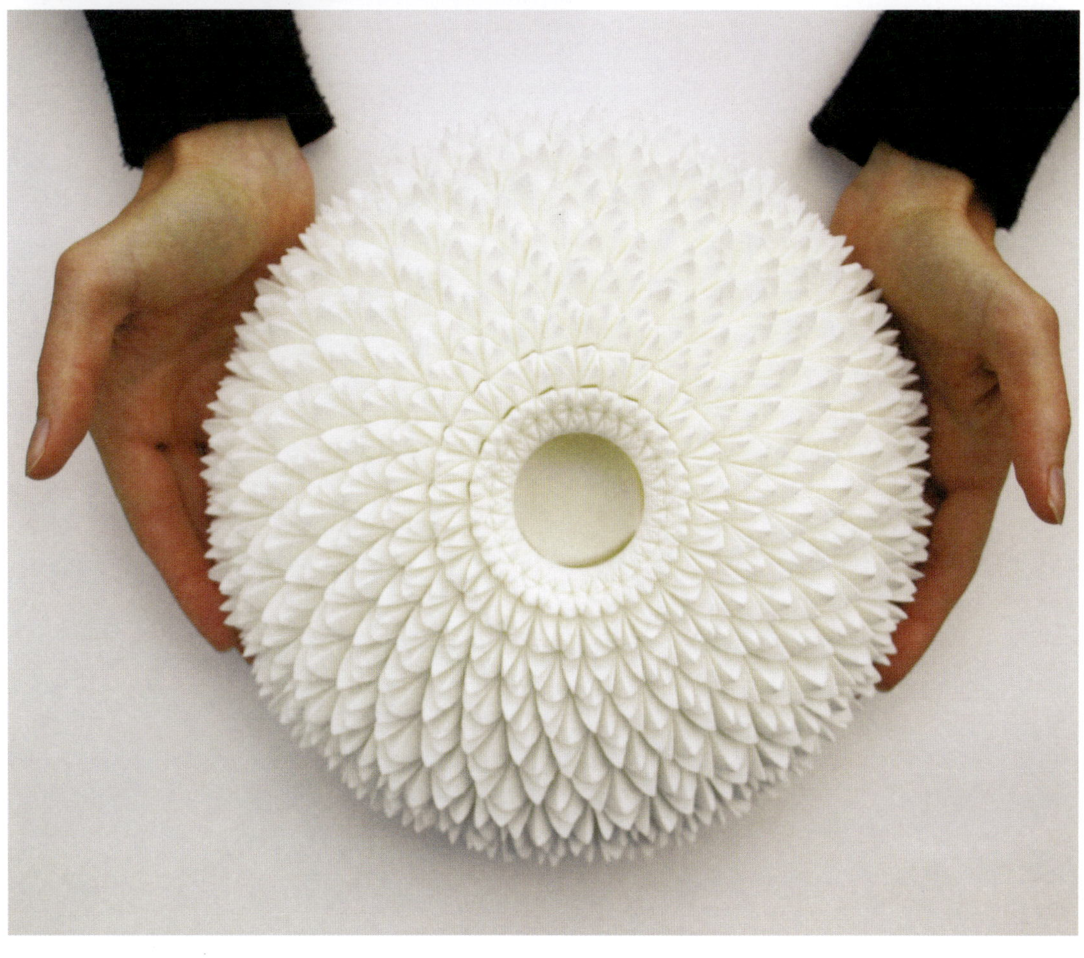

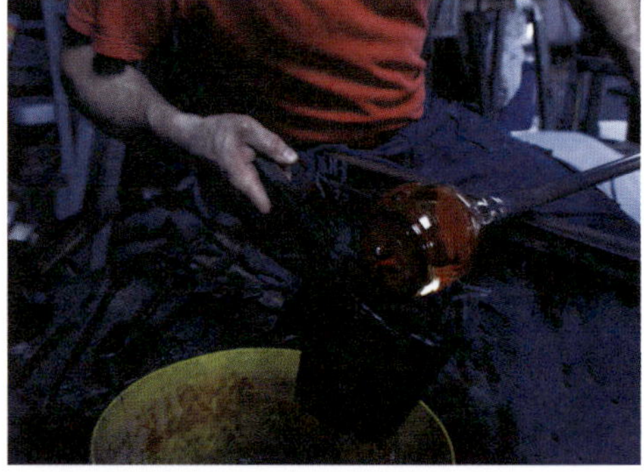

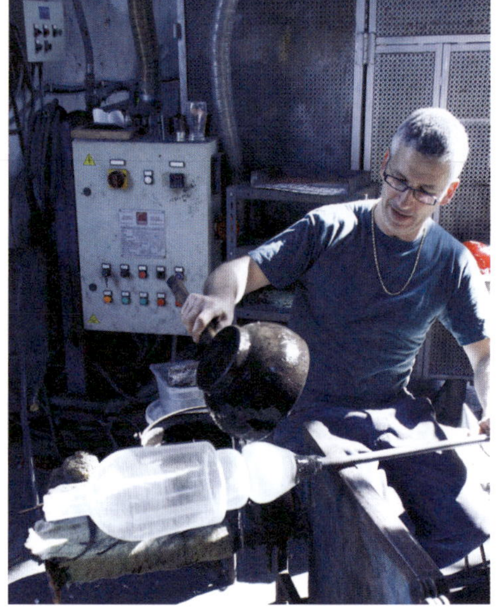

TRAP LIGHT

DESIGNERS
Gionata Gatto & Mike Thompson

PHOTOGRAPHY
Gionata Gatto

By utilizing photoluminescent pigments to capture escaping light, Trap Light converts waste energy back into visible light. Photoluminesence is a process in which energy absorbed by a substance is gradually released as light.
Using the Murano glassblowing technique, the designers were able to embed photoluminescent pigments into the glass body of the lamp. A thirty-minute "charge" of recycled light from a traditional incandescent or LED lightbulb provides up to eight hours of ambient lighting.

FRA
Grâce à des pigments photoluminescents qui captent la lumière qui s'échappe, Trap Light transforme la déperdition d'énergie en lumière visible. La photoluminescence est un processus au cours duquel l'énergie absorbée par une substance est restituée ensuite progressivement sous forme de lumière. Les designers ont employé la technique du verre soufflé des artisans de Murano pour incruster des pigments photoluminescents dans le corps de la lanterne. Une « charge » de trente minutes d'éclairage provenant d'une ampoule incandescente ou LED fournit plus de huit heures de lumière d'ambiance.

ESP
La lámpara Trap Light utiliza pigmentos fotoluminiscentes para capturar la luz que se escapa y convertir la energía despilfarrada en luz visible.
La fotoluminiscencia es un proceso en el que la energía que absorbe una sustancia se emite gradualmente en forma de luz. Los diseñadores aplicaron la técnica de soplado de cristales de Murano con el fin de insertar pigmentos fotoluminiscentes en el cuerpo cristalino de esta lámpara. Con una «carga» de treinta minutos de luz reciclada de una bombilla LED o incandescente tradicional se disfrutan hasta treinta horas de luz de ambiente.

POR
A luminária Trap Light utiliza pigmentos fotoluminescentes para capturar a luz que escapa e para transformar a energia desperdiçada em luz visível.
A fotoluminescência é um processo pelo qual a energia absorvida por uma substância vai sendo emitida gradualmente em forma de luz. Os designers aplicaram a técnica de sopro de vidros de Murano a fim de inserir pigmentos fotoluminescentes no corpo cristalino desta luminária. Com uma «carga» de trinta minutos de luz reciclada de uma lâmpada LED ou incandescente tradicional, pode-se usufruir até trinta horas de luz ambiente.

FYR

DESIGN FIRM
Ida Noemi & Studio Vibeke Skar

DESIGNERS
Ida Noemi & Vibeke Skar

PHOTOGRAPHY
Ida Noemi & Kaja Bruskeland

Fyr is Norwegian for lighthouse, which since old times have helped sailors to find their way home. Inspired by the many lighthouses along the coast, Fyr is a warm flame to guide you in the dark. The table lantern comes in two versions: the one-piece classic version and the open version with a glass top and a base made from Corian. Having a separate top and base makes it easy to access the candle.

FRA

Fyr est un mot norvégien signifiant « phare », ce point de repère qui depuis des temps immémoriaux permet aux marins de rentrer à bon port. La flamme du photophore Fyr, qui s'inspire des multiples phares qui jalonnent les côtes du pays, saura vous guider dans l'obscurité. Le photophore existe en deux versions, la classique, formée d'une seule pièce et la moderne avec un corps en verre et un socle en Corian, qui est plus pratique pour accéder à la bougie.

ESP

Fyr significa «faro» en noruego. Así, esta creación se inspira en numerosos faros de la costa, que desde hace siglos señalan a los marineros el camino de regreso a casa, adoptando la forma de una llama cálida que alumbra cuando está oscuro. Este farol de sobremesa está disponible en dos versiones: la versión clásica de una sola pieza y la versión abierta con superficie cristalina y una base de Corian. La vela tiene fácil acceso, ya que la superficie y la base están separadas.

POR

Fyr significa «farol» em norueguês. Por isso, esta criação inspira-se em numerosos faróis da costa, que desde há séculos indicam aos marinheiros o caminho de regresso à casa, adotando a forma de uma chama cálida que ilumina quando está escuro. Este farol de mesa está disponível em duas versões: a versão clássica de uma única peça e a versão aberta, com superfície cristalina e uma base de Corian. A vela é de fácil acesso, já que a superfície e a base são separadas.

KYUDO

DESIGN FIRM
Hansandfranz

DESIGNERS
Konstantin Landuris & Horst Wittmann

PHOTOGRAPHY
Kundalini

CLIENT
Kundalini

Kyudo, a creation of talented young designers Konstantin Landuris and Horst Wittmann, was inspired by the ancient Japanese art of archery. It's a thin and flexible light arc designed to communicate elegance, balance, and harmony.
LED technology creates a luminous ribbon along one of the two arcs of the lamp structure. The arcs slide over one other, allowing both the lamp and the luminous ribbon to extend and therefore be adjusted to the user's liking

FRA
Le lampadaire Kyudo, créé par les talentueux jeunes designers Konstantin Landuris et Horst Wittmann, s'inspire de l'art du tir à l'arc du Japon d'autrefois. Le corps du lampadaire est un arc souple et léger conçu pour exprimer élégance, équilibre et harmonie. La technologie LED a permis de doter la partie mobile du lampadaire d'un ruban lumineux en LED. Celle-ci glisse sur l'arc fixe pour que l'on puisse ajuster la position du faisceau de lumière à sa convenance.

ESP
Kyudo, fruto del talento de los jóvenes diseñadores Konstantin Landuris y Horst Wittmann, se inspira en el antiguo arte japonés de la arquería. Así, consiste en un delgado y flexible arco luminoso que transmite elegancia, equilibrio y armonía. La tecnología LED crea una franja luminosa que recorre uno de los dos arcos que componen la estructura de la lámpara; estos arcos se deslizan el uno sobre el otro, permitiendo que la lámpara y la franja luminosa se extiendan para adaptarse al gusto del usuario.

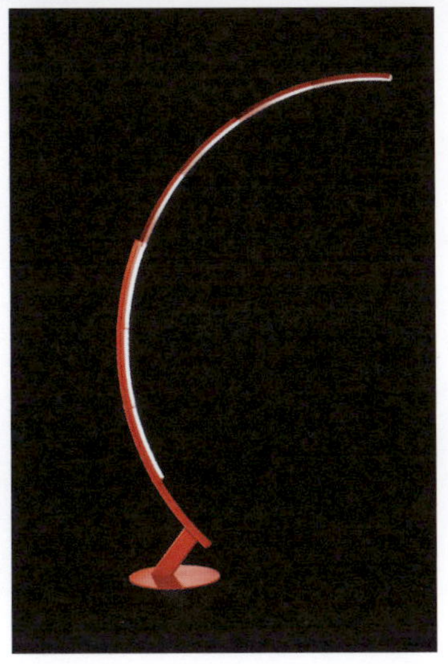

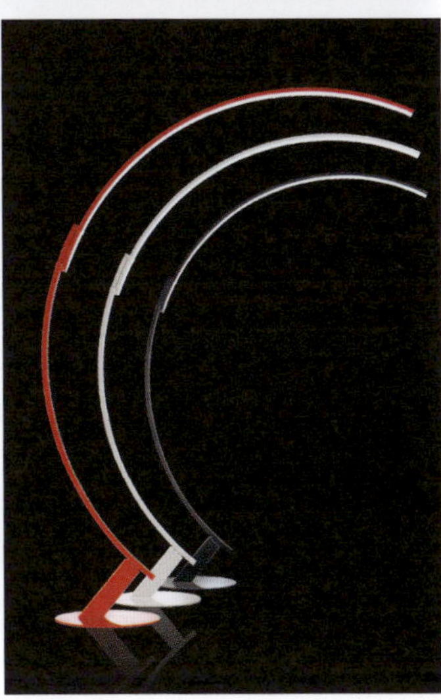

POR
Kyudo, fruto do talento dos jovens designers Konstantin Landuris e Horst Wittmann, inspira-se na antiga arte japonesa do arco. Trata-se de um fino e flexível arco luminoso que transmite elegância, equilíbrio e harmonia. A tecnologia LED cria uma franja luminosa que percorre um dos dois arcos que compõem a estrutura da luminária; estes arcos deslizam um sobre o outro, permitindo que a luminária e a franja luminosa se estendam para se adaptarem ao gosto do usuário.

LIGHTNESS OF BEING

DESIGN FIRM
Studio Pepe Heykoop

DESIGNER
Pepe Heykoop

PHOTOGRAPHY
Studio Pepe Heykoop

The way in which Lightness of Being is adjusted is based on the reaction of flowers to light. Flowers seem to hardly move at all, but when they are filmed using time-lapse photography it is clear that they move a great deal as they follow the sun. When plants receive light from only one side they can bend in spectacular ways, and so can this 3.5-meter-long lamp.

FRA
Le lampadaire Lightness of Being réagit à la lumière comme les fleurs, qui semblent rester immobiles, mais bougent en réalité pour suivre la course du soleil, ce que l'on constate lorsqu'on les filme en accéléré. Lorsqu'une plante ne reçoit de la lumière que d'un côté seulement, elle est capable des pires contorsions pour s'exposer tout entière. C'est exactement ce qui se passe avec ce lampadaire qui mesure 3,5 m de long.

ESP
Los ajustes de Lightness of Being se basan en la reacción de las flores frente al sol; aunque aparentemente apenas se mueven, cuando se filman mediante fotografía de intervalo comprobamos que en efecto se mueven mucho siguiendo al sol y cuando solo se iluminan desde un lado se inclinan de forma espectacular, al igual que esta lámpara de tres metros y medio de largo.

POR
Os ajustes de Lightness of Being baseiam-se na reação das flores diante do sol; ainda que, aparentemente, quase não se movam, quando são filmadas com fotografia com intervalos constatamos que de fato se movimentam muito seguindo o sol, e quando são iluminadas só por um lado, inclinam-se de forma espetacular, assim como esta luminária de três metros e meio de comprimento.

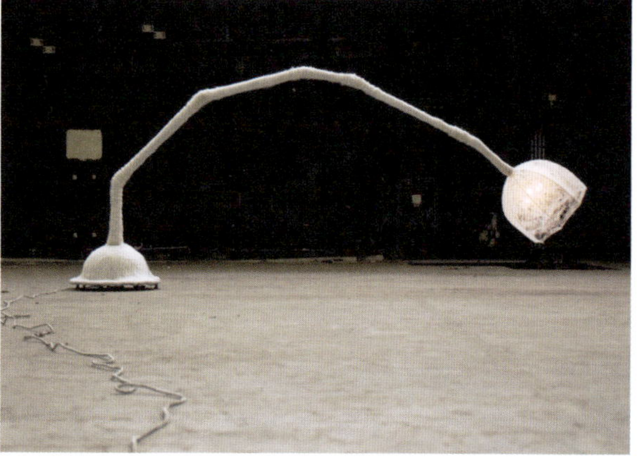

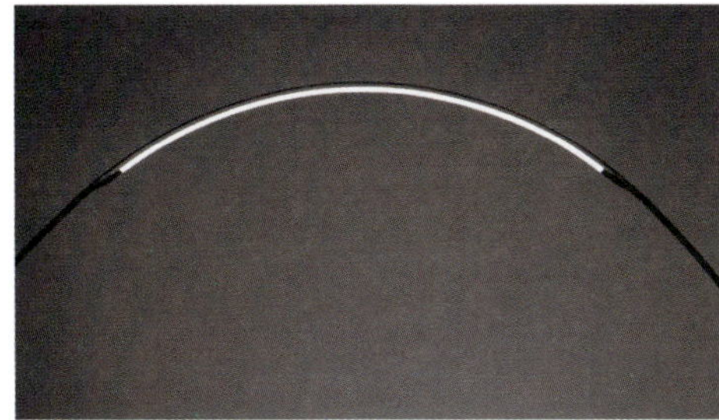

HALLEY

DESIGN FIRM
Vibia

DESIGNERS
Jordy Vilardell & Meritxell Vidal

PHOTOGRAPHY
Ferran Val & Albert Font

Halley, designed by Jordy Vilardell and Meritxell Vidal, achieves a combination of enormous sensitivity, high technology, and excellent functionality. Halley is visually a very light piece, concealing a high-tech luminaire which meets the highest quality standards. Halley conforms to IP64, which guarantees it can withstand outdoor wet-weather conditions.

FRA
Halley, conçu par Jordy Vilardell et Meritxell Vidal, combine extrême sensibilité, haute technologie et excellente fonctionnalité. Visuellement, Halley est très discret et léger. Il renferme un système d'éclairage haute technologie conforme aux plus hauts standard de qualité et à la norme IP64, qui garantit son utilisation à l'extérieur même lorsqu'il pleut.

ESP
Halley, una creación de Jordy Vilardell y Meritxell Vidal, es una combinación de gran delicadeza, alta tecnología y excelente rendimiento. Se trata de una obra visualmente muy ligera que oculta un farol de alta tecnología que satisface los criterios más exigentes. Halley cumple el estándar IP64, lo que garantiza que es resistente a los ambientes exteriores húmedos.

POR
Halley, uma criação de Jordy Vilardell e Meritxell Vidal, é uma combinação de grande delicadeza, alta tecnologia e excelente rendimento. Trata-se de uma obra visualmente muito leve, que oculta um farol de alta tecnologia que atende aos critérios mais exigentes. Halley obedece ao padrão IP64, o que garante que seja resistente aos ambientes exteriores úmidos.

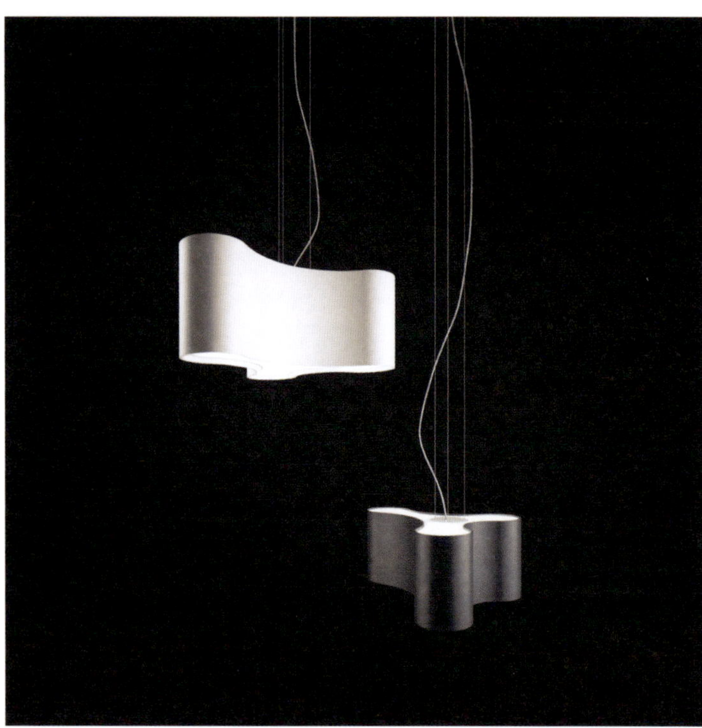

AMEBA

DESIGN FIRM
Vibia

DESIGNER
Pete Sans

PHOTOGRAPHY
Ferran Val & Albert Font

Ameba is a new pendant concept that can adapt to every space, need, and preference. Ameba is formed out of five different shapes that can be combined, allowing it to offer an infinite range of compositions. The Prestigious US magazine Interior Design included Ameba in its annual Best of Year Awards, selecting it as the best hanging lamp of 2009. Ameba was also the winner of the Hospitality Design Award presented by the International Interior Design Association.

FRA
Ameba est un tout nouveau concept de lustre qui s'adapte à tous les espaces, besoins et goûts. Il se compose de cinq modules de formes différentes que l'on peut combiner à volonté pour créer un nombre infini de variantes. Le prestigieux magazine américain Interior Design a inclu Ameba dans son classement annuel des meilleurs produits et l'a déclaré lustre de l'année 2009. Ameba a également remporté le prix « Hospitality Design » de l'Association internationale de décoration intérieure.

ESP
Presentamos un nuevo concepto de lámpara colgante que se adapta a todos los espacios, gustos y necesidades. Ameba consiste en cinco formas diferentes que se combinan, ofreciendo una gama infinita de composiciones. En 2009 la prestigiosa revista norteamericana Interior Design incluye esta creación en sus premios anuales y la selecciona como la mejor lámpara colgante del año. Ameba también ha sido galardonada con el premio Hospitality Design que otorga la International Interior Design Association.

POR
Apresentamos um novo conceito de luminária pendente que se adapta a todos os espaços, gostos e necessidades. Ameba é feita de cinco formas diferentes que se combinam, oferecendo uma gama infinita de composições. Em 2009, a famosa revista norte-americana *Interior Design* inclui esta criação em seus prêmios anuais e a seleciona como a melhor luminária pendente do ano. Ameba também foi agraciada com o prêmio Hospitality Design e conferido pela International Interior Design Association.

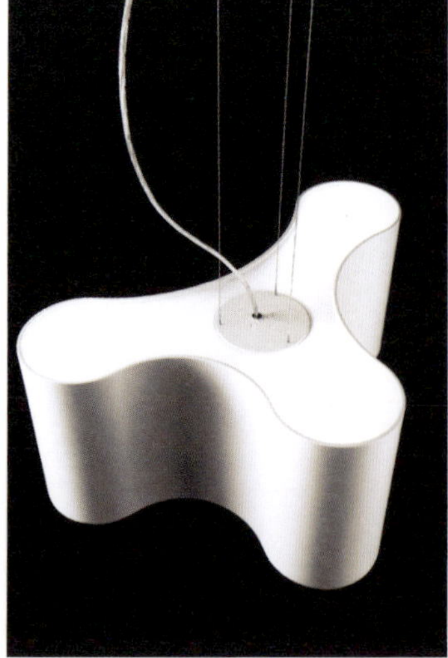

FIELD OF LIGHT

DESIGNER
Bruce Munro

PHOTOGRAPHY
Mark Pickthall

CLIENT
The Eden Project

Field of Light is made of six thousand acrylic stems, through which fiber-optic cables run, and each is crowned with a clear glass sphere. Like dry desert seeds lying in wait for the rain, the sculpture's fiber-optic stems lie dormant until darkness falls, and then under a blazing blanket of stars they flower with gentle rhythms of light. Field of Light uses recycled materials and low-energy light sources such as LED projectors and light, fiber-optic pieces.

POR

Field of Light é composta por seis mil caules acrílicos percorridos por cabos de fibra ótica arrematadas por esferas de vidro transparente. Como as sementes secas do deserto que aguardam a chuva, os caules de fibra ótica da escultura dormem até que cai a noite e então, sob um deslumbrante manto de estrelas, florescem com suaves cadências luminosas. Field of Light utiliza materiais reciclados e fontes de baixa potência, como projetores LED e componentes leves de fibra ótica.

FRA

Field of Light est composé de six mille tiges en acrylique terminées par une sphère en verre transparent abritant des câbles en fibre optique. À l'image des graines dans le désert qui attendent la pluie pour se manifester, la sculpture en fibre optique sommeille jusqu'à la tombée du jour où ses fleurs éclosent dans des galaxies de lumières colorées qui font concurrence aux étoiles du ciel. Field of Light utilise des matériaux recyclés et des sources d'énergie de basse tension comme des projecteurs, des ampoules LED et de la fibre optique.

ESP

Field of Light consiste en seis mil tallos acrílicos que recorren cables de fibra óptica rematadas en esferas de cristal transparente. Al igual que las semillas secas del desierto que aguardan la lluvia, los tallos de fibra óptica de la escultura duermen hasta que cae la noche y entonces, bajo un deslumbrante manto de estrellas, florecen con suaves cadencias luminosas. Field of Light emplea materiales reciclados y fuentes de baja potencia como proyectores LED y componentes de fibra óptica ligeros.

DUNE

DESIGN FIRM
Studio Roosegaarde

DESIGNER
Daan Roosegaarde

PHOTOGRAPHY
Studio Roosegaarde

CLIENT
CBK Rotterdam

Dune is a landscape that interacts with human behavior. This hybrid of nature and technology has been created using fibers that brighten according to the sounds and motions of passing visitors. The most recent version is filled with hundreds of interactive lights and sounds. Dune is a futuristic investigation of nature's relationship with urban space by means of looking, walking, and interacting.

FRA
Dune est un paysage qui interagit avec les gens. Hybride entre nature et technologie, Dune est fabriqué avec des fibres qui s'éclairent en réaction aux sons et aux mouvements des visiteurs qui passent. La toute dernière version de Dune compte des centaines de lumières et de sons interactifs. Dune est un projet futuriste sur la relation de la nature avec l'espace urbain qui associe observation, déplacement et interaction.

ESP
Dune es un paisaje que interactúa con el comportamiento humano. Este híbrido de la naturaleza y la tecnología está hecho de fibras que se iluminan frente a los sonidos y los movimientos de los visitantes. La última versión dispone de cientos de sonidos y luces interactivas. Se trata de una investigación futurista de la relación que mantiene la naturaleza con el espacio urbano a través de la mirada, el movimiento y la interacción.

POR
Dune é uma paisagem que interage com o comportamento humano. Este híbrido de natureza e tecnologia é feito de fibras que se iluminam perante os sons e os movimentos dos visitantes. A última versão dispõe de centenas de sons luzes interativas. Trata-se de uma pesquisa futurista da relação que a natureza mantém com o espaço urbano através do olhar, o movimento e a interação.

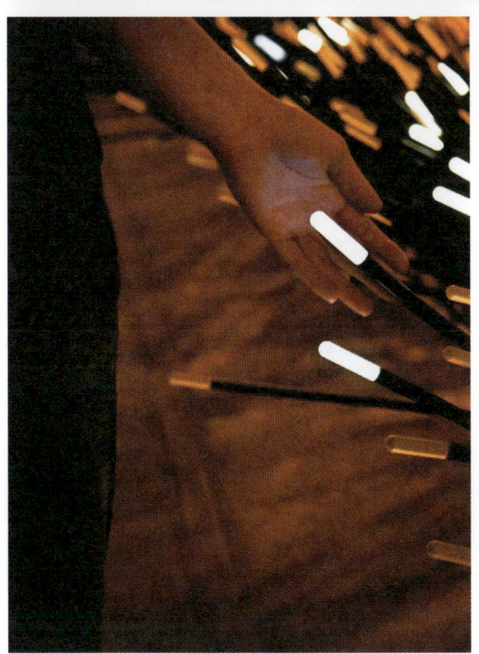

LOTUS 7.0

DESIGN FIRM
Studio Roosegaarde

DESIGNER
Daan Roosegaarde

PHOTOGRAPHY
Studio Roosegaarde

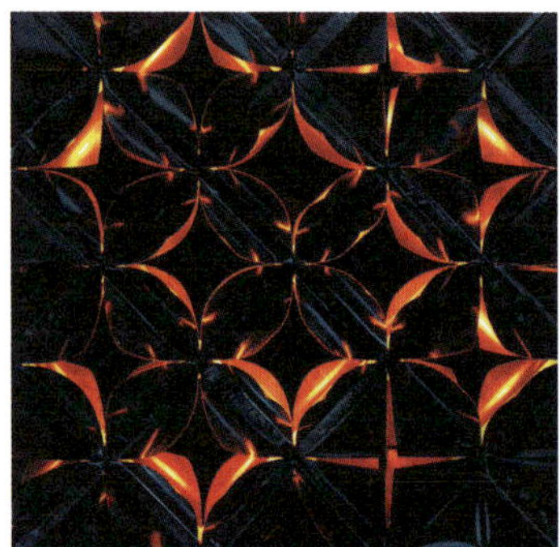

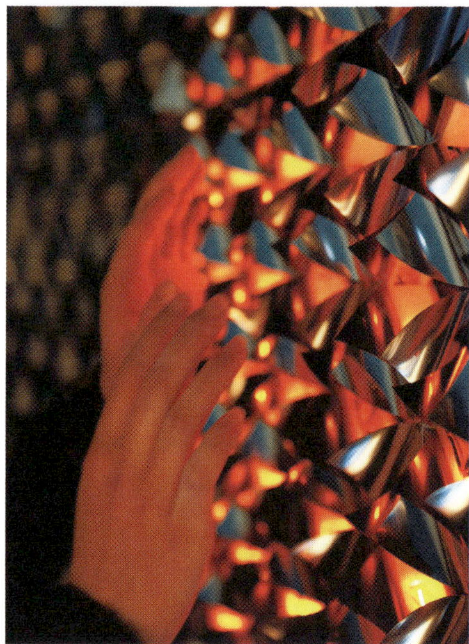

Lotus 7.0 is a living wall made out of smart foil that folds open in response to human behavior. As you walk by Lotus 7.0 hundreds of pieces of aluminum foil unfold themselves in an organic way, generating transparent voids between private and public spaces. With Lotus, physical walls are made immaterial, giving way to a poetic morphing of space and people.

FRA

Lotus 7.0 est un mur vivant composé d'alvéoles intelligentes en feuille d'aluminium qui s'ouvrent en réponse au comportement humain. Lorsqu'une personne passe près de Lotus 7.0, des centaines de morceaux de feuille d'aluminium se déplient comme des pétales, découvrant des ouvertures qui laissent voir ce qui se passe de l'autre côté de la cloison, rapprochant ainsi espace public et sphère privée. Avec Lotus, les murs s'ouvrent et transportent l'espace et les gens vers une autre dimension où règne la poésie.

ESP

Lotus 7.0 es una pared viviente de papel de aluminio inteligente que se abre en respuesta al comportamiento humano. Así, cuando alguien pasa frente a ella se despliegan de forma orgánica cientos de fragmentos de papel de aluminio inteligente con los que se generan abismos transparentes entre el espacio público y privado.
Con Lotus 7.0 las paredes físicas se vuelven inmateriales, dando paso a una metamorfosis poética del espacio y las personas.

POR

Lotus 7.0 é uma parede vivente de papel de alumínio inteligente que se abre em resposta ao comportamento humano. Deste modo, quando alguém passa em frente a ela, desdobram-se de forma orgânica centenas de fragmentos de papel de alumínio inteligente e com isto geram-se abismos transparentes entre o espaço público e o privado.
Com Lotus 7.0 as paredes físicas se tornam imateriais, dando lugar a uma metamorfose poética do espaço e das pessoas.

LUNAR

DESIGN FIRM
Studio Roosegaarde

DESIGNER
Daan Roosegaarde

PHOTOGRAPHY
Studio Roosegaarde

CLIENT
Mental Health Care GGZ Breda

This interactive artwork installed at the Youth Division of Mental Health Care GGZ in the Netherlands features a series of light objects. Filled with LEDs and interactive technologies, these objects are designed to come to life by emitting sounds and color upon detection of a child's touch. By interacting with the existing architecture, Lunar creates an informal interplay between children, their therapy, and the building.

ESP
Esta obra de arte interactiva instalada en el Departamento de Juventud del Centro de Enfermedades Mentales GGZ de Holanda consiste en una serie de objetos luminosos que incorporan luces LED y tecnologías interactivas que cobran vida emitiendo sonidos y colores cuando detectan el contacto de los niños. Lunar establece una relación informal entre los niños, la terapia y el edificio interactuando con la estructura existente.

FRA
Cette œuvre d'art interactive composée d'objets lumineux est installée dans la division réservée aux jeunes du centre de santé mentale GGZ aux Pays-Bas. Ces objets, qui renferment des LED et un système de technologie interactive, sont conçus pour prendre vie et émettre des sons et des couleurs lorsqu'un enfant les touche. Lunar s'intègre parfaitement à l'architecture du lieu et crée une interaction ludique entre les enfants, leur thérapie et le bâtiment.

POR
Esta obra de arte interativa instalada no Departamento de Juventude do Centro de Doenças Mentais GGZ da Holanda é constituída por uma série de objetos luminosos que incorporam lâmpadas LED e tecnologias interativas que ganham vida emitindo sons e cores quando detectam o contato das crianças. Lunar estabelece uma relação informal entre as crianças, a terapia e o edifício, interagindo com a estrutura existente.

FRA

AUTRES APPROCHES ÉCOLOGIQUES

Par écoconception on entend la prise en compte de l'impact sur l'environnement d'un produit pendant toute sa durée de vie dès l'étape de son élaboration. Dans les chapitres précédents nous avons vu différentes facettes de l'écoconception comme le recyclage, le réemploi, l'utilisation de matériaux naturels, les apports de la technologie et la fabrication artisanale. Il existe aussi d'autres façons de créer des produits respectueux de l'environnement, comme l'exploitation de matériaux disponibles sur place, l'emploi de matières brutes provenant de sources à gestion durable et la capacité d'économie d'énergie et d'autosuffisance.

ESP

OTRAS TENDENCIAS ECOLÓGICAS

El término «diseño ecológico» se aplica a todas las actitudes que durante el diseño de un objeto determinado tienen en cuenta especialmente el impacto que dicho objeto causará en el medio ambiente durante toda su vida. Además de las modalidades de diseño ecológico que hemos incluido en los capítulos anteriores sobre el reciclaje y la reutilización, los materiales naturales y la tecnología y la artesanía, existen muchas otras maneras de crear diseños respetuosos con el medio ambiente, como por ejemplo utilizar materiales locales y materias primas procedentes de fuentes gestionadas de manera sostenible y aplicar conceptos como el ahorro de energía pasivo y la autosostenibilidad.

POR

OUTROS ENFOQUES ECO

O termo «design ecológico» aplica-se a todas as atitudes que durante o projeto de um determinado objeto levam em conta, especialmente, o impacto que tal objeto causará no meio ambiente durante toda a sua vida. Além das modalidades de design ecológico que incluímos nos capítulos anteriores sobre a reciclagem e a reutilização, os materiais naturais, a tecnologia e o artesanato, existem muitas outras maneiras de criar designs que respeitam o meio ambiente, como, por exemplo, utilizar materiais locais e matérias primas procedentes de fontes administradas de maneira sustentável e aplicar conceitos como a economia de energia passiva e a autosustentabilidade.

04

136-155

OTHER ECO APPROACHES

Eco design is any approach to product design that takes special consideration of the environmental impact of the product during its whole lifecycle. In addition to the types of eco design covered in the previous chapters on recycling and reuse, natural materials, and technology and crafts, there are many other ways to create eco-friendly designs, such as working with locally sourced materials, using raw materials that come from sustainably managed sources, and making use of concepts such as passive energy saving and self-sustainability.

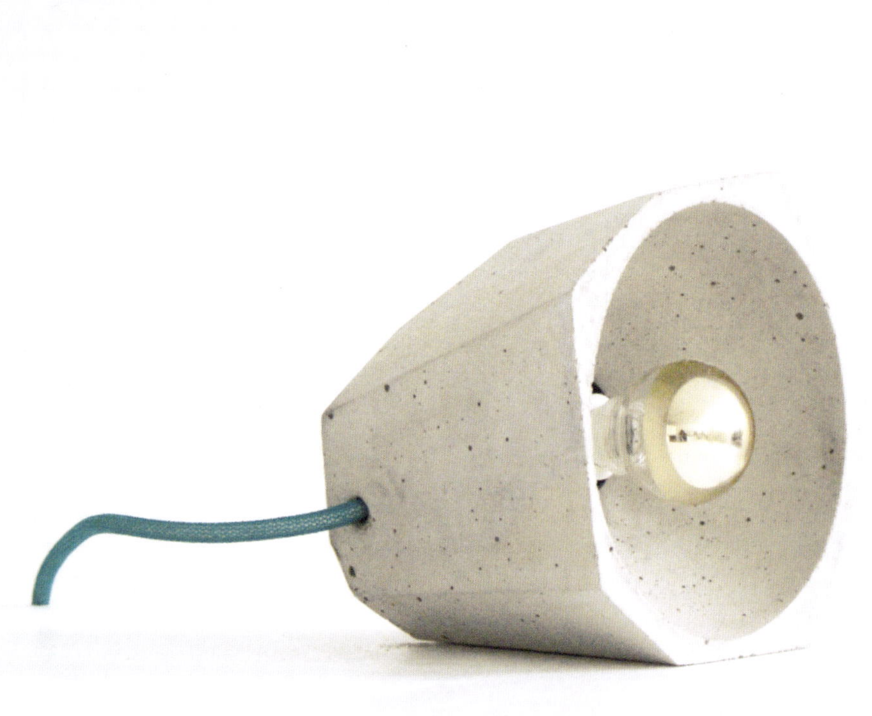

TILT LAMP

DESIGN FIRM
lokolo

DESIGNERS
Jonathan Markus & Sam Liu

PHOTOGRAPHY
lokolo

The ecological aspect of this project lies in its use of local and custom/on-demand production. Unlike mass production carried out by exploiting cheap labor or resources in a remote country, local production not only reduces the carbon footprint of our products, but also brings benefits to the productive industries of the local economy.

FRA
Cette lampe est écologique dans la mesure où nous avons opté pour une production sur place et à la demande. Contrairement à la production de masse où l'on exploite de la main d'œuvre ou des ressources bon marché de pays reculés, la production sur place réduit nos seulement l'empreinte carbone des produits, mais profite aussi à l'industrie et à l'économie locales.

ESP
El aspecto ecológico de este proyecto consiste en la producción local y personalizada; en otras palabras, a petición del cliente. Al contrario que la fabricación en serie con la que se explotan la mano de obra barata y los recursos de países lejanos, la producción local no solo reduce la huella de carbono de nuestros productos, sino que también beneficia a las industrias locales.

POR
O aspecto ecológico deste projeto consiste na produção local e personalizada; em outras palavras, por encomenda do cliente. Ao contrário da fabricação em série, com a qual se exploram a mão de obra barata e os recursos de países longinquos, a produção local não só reduz a pegada de carbono dos nossos produtos, mas também beneficia as indústrias locais.

NAÏVE SHADE

DESIGN FIRM
Fargo Design

DESIGNER
Michal Fargo

PHOTOGRAPHY
Svetlana Yorchenko & Liran Fisher

The Naïve Shade is produced from porcelain and is designed using the aesthetics of an old-school lampshade and a basic bulb. In designing the Naïve Shade Michal Fargo created an object which mediates between the necessity of an eco-friendly bulb and the authenticity and nostalgia embodied in the Naïve Shade's aesthetics. This porcelain lampshade's mountainous pattern is an important part of the structure as it helps to prevent the porcelain getting distorted.

FRA
Le lustre Naïve Shade, fabriqué en porcelaine, s'inspire de l'abat-jour à l'ancienne éclairé par une ampoule à filament. Avec Naïve Shade, son designer Michal Fargo a su trouver un compromis entre la nécessité d'utiliser une ampoule écologique et la nostalgie du passé. L'esthétique en strates et franges du lustre est un aspect important de la structure parce qu'elle empêche la porcelaine de se déformer.

ESP
La Naïve Shade está hecha de porcelana y aplica una estética consistente en una pantalla de la vieja escuela y una simple bombilla. Michal Fargo la ha diseñado como un objeto que media entre la necesidad de una bombilla respetuosa con el medio ambiente y la autenticidad y la nostalgia que encarna la estética de la lámpara. El contorno montañoso de la pantalla constituye una parte significativa de la estructura, ya que impide que se deforme la porcelana.

POR
A Naïve Shade é feita de porcelana e aplica uma estética consistente numa cúpula da velha escola e uma simples lâmpada. Michal Fargo desenhou-a como um objeto que medeia entre a necessidade de uma lâmpada que respeita o meio ambiente e a autenticidade e nostalgia que encarna a estética da luminária. O contorno montanhoso da cúpula constitui uma parte significativa da estrutura, já que impede que se a porcelana se deforme.

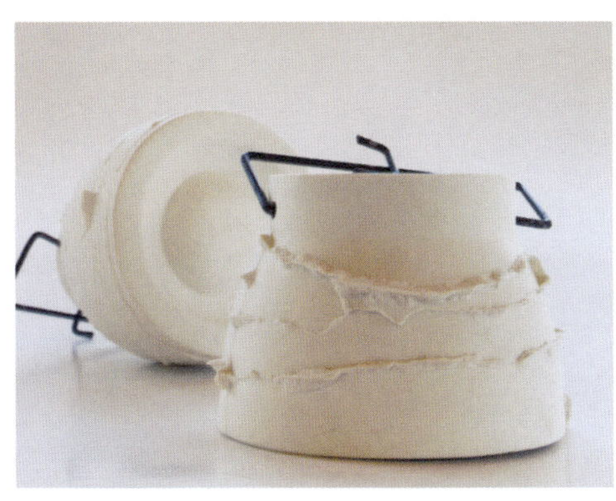

MUSHROOM LAMP

DESIGN FIRM
h220430

PHOTOGRAPHY
h220430

There are tens of thousands of nuclear weapons in the world, in spite of the end of the Cold War. For those who dream of a nuclear-free world it is important to display concern about this issue, deepen people's understanding of the subject, and continue to advocate the elimination of nuclear weapons. h220430 would like to create a catalyst for these goals through people incorporating the Mushroom Lamp into their daily lives, and help to lighten the hearts of those who hope for peace in the world.

ESP
Aunque la Guerra Fría ha concluido, en el mundo todavía existen decenas de miles de armas nucleares. Los que sueñan con un mundo sin armas nucleares sienten la obligación de manifestar esta preocupación, explicársela a los demás y apostar por la desaparición de las armas nucleares. A h220430 le gustaría que la incorporación de la lámpara Mushroom a la vida cotidiana de los usuarios catalizara estos objetivos y reconfortara a quienes desean la paz en el mundo.

FRA
En dépit de la fin de la Guerre froide, il existe des milliers d'armes nucléaires sur la planète. Pour ceux qui rêvent à un monde libéré du nucléaire, il est important d'exprimer leurs inquiétudes face à cette menace, de les informer des divers aspects de cette énergie et de demander l'élimination de toutes les armes nucléaires. À cet égard, la lampe h220430 souhaite jouer le rôle de catalyseur. En intégrant la lampe Mushroom dans leur univers quotidien, les gens qui souhaitent la paix dans le monde se sentiront soutenus dans leur démarche.

POR
Ainda que a Guerra Fria tenha terminado, ainda existem no mundo dezenas de milhares de armas nucleares. Os que sonham com um mundo sem armas nucleares sentem a obrigação de manifestar esta preocupação, de explicá-la aos demais e de apostar na desaparição das armas nucleares. A h220430 gostaria que a incorporação da luminária Mushroom à vida cotidiana dos usuários catalisasse estes objetivos e reconfortasse aos que desejam a paz no mundo

2D LED

DESIGN FIRM
DING3000

DESIGNERS
Sven Rudolph, Ralf Webermann & Carsten Schelling

PHOTOGRAPHY
SKITSCH

CLIENT
SKITSCH

A quick hand sketch of an archetypical lamp was the inspiration for 2D LED. By means of modern LED technology it is possible to keep the body of the lamp as thin as possible, which gives the luminaire the appearance of a sketched line. The sheathed metal hose within the foot provides an adjustable hood. 2D LED is available as a table or a floor lamp. In 2011 the 2D LED family was enlarged with the addition of a pendant version.

ESP
2D LED se inspira en un boceto apresurado de una lámpara arquetípica. El cuerpo es tan delgado gracias a la moderna tecnología LED, que le confiere la apariencia de una línea abocetada. Asimismo, dispone de una cubierta ajustable gracias a la barra metálica recubierta del pie. 2D LED está disponible como lámpara de pie o de sobremesa. En 2011 la familia 2D LED aumenta con la incorporación de una versión colgante.

POR
2D LED inspira-se num esboço apressado de uma luminária arquetípica. O corpo é tão fino graças à moderna tecnologia LED, que lhe confere a aparência de uma linha esboçada. Igualmente, dispõe de uma cobertura ajustável graças à barra metálica recoberta do pé. 2D LED está disponível como luminária de pé ou de mesa. Em 2011, a família 2D LED aumenta com a incorporação de uma versão pendente.

FRA
La série 2D LED est née d'une esquisse représentant l'archétype même du luminaire. La technologie LED permet d'avoir une structure extrêmement mince ressemblant à un croquis. Le tube gainé en métal intégré au pied peut se tordre de façon à orienter le faisceau lumineux selon les besoins. 2D LED est disponible en version lampe, lampadaire et lustre, cette dernière étant proposée depuis 2011.

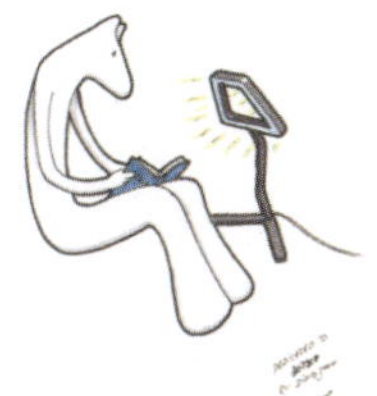

ICHI-GO

DESIGN FIRM
Freyja

DESIGNER
Freyja Sewell

PHOTOGRAPHY
Freyja Sewell

Ichi-Go is a light that arrives as a pristine sphere that you have to smash to transform into a functional object. The smashed pieces are held in suspension beneath the light via chains which are hidden within the sphere. The light will forever be a memorial of this unique moment of destruction/creation, as the pattern will vary depending on the angle and strength of the break.

FRA
Ichi-Go est livré sous forme de sphère parfaite que l'on doit briser pour la transformer en objet fonctionnel. Les éclats restent suspendus à la sphère par des chaînes cachées à l'intérieur du lustre, qui représentera pour toujours le précieux moment de destruction/création qui l'a façonné. Le résultat dépendra de l'angle et de la force du coup porté.

ESP
Ichi-Go es una lámpara en forma de esfera pristina que debe destruirse para transformarse en un objeto práctico. Los fragmentos se mantienen suspendidos bajo la luz mediante cadenas que se ocultan dentro de la esfera. Así, la lámpara será siempre un recuerdo de este efímero momento de destrucción/creación, ya que el patrón cambia en función del ángulo y la fuerza de la ruptura.

POR
Ichi-Go é uma luminária em forma de esfera prístina que deve destruir-se para se transformar num objeto prático. Os fragmentos se mantêm suspensos sob a luz por meio de correntes que se ocultam dentro da esfera. Desta forma, a luminária será sempre uma recordação deste efêmero momento de destruição/criação, já que o padrão muda em função do ângulo e da força da ruptura.

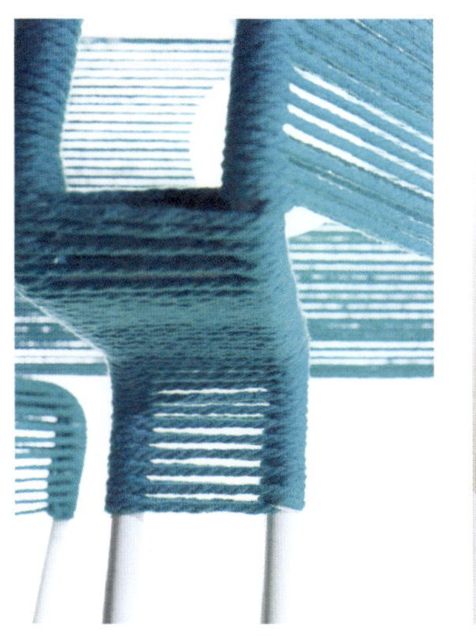

CLOVER LAMP

DESIGN FIRM
Mut Design

DESIGNER
Alberto Sánchez

PHOTOGRAPHY
Syncro Fotografía

CLIENT
Mut Shop

This collection combines a zinc-coated steel structure with ecological string to create lamps that come in a range of colors. True to their designer's commitment to the environment and using nature as a source of inspiration, this collection of lamps was influenced by the shape of clovers. Consisting of three identical structures onto which colored string is woven, Clover Lamps can be customized by offering numerous possible color combinations.

ESP

Esta colección, disponible en una amplia gama de colores, combina una estructura de acero recubierta de zinc con una cuerda ecológica. En consonancia con el compromiso del diseñador con el medio ambiente y tomando la naturaleza como fuente de inspiración, esta colección de lámparas acusa la influencia de la forma de los tréboles. Las lámparas Clover, consistentes en tres estructuras idénticas que se recubren con una cuerda coloreada, pueden personalizarse para ofrecer numerosas combinaciones de colores.

FRA

Cette collection associe une structure en acier revêtue d'une couche de zinc ornée de corde écologique de différentes couleurs. Conforme à l'objectif de son designer, qui souhaitait créer des luminaires écologiques s'inspirant de la nature, la collection reprend la forme du trèfle. Chaque luminaire Clover est constitué de trois structures identiques sur lesquelles est tissée une corde de couleur. Clover peut être adapté au goût du client grâce aux multiples combinaisons de couleurs possibles.

POR

Esta coleção, disponível em ampla variedade de cores, combina uma estrutura de aço recoberta de zinco com uma corda ecológica. Em consonância com o comprometimento do designer com o meio ambiente, e tomando a natureza como fonte de inspiração, esta coleção de luminárias revela influência da forma dos trevos. As luminárias Clover, feitas com três estruturas idênticas que se recobrem com uma corda colorida, podem ser personalizadas para oferecer numerosas combinações de cores.

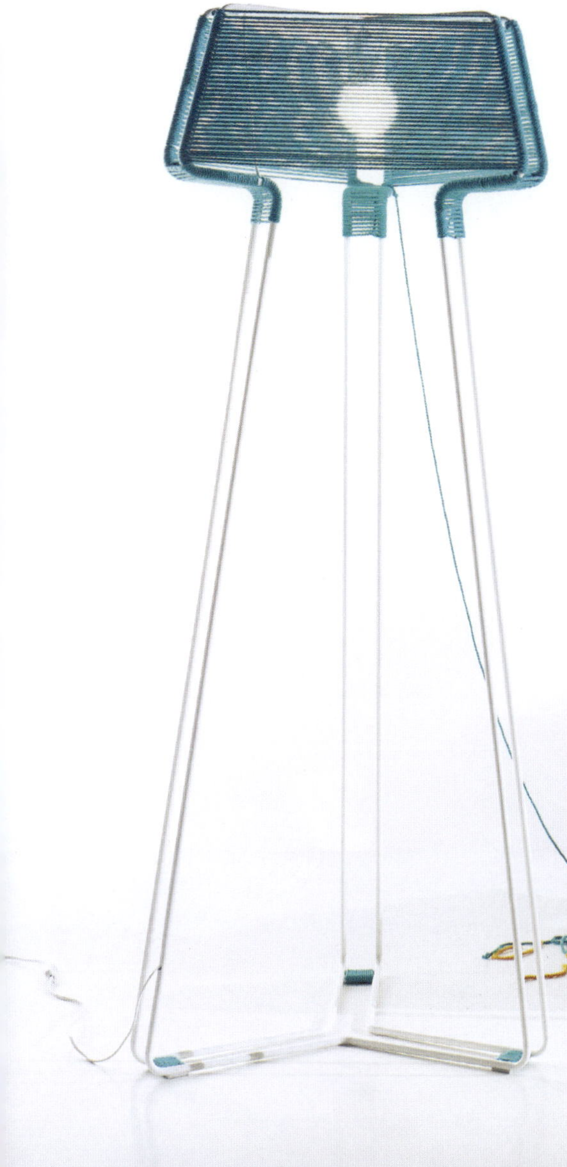

THE DUCK LAMP

DESIGNER
Sebastian Errazuriz

PHOTOGRAPHY
Sebastian Errazuriz

Rescued from the trashcan of an old taxidermy museum, this stuffed bird with a broken neck has been given a new life through being turned into a lamp. The Duck Lamp by New York-based artist and designer Sebastian Errazuriz is an eerie yet funny and beautiful object that explores the borders between sculptural and functional forms in both art and design.

ESP
Este pájaro disecado con el cuello roto, encontrado en la papelera de un antiguo museo de taxidermia, ha cobrado nueva vida al convertirse en lámpara. La lámpara Duck del artista y diseñador afincado en Nueva York Sebastián Errazuriz es un objeto divertido y hermoso al tiempo que escalofriante que explora las fronteras entre las formas esculturales y funcionales tanto en el arte como en el diseño.

FRA
Récupéré dans les poubelles d'un vieux musée de taxidermie, ce canard sans tête empaillé reprend du service comme lampe de bureau. Créé par le designer new-yorkais Sebastian Errazuriz, cet objet à la fois étrange et magnifique explore la frontière entre sculpture et fonctionnalité, tant au niveau de l'art pur que du design.

POR
Este pássaro dissecado e sem o pescoço, encontrado no cesto dos papéis de um antigo museu de taxidermia, ganhou nova vida ao transformar-se em luminária. A luminária Duck do artista e designer estabelecido em Nova York, Sebastián Errazuriz, é um objeto divertido, bonito e, ao mesmo tempo, assustador, que explora as fronteiras entre as formas esculturais e funcionais, tanto na arte como no design.

E.T.A. BABY

DESIGN FIRM
Studio Guglielmo Berchicci

PHOTOGRAPHY
Kundalini

DESIGNER
Guglielmo Berchicci

CLIENT
Kundalini

E.T.A. Baby (Extra-Terrestrial Angel) was designed by Guglielmo Berchicci. Its iconic diffuser is made by hand using ecological fiberglass, a highly durable and recyclable material. The lamp's inner structure is metallic.

ESP
E.T.A. Baby (o Extra-Terrestrial Angel, «ángel extraterrestre») es un diseño de Guglielmo Berchicci. El icónico difusor está hecho a mano con fibra de vidrio ecológica, un material altamente duradero y reciclable. La estructura interna de la lámpara es metálica.

FRA
E.T.A. Baby (initiales de l'expression « ange extra-terrestre » en anglais) est une création du designer Guglielmo Berchicci. La lampe, fidèle au style de son créateur, est fabriquée à la main à partir de fibre de verre écologique, matière hautement durable et recyclable. La structure interne de la lampe est en métal.

POR
E.T.A. Baby (o Extra-Terrestrial Angel, «anjo extraterrestre») é um projeto de Guglielmo Berchicci. O icônico difusor é feito à mão, com fibra de vidro ecológica, um material altamente duradouro e reciclável. A estrutura interna da luminária é metálica.

SELF COMPILING LAMP

DESIGN FIRM
Milos Design

DESIGNER
Milos Jovanovic

PHOTOGRAPHY
Milos Jovanovic

This is the standard classic chandelier adapting to the times through contemporary forms and the use of ecological material. It reflects the designer's passion for the textures, organic shapes, and patterns found in nature. The lamp is designed so that the customer can compile it by him or herself according to the instructions. The lamp is made of PVC material and consists of six elements. In unfolded form these elements are no bigger than a sheet of A4 paper, which reduces transportation costs to a minimum.

FRA
Voici une version moderne du lustre classique fabriquée dans un matériau écologique. Cet objet reflète la passion du designer Milos Jovanovic pour les textures, les formes et les motifs que l'on trouve dans la nature. Le lustre est conçu pour que le client le monte lui-même. Il est en PVC et compte six éléments. Avant son montage, l'ensemble des composants du lustre ne dépasse pas la taille d'une feuille A4, ce qui réduit au minimum les coûts de transport.

ESP
Presentamos una adaptación de la araña clásica a los nuevos tiempos mediante formas contemporáneas y materiales ecológicos en la que se refleja la pasión del diseñador por las texturas, las formas orgánicas y los contornos que se encuentran en la naturaleza. La lámpara está concebida para que el usuario la monte siguiendo las instrucciones. Está hecha de PVC y se compone de seis elementos que cuando se despliegan no son más grandes que una hoja de papel A4, de manera que los gastos de transporte son mínimos.

POR
Apresentamos uma adaptação do lustre clássico aos novos tempos através de formas contemporâneas e materiais ecológicos em que se reflete a paixão do designer pelas texturas, pelas formas orgânicas e pelos contornos da natureza. A luminária foi concebida para que o usuário a monte, seguindo as instruções. É feita de PVC e se compõe de seis elementos que, quando se desdobram, não são maiores grandes que uma folha de papel A4, de maneira que os custos de transporte são mínimos.

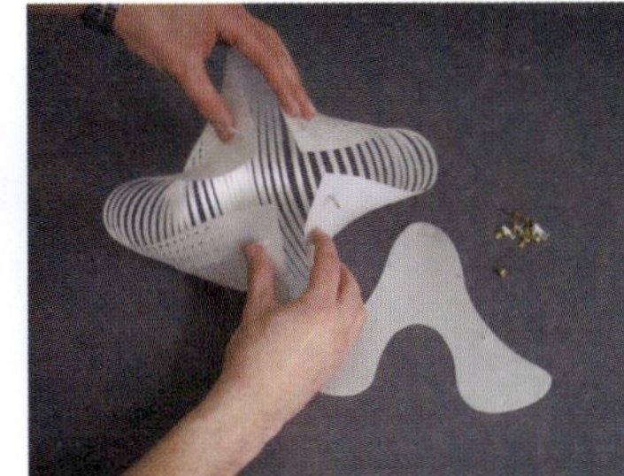

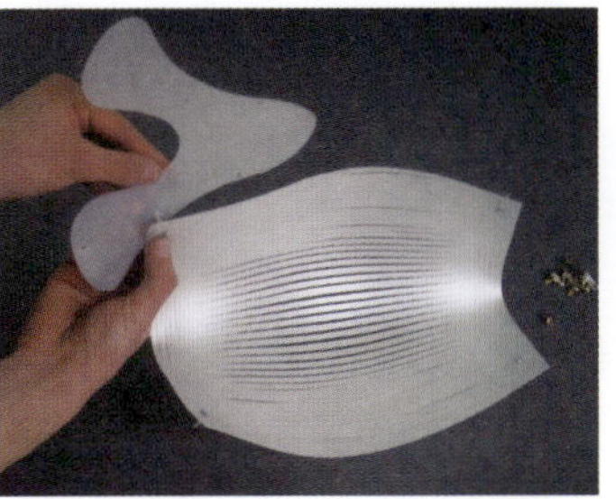

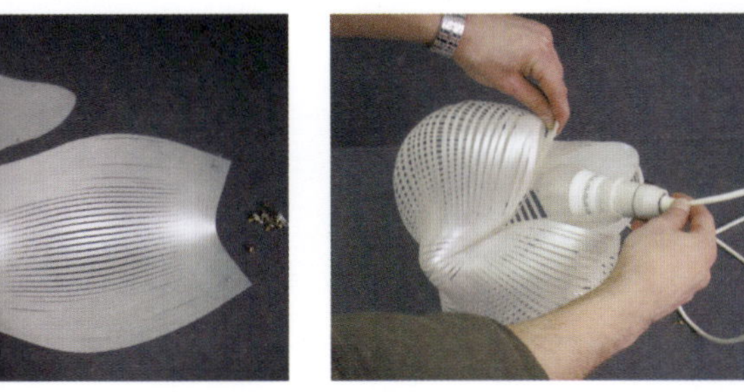

LIBERTY

DESIGN FIRM
Danny Kuo

DESIGNER
Danny Kuo

PHOTOGRAPHY
Thomas Pleeging & Bas van der Veer

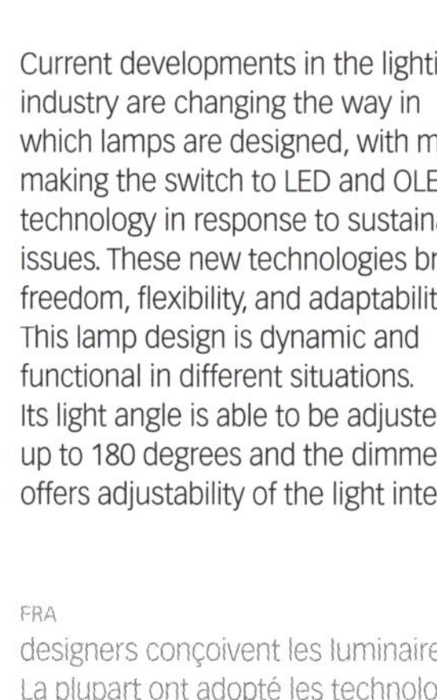

Current developments in the lighting industry are changing the way in which lamps are designed, with many making the switch to LED and OLED technology in response to sustainability issues. These new technologies bring freedom, flexibility, and adaptability. This lamp design is dynamic and functional in different situations. Its light angle is able to be adjusted up to 180 degrees and the dimmer offers adjustability of the light intensity.

ESP

Las innovaciones actuales en la industria de las lámparas están cambiando los diseños de estas, que en muchos casos adoptan las tecnologías LED y OLED en respuesta a criterios sostenibles. Gracias a estas nuevas tecnologías disfrutamos de creaciones más libres, flexibles y adaptables. Así, este diseño es sumamente dinámico y se amolda a situaciones diversas. El ángulo de la lámpara llega hasta 180 grados y el reductor nos ofrece distintas intensidades.

FRA

designers conçoivent les luminaires. La plupart ont adopté les technologies LED et OLED pour répondre aux exigences en matière d'écologie et de durabilité. Ces nouvelles technologies apportent liberté, souplesse et adaptabilité. Le design de ce lustre est dynamique et fonctionnel, ce qui lui permet de s'adapter à différentes situations. L'angle d'éclairage peut être réglé jusqu'à 180° et son intensité est modulable grâce au variateur intégré.

POR

A inovações atuais na indústria das luminárias estão mudando os seus designs, que, em muitos casos, adotam as tecnologias LED e OLED como resposta a critérios de sustentabilidade. Graças a estas novas tecnologias, desfrutamos de criações mais livres, flexíveis e adaptáveis. Assim, este design é extremamente dinâmico e se adapta a situações diversas. O ângulo da luminária chega a 180 graus e o redutor nos oferece diferentes intensidades.

LIGHTMATE

DESIGN FIRM
Lanzavecchia + Wai Design Studio

DESIGNER
Francesca Lanzavecchia

PHOTOGRAPHY
Davide Farabegoli

Can electrical energy fill the void of human absence? Lightmates are soft, anthropomorphic pillows and warming lamps. These attractive creatures heat, light, and provide company. Their different sizes respond to everyone's need for warmth. They are a mate to hug or a huge companion you can lie on.

FRA
L'énergie électrique peut-elle remplir le vide laissé par l'absence des êtres humains ? Lightmate est tout à la fois une lampe et un coussin de forme anthropomorphe. Cette agréable créature réchauffe, éclaire et tient compagnie. Lightmate existe en différentes tailles pour répondre aux besoins de chacun. C'est un complice que l'on peut enlacer ou sur lequel on peut s'allonger.

ESP
¿La energía eléctrica llena el hueco que deja la ausencia humana? Las lámparas Lightmates son almohadas blandas y antropomórficas al tiempo que calefactoras. Estas atractivas criaturas calientan, iluminan y nos hacen compañía. Los distintos tamaños obedecen a las necesidades de todos. Podemos abrazarlas como a un amante o recostarnos sobre ellas como si fueran un fornido compañero.

POR
A energia elétrica preenche o vazio que deixa a ausência humana? As luminárias Lightmates são almofadas macias e antropomórficas e, ao mesmo tempo, aquecedoras. Estas atraentes criaturas aquecem, iluminam e nos fazem companhia. Os diversos tamanhos atendem às necessidades de todos. Podemos abraçá-las como a um amante ou recostar-nos sobre elas como se fossem um musculoso companheiro.

LIGHT_NESS

DESIGN FIRM
UXUS

DESIGNER
UXUS

MANUFACTURER
The Set Company

PHOTOGRAPHY
Dim Balsem

UXUS have developed the concept of the user and the designer's roles becoming interchangeable, with the consumer dictating what the product should look like and the designer being limited to simply providing the materials. LIGHT_NESS lamps are assembled by putting the frame together, attaching the cord to the desired position, and lastly taping the frame with the neon-orange tape provided to create the lampshade. The result is a whimsical and highly individualized collection of designs that expresses the maker's personality.

FRA
UXUS a mis au point un nouveau concept où les rôles du designer et du client sont interchangeables et où le consommateur décide de l'aspect du produit, le créateur se contentant de lui fournir les matériaux nécessaires. Les lustres LIGHT_NESS se montent en assemblant les différents éléments de sa structure, en fixant le cordon électrique à l'endroit souhaité et en entourant l'armature avec le ruban adhésif orange fluo fourni de manière à créer l'abat-jour. Le résultat est une collection amusante et variée de designs qui expriment la personnalité du créateur.

ESP
UXUS ha desarrollado la idea de que los papeles del diseñador y el usuario son intercambiables y que el consumidor determina la apariencia del producto mientras que el diseñador se limita a facilitarle los materiales. Las lámparas LIGHT_NESS se montan ensamblando la estructura, instalando el cable en la posición que se desea y finalmente uniendo el armazón con la cinta naranja fosforescente que se incluye, obtenido de esta forma la pantalla. El resultado es una colección de diseños caprichosos y altamente individualizados que expresan la personalidad del creador.

POR
UXUS desenvolveu a ideia de que os papéis do designer e do usuário são intercambiáveis e de que o consumidor determina a aparência do produto, enquanto o designer se limita a facilitar-lhe os materiais. As luminárias LIGHT_NESS são montadas juntando a estrutura, instalando o fio na posição que se deseja e, finalmente, unindo a armação com a fita laranja fosforescente inclusa, obtendo assim a cúpula. El resultado é uma coleção de desenhos caprichosos e altamente individualizados, que expressam a personalidade do criador.

LIGHTPAINTINGS

PROJECT
Lightpaintings

DESIGNER
Stephen Knapp

PHOTOGRAPHY
Stephen Knapp

Deriving inspiration from his studies of light, color, dimensions, space, and perception, artist Stephen Knapp has been creating art that interacts with and is transformed by light for over thirty years. Existing at the intersection of abstract painting, sculpture, and technology, Lightpaintings are created with light—considered by some to be the first new art medium of the twenty-first century—as well as treated glass and stainless steel mounts.

FRA
Depuis plus de trente ans, l'artiste Stephen Knapp crée des œuvres qui interagissent avec la lumière et la transforme. Il tire son inspiration de ses études sur la lumière, la couleur, l'espace et la perception. À la frontière entre la peinture abstraite, la sculpture et la technologie, Lightpaintings est créé avec de la lumière — que certains artistes considèrent comme le nouveau matériau du XX0 siècle —ainsi que du verre traité et des cadres en acier inoxydable.

ESP
Desde hace más de treinta años, el artista Stephen Knapp ha creado obras de arte que interactúan con la luz y son transformadas por ella, inspirándose en los estudios que ha realizado sobre la luz, el color, las dimensiones, el espacio y la percepción. Las lámparas Lightpaintings, que se encuentran en la intersección de la pintura abstracta, la escultura y la tecnología, están hechas de luz (que en opinión de algunos es el primer medio artístico nuevo del siglo XXI), cristales tratados y monturas de acero inoxidable.

POR
Desde há trinta anos, o artista Stephen Knapp vem criando obras de arte que interagem com a luz e são transformadas por ela, inspirando-se nos estudos que realizou sobre a luz, a cor, as dimensões, o espaço e a percepção. As luminárias Lightpaintings, que estão na intersecção da pintura abstrata, com a escultura e a tecnologia, são feitas de luz (que na opinião de alguns é o primeiro meio artístico novo do século XXI), vidros tratados e montagens de aço inoxidável.

FREAKSHOW

DESIGNER
Kobo Sin

PHOTOGRAPHY
Kobo Sin

Freakshow explores our relationship with nature and our loss of touch with the natural world around us. The aim of this project is to confront and shock people and turn unwanted and unused parts of nature into provocative products that pull nature back into people's minds by incorporating elements of the animal world—especially those parts that are normally thrown away or ignored—into a whole series of decorative furniture and lighting.

FRA
Freakshow explore notre relation avec la nature, et notre perte de contact avec le monde qui nous entoure. Le but du projet est d'une part d'interpeller et de provoquer et, d'autre part, de transformer des éléments de la nature dont personne ne veut, en produits chocs qui redonneront conscience aux gens de son existence. Le designer Kobo Sin a ainsi incorporé à ses luminaires et ses meubles des bribes du monde animal — en particulier des morceaux que l'on jette ou préfère ignorer.

ESP
Freakshow ahonda en la relación que mantenemos con la naturaleza y nuestro distanciamiento del mundo que nos rodea. El objetivo de este proyecto es que el público se sienta escandalizado y ofendido, convirtiendo elementos indeseables e inútiles de la naturaleza en productos provocadores que nos recuerdan la naturaleza incorporando elementos del mundo animal (sobre todo los elementos que normalmente se tiran o se ignoran) en una serie de luces y muebles decorativos.

POR
Freakshow aprofunda na relação que mantemos com a natureza e em nosso distanciamento do mundo que nos rodeia. O objetivo deste projeto é que o público se sinta escandalizado e ofendido, transformando elementos indesejáveis e inúteis da natureza em produtos provocativos que, ao incorporar elementos do mundo animal (sobretudo os elementos que normalmente são descartados ou ignorados) numa série de luminárias e móveis decorativos, nos recordam a natureza.

STORM

DESIGNER
Tanya Clarke

PHOTOGRAPHY
Lisa Gizara

Tanya Clarke's on-going Liquid Light series experiments with the fusion of art, function, and environmental consciousness by creating a visual reminder of water's status as a precious commodity and our need to protect this natural resource. The piece is grounded in a zero-carbon-footprint philosophy and combines LED lights, reclaimed copper, brass, and galvanized-steel plumbing and hardware.

FRA

La série Liquid Light de Tanya Clarke, qui ne cesse de s'agrandir, fusionne l'art, la fonction et la conscience écologique pour nous rappeler que l'eau est une précieuse ressource naturelle que nous devons sauvegarder. Cette œuvre, tout à fait dans le ton d'une empreinte carbone zéro, combine ampoules LED, articles de plomberie et de quincaillerie de récupération en cuivre, en laiton et en acier galvanisé.

ESP

La serie en desarrollo Liquid Light de Tanya Clarke experimenta con la fusión del arte, la función y la conciencia del medio ambiente y nos recuerda visualmente que el agua es un recurso muy valioso y debemos protegerlo. Esta creación está arraigada en una filosofía de huella de carbono cero y combina luces LED, cobre reciclado, latón, componentes electrónicos y tuberías de acero galvanizado.

POR

A série em desenvolvimento Liquid Light de Tanya Clarke faz experiências com a fusão da arte, a função e a consciência do meio ambiente, e nos recorda visualmente que a água é um recurso muito valioso, que devemos proteger. Esta criação está arraigada numa filosofia de pegada de carbono zero e combina lâmpadas LED, cobre reciclado, latão, componentes eletrônicos e tubos de aço galvanizado.

STRUCTEND LIGHT

DESIGNER
Cláudio Cigarro

PHOTOGRAPHY
Cláudio Cigarro

Structend Light is based on tent structures and the way in which they emit light at night. When tents are illuminated from within their structures become visible due to them casting a shadow. Structend consists of a structure, internal lighting, and an outer layer, just like a tent. The outer layer adapts to the shape of the structure and can be removed for replacement—perhaps for a different color—or cleaned.

FRA
Structend s'inspire de la structure des tentes de camping et de la façon dont elles diffusent la lumière la nuit. Lorsqu'une tente est éclairée de l'intérieur, les éléments de sa structure deviennent apparents parce qu'ils projettent une ombre. Structend, à la manière d'une tente, est constitué d'une structure, d'un éclairage intérieur et d'une toile. La forme de celle-ci épouse parfaitement l'armature et on peut la retirer soit pour la remplacer par une autre d'une couleur différente, soit pour la nettoyer.

ESP
Structend Light se basa en la estructura de las tiendas de campaña y la forma en la que estas emiten luz durante la noche. Cuando el interior se ilumina la estructura arroja una sombra y de esta forma se hace visible. Así, Structend se compone de una estructura, una luz interna y una capa externa, como si fuera una tienda de campaña. La capa externa se adapta a la forma de la estructura y se retira para limpiarla o cambiarla (quizá por otra de un color distinto).

POR
Structend Light baseia-se na estrutura das tendas de campanha e na forma como estas emitem luz durante a noite. Quando o interior se ilumina, a estrutura lança uma sombra e desta forma se torna visível. Assim, Structend compõe-se de uma estrutura, uma luz interna e uma capa externa, como se fosse uma tenda de campanha. A capa externa se adapta à forma da estrutura e é retirada para limpá-la ou trocá-la (talvez por outra de cor diferente).

LACE LIGHT

DESIGNER
Vladimir Usoltsev

PHOTOGRAPHY
Vladimir Usoltsev

CLIENT
Thorsten Van Elten

The idea behind the Lace Light was to create a light that had a unique and one-off or handmade feel and would bring an atmosphere of intimacy to the environment in which it is installed. This was achieved by subverting the stereotypical image of stockings and using them as a shade for the light. The intricate lace patterns that let through light help to blur the boundary between a functional object and a piece of art.

ESP
Lace Light es fruto del intento de crear una lámpara que inspire una sensación irrepetible y única o artesanal, insuflando una atmósfera íntima en el entorno donde se instala. Para ello subvierte la imagen estereotipada de las medias y las usa a modo de pantalla. Los intrincados diseños de encaje que atraviesa la luz contribuyen a difuminar la frontera entre el objeto funcional y la obra de arte.

FRA
Le but du projet était de créer un luminaire original qui ait un « look » artisanal tout en conférant une ambiance chaleureuse et intime à l'espace environnant. C'est ce que le designer Vladimir Usoltsev a réussi à obtenir en détournant les bas de leur usage courant pour en faire des abat-jour. Le motif élaboré de la dentelle filtre la lumière de telle sorte que l'objet fonctionnel devient une œuvre d'art.

POR
Lace Light é fruto da tentativa de criar uma luminária que inspire uma sensação irrepetível e única ou artesanal, insuflando uma atmosfera íntima no ambiente onde é instalada. Para isso, subverte a imagem estereotipada das meias usando-as como cúpula. Os intrincados desenhos rendados que a luz atravessa contribuem para esvair a fronteira entre o objeto funcional e a obra de arte.

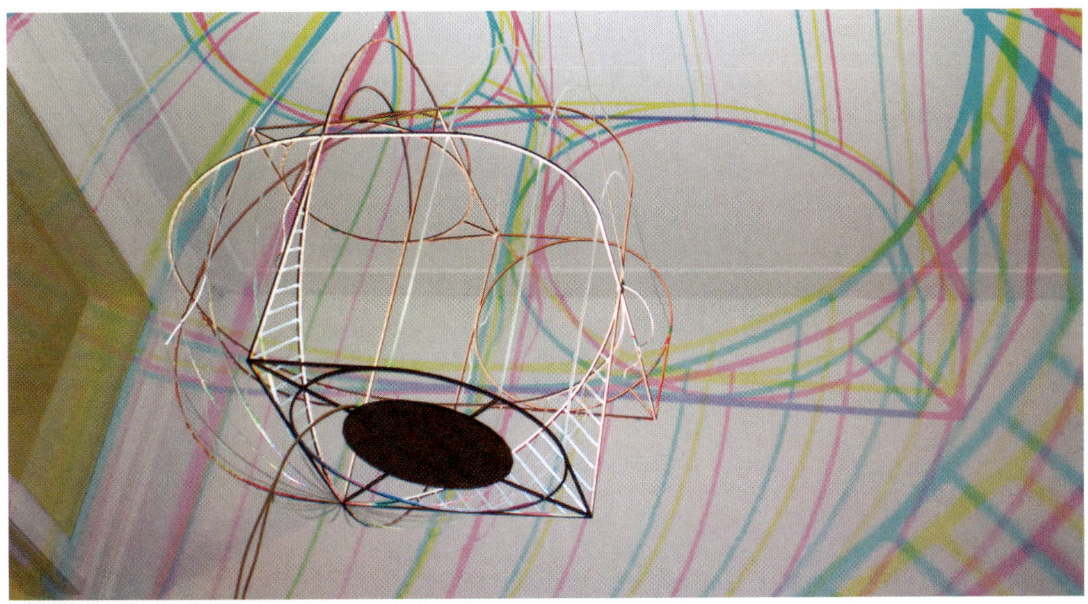

CMYK LAMP

DESIGNER
Dennis Parren

PHOTOGRAPHY
Dennis Parren & Galerie VIVID

CMYK Lamp plays with the mystery of light and color by casting an elusive network of lines of cyan, magenta, and yellow light on the ceiling. LED technology has revolutionized lighting. Its popularity and range of applications are increasing rapidly due to the remarkable properties that LEDs have, which have enabled designers to show how the primary colors of light on the one hand and pigment colors on the other interact.

FRA

Le lustre CMYK joue avec le mystère de la lumière et de la couleur en projetant sur le plafond un réseau de lignes cyans, magentas et jaunes. La technologie LED a résolument révolutionné l'éclairage. Sa popularité et ses applications ne cessent de s'étendre grâce aux propriétés remarquables des LED qui permettent de montrer l'interaction entre les couleurs en synthèse soustractive et additive.

ESP

La lámpara CMYK juega con el misterio de la luz y el color proyectando un elusivo entramado de líneas turquesa, magenta y amarilla sobre el techo. La tecnología LED ha revolucionado el mundo de las lámparas. Su popularidad y su gama de aplicaciones están aumentando rápidamente debido a sus excelentes características, con las que los diseñadores nos muestran la interacción entre los colores primarios de la luz y los colores de los pigmentos.

POR

A luminária CMYK joga com o mistério da luz e da cor projetando uma elusiva trama de linhas turquesa, magenta e amarela sobre o teto. A tecnologia LED revolucionou o mundo das luminárias. Sua popularidade e sua variedade de aplicações estão aumentando rapidamente devido às suas excelentes características, com as quais os designers nos mostram a interação entre as cores primárias da luz e as cores dos pigmentos.

A / Z

ALICJA WASIELEWSKA

Warsaw, Poland
www.wasielewska.com
+48 784 940 664
a.wasielewska@hotmail.com

ANDREAS KOWALEWSKI

Veembroederhof 122, 1019 HC Amsterdam, the Netherlands
www.andreaskowalewski.com
+31 (0)20 7726889
mail@andreaskowalewski.com

ANGO

53 / 20 Soi Suparaht 1, Phaholyothin Road, Payathai, Bangkok 10400, Thailand
www.angoworld.com
+ 66 (0) 2 873 0167
contact@angoworld.com

ANNE-CÉCILE RAPPA

Lausanne, Switzerland
www.annececile-rappa.ch
+41 (0)79 238 34 90
contact@annececile-rappa.ch

ANTHONY DICKENS

London, UK
www.anthonydickens.com
+44 (0) 207 3789399
studio@anthonydickens.com

AURA

Paris & Lausanne
www.aura-lamp.com
info@aura-lamp.com

BRUCE MUNRO

Wiltshire, Endland
www.brucemunro.co.uk
(0)1985 845 228
info@brucemunro.co.uk

CAROLINA FONTOURA ALZAGA

Los Angeles, CA
www.facaro.com
+213 570 9819
caro@kein.org

CLÁUDIO CIGARRO

Lisbon, Portugal
www.cargocollective.com/claudiocigarro
claudio.cigarro@gmail.com

DAAN ROOSEGAARDE

Rotterdam, Holland
www.studioroosegaarde.net
mail@studioroosegaarde.net

DAISUKE HIRAIWA

London/Stockholm
www.gdotplus.com; www.daisukehiraiwa.com
+46 -(0)72949231
d@gdotplus.com

DAMIAN O'SULLIVAN

Rotterdam, the Netherlands
www.damianosullivan.com
+31 (0)10 842 7364
info@damianosullivan.com

DANA BACHAR

Tel-Aviv, Israel
www.danabachar.com
+972 54 5888255
danabachar@gmail.com

DANNY KUO

F.v. Pruisenweg 14a, 5616 AV Eindhoven, the Netherlands
www.dannykuo.com
+31 611 308 506
info@dannykuo.com

DARSHAN ALATAR PATEL

New York City, USA
www.darshan-alatar.com
+1 732 331 6124
darshan.alatar@gmail.com

DAVID KRYNAUW

Madola farm, Piet Retief, Mpumalanga, South Africa
www.davidkrynauw.com
+27 84 626 3807
david@davidkrynauw.com

DECORKUZNETSOV

Dnepropetrovsk city, Ukraine
www.decorkuznetsov.com
+38 067 633 7890
we@decorkuznetsov.com

DENNIS PARREN

Eindhoven, the Netherlands
dennisparren.nl
+31 614355696
dennisparren@me.com

DIALOGUEMETHOD DESIGN STUDIO

Lotte castle first apt. 120-2701, Am-sa dong, Gang-dong gu, Seoul, Korea
www.dialoguemethod.com
+82 10 7366 6814
dialoguemethod@gmail.com

DIK SCHEEPERS

Heerlen, the Netherlands
www.dikscheepers.nl
+31(0)611396977
info@dikscheepers.nl

DIMITRIOS STAMATAKIS

Athens, Greece
www.thetemporarymrdmtrsstmtks.tumblr.com
+30 6973968155
di.stamatakis@gmail.com

DING3000

Ratswiese 18, 30453 Hannover, Germany
www.ding3000.com
+49 511 3539376

DROR

New York, USA
www.studiodror.com
+ 212 929 2196
melanie@studiodror.com

D-VISION

6 Ramat Yam, Herzliya 46851, Israel
www.d-vision.co.il
+972 9 9626408
Email: d-vision@keter.co.il

ENRICO ZANOLLA

Gorizia, Italy
www.enricozanolla.com
+39 392 8424081
info@enricozanolla.com

ENRIQUE ROMERO DE LA LIANA

Madrid & Barcelona, Spain
www.romerodelallana.com
+34 607 729 970
enrique@romerodelallana.es

ETT LA BENN

Berlin, Germany
www.ettlabenn.com
+49 (0)30 40576794
d.duerler@ettlabenn.com

EVA MENZ DESIGN

Eva Menz Design, 10 Clarendon Cross, London, W11 4AP, UK
www.evamenz.com
+44(0) 207 243 8292
info@evamenz.com

EWA SENDECKA

Kraków, Poland
www.ewasendecka.com
+48 691 575 692
info@ewasendecka.com

FANSON MENG

Taipei, Taiwan
www.be.net/fansonmeng
+886 35784022; +886 952758927
fanson_meng@hotmail.com

FARGO DESIGN

Tel Aviv, Israel
www.wix.com/kiltbanana/fargo
+972542549336
design.fargo@gmail.com

FRANK NEULICHEDL

Vancouver, Cananda
www.frankie.bz
info@frankie.bz

FREYJA SEWELL

London, UK
www.freyjasewell.co.uk
freyja@freyjasewell.co.uk

GIONATA GATTO

Kronehoefstraat 1, 5612 HK Eindhoven, the Netherlands
www.atuppertu.com
+31 (0) 626 047 267
gionatagatto@atuppertu.com

GREAT THINGS TO PEOPLE

Santiago, Chile
www.gt2p.com
info@gt2p.com

H220430

Tokyo, Japan
www.h220430.jp
+81-3-3555-5877
info@h220430.jp

H COMMA

321, DMC HI-Tech Industry Center,1580, Sangam-dong, Mapo-gu, Seoul, Korea
www.hcomma.com
+82 10 6278 1519
info@hcomma.com

IDA NOEMI

Oslo, Norway
www.idanoemi.no
+47 470 74 142
post@idanoemi.no

IDEA

Sofia, Bulgaira
www.idea.bg
+359896606000
alex@idea.bg

INNOVO DESIGN

Hangzhou,China.
www.innovo-design.com; www.pinwu.net
+86 571 85850202
innovo.com@gmail.com

JASON KRUGMAN

Brooklyn, New York
www.jasonkrugman.com/projects/treble
+001-617-571-9442
jasonkrugman@gmail.com

JEANNINE VAN ERK

Berlin, Germany
www.bel-bo.net
www.schubLaden.de
+49 (0)30 61 65 11 49
j.vanerk@schubLaden.de

JEROEN VERHOEVEN

Marconistraat 52, 3029 AK Rotterdam, the Netherlands
www.demakersvan.com; www.blainsouthern.com
+31 (0) 10-2447474
info@demakersvan.com; info@blainsouthern.com

JESPER JONSSON

Gothenburg, Sweden
www.jesperj.se
+46 (0)73 72 06 005
hello@jesperj.se

JORDI MILÀ

Barcelona, Spain
www.jordimila.com
+34 935 938 185
contact@jordimila.com

KIESER SPATH

Darmstadt
www.kieserspath.de
mail@kieserspath.de

KIM HYUNJOO

77-67, heukSuk-dong, DongJak-gu, Seoul, South Korea
www.kimhyunjoo.com
+82 10 5617 0559
studio@uundesign.com

KOBO SIN

Hong Kong, London
www.kobosin.com
+852 60200456; +44 7530662991
kobo.sin@hotmail.com

KOZO LAMP

Tel Aviv, Israel
www.kozo-lamp.com
+972 (0) 508 264746
contact@kozo-lamp.com

KULLA STUDIO

Tel-Aviv, Israel
www.kulladesign.com
+972 54 5636346
studio@kulladesign.com

KUNDALINI

Milan, Italy
www.kundalini.it
+39 02 36538950
info@kundalini.it

KYOUEI DESIGN

1326-15 Kusanagi, Shimizu-ku, Shizuoka City, Shizuoka, Japan.
www.kyouei-ltd.co.jp
+81 54 347 0653
info@kyouei-ltd.co.jp

LANZAVECCHIA + WAI

Italy & Singapore
www.lanzavecchia-wai.com
info@lanzavecchia-wai.com

LATORRE CRUZ

London, UK
www.latorrecruz.com
+44 (0)7795 141176
mail@latorrecruz.com

LOKOLO

Berlin, Germany
www.lokolo.eu
+493053162623
info@lokolo.eu

LOUIE RIGANO

New York, NY, USA
www.louierigano.com
lrigano@g.risd.edu

MACMASTER

London, UK
www.macmasterdesign.com
+44 (0) 208 316 4006
info@macmasterdesign.com

MAMMALAMPA

Riga, Latvia
www.mammalampa.com
info@mammalampa.com

MARKUS JOHANSSON

Stockholm, Sweden
www.claessonkoivistorune.se
Tel: +46 8644 58 63
all@ckr.se

MAURO SODDU

Cagliari, Italy
www.maurosoddu.com
+393492168169
info@maurosoddu.com

MICHAEL KONSTANTIN WOLKE

Köln, Germany
www.herrwolke.com
+0221 29025551
post@herrwolke.com

MICHAELLA JANSE VAN VUUREN

Pretoria, South Africa
www.nomili.co.za
+27(0)731730750
info@nomili.co.za

MIKE THOMPSON

Kronehoefstraat 1, 5612 HK Eindhoven, the Netherlands
www.miket.co.uk
+31 (0) 638 584 931
info@miket.co.uk

MILOS JOVANOVIC

Kralja Petra I 6 11320 Velika Plana, Serbia
www.milos-design.com
+381643088242

MISCHER'TRAXLER

Vienna, Austria
www.mischertraxler.com
we@mischertraxler.com

MOLO

British Columbia, Canada
www.molodesign.com
+1 604 696 2501
info@molodesign.com

MUT DESIGN

Valencia, Spain
www.mutdesign.com
+0034 96 394 26 85;
+0034 693 494 696
info@mutdesign.com

NICK SAYERS

Brighton & Hove, UK
www.nicksayers.com;
www.flickr.com/nicksayers
+44 (0) 7812 036415
mail@nicksayers.com

NIELS GRUBAK

Aarhus, Danmark
www.nielsgrubak.com
+45 2226 5832
Niels@grubakdesign.com

NIR MEIRI

Tel Aviv, Israel
www.nirmeiri.com
+972 54 4740865
nirmeiri.com@gmail.com

NISTOR&NISTOR

Paris, France
www.ggnistor.com
+972 52 4040977
ggnistor@gmail.com

NONDESIGNS

California, USA
www.nondesigns.com
+626 616 0796
info@nondesigns.com

PEPE HEYKOOP

Amsterdam, the Netherland
www.pepeheykoop.nl
pepeheykoop@gmail.com

PIA WUSTENBERG

London, UK
www.piadesign.eu
+44(0)7917182471
pia@piadesign.eu

PRZEMYSLAW KRAWCZYNSKI

Lodz city, Poland
www.calabarte.com
calabarte@gmail.com

RAW-EDGES

London, UK
www.raw-edges.com
+44 78 9056 9470

RELEVÉ DESIGN

Brooklyn, NY, USA
www.relevedesign.com
+1 646 484 8007
info@relevedesign.com

RICK TEGELAAR

Arnhem, the Nederland
www.ricktegelaar.nl
+31 6 309 848 09
info@ricktegelaar.nl

SAM BARON

Treviso, Italy.
www.fabrica.it
+39 4 22 51 6260
samuelbaron@gmail.com

SANDER MULDER

Veldhoven, the Netherlands
www.sandermulder.com
+31 (0)40 - 21 22 900
press@sandermulder.com

SEBASTIAN ERRAZURIZ

Santiago, Chile
www.meetsebastian.com
info@meetsebastian.com

STEPHEN KNAPP

Massachusetts, USA
www.lightpaintings.com
sk@stephenknapp.com

STEVEN HAULENBEEK

Chicago, USA
www.stevenhaulenbeek.com
+1 616 405 2469

STUDIO KLASS

Milan, Italy
www.studioklass.com
+39 338 10 37 236
info@studioklass.com

STUDIO SCHNEEMANN

Overschiesedorpstraat 83, 3043CP Rotterdam, the Netherlands
www.studioschneemann.com
+0031615066653
info@studioschneemann.com

STUDIO WM.

Loods Holland 1, 3024 WB,
Rotterdam, the Netherlands
www.wendymaarten.com
+31 (0) 108410829
info@wendymaarten.com

SVETLANA KOZHENOVA

Prague, Czech Republic
www.svetlanakozhenov.com
+00420776044243
svetlanakozhenov@gmail.com

TANYA CLARKE

California, USA
www.liquidlightsite.com.
tanyacclarke@yahoo.com

TOM RAFFIELD DESIGN

Cornwall, UK
www.tomraffield.com
+44 (0)7968 621955

UXUS

Amsterdam, the Netherlands
www.uxusdesign.com
+31 20 623 3114
info@uxusdesign.com

VIBEKE SKAR

Oslo, Norway
www.vibekeskar.com
+47 410 40 710
info@vibekeskar.com

VIBIA

Barcelona, Spain
www.vibia.com
+ 34 934796971
directmarketing@grupo-t.com

VICTOR WAYNE VETTERLEIN

44 Remsen Street, #9, Brooklyn, NY 11201, USA
www.victorvetterlein.com
+1 646 228 1616

VLADIMIR USOLTSEV

Moscow, Russia
www.betamedium.com
+7 916 671 27 00
vlad@betamedium.com

WOODLABO

Bordeaux, France / Turku, Finland
mywoodlabo.com
+06 14 80 02 06
gael@mywoodlabo.com

YU JORDY FU

London, UK
www.jordyfu.com;
www.jordyfu.co.uk/shop
+66 850598978
jordyfu@mac.com